Pierre Blot

What to eat, and how to cook it

containing over one thousand Receipts

Pierre Blot

What to eat, and how to cook it
containing over one thousand Receipts

ISBN/EAN: 9783744789554

Printed in Europe, USA, Canada, Australia, Japan

Cover: Foto ©Lupo / pixelio.de

More available books at **www.hansebooks.com**

HOW TO COOK IT:

CONTAINING

OVER ONE THOUSAND RECEIPTS,

SYSTEMATICALLY AND PRACTICALLY ARRANGED, TO ENABLE THE HOUSEKEEPER TO PREPARE THE MOST DIFFICULT OR SIMPLER DISHES IN THE BEST MANNER.

BY

PIERRE BLOT,

EDITOR OF THE "ALMANACK GASTRONOMIQUE," OF PARIS, AND OTHER GASTRONOMICAL WORKS.

"Feed me with food convenient for me."—BIBLE.

NEW YORK:
D. APPLETON AND COMPANY,
443 & 445 BROADWAY.
LONDON: 16 LITTLE BRITAIN.
1863.

D. APPLETON AND COMPANY,
In the Clerk's Office of the District Court of the United States for the Southern District of New York.

PREFACE.

IMPROVEMENTS of every kind are daily introduced in almost every branch of labor; why not introduce them in the culinary department as well, and especially when these improvements have for their object economy, celerity, taste, and health?

The division of the art of cooking, and the system of arranging bills of fare, contained in these pages, solve that great and perplexing question, especially for ladies, how to arrange a bill of fare for every season of the year, to suit any number of guests, at a greater or less expense, as they may desire.

No matter how inexperienced some of our housekeeping readers may be, by carefully following our directions, they will be able to live as well and economically as possible, and also serve a dinner in as orderly a manner as any steward could do.

Some think that good cooking is expensive, that money alone makes good dishes; but this is not true. A good cook spends much less than a poor one in preparing the same dish, and prepares it much better.

It will not only be easy to order a suitable dinner at all times, but also a breakfast, lunch, or supper; and any housekeeper may superintend her culinary department and direct her cook, making proper observations whenever necessary, without the least trouble.

In our directions, gastronomy is blended with economy, and although everything prepared according to these receipts will be in the highest and best style, it will still be cheaper than if prepared in the poorest way, as nothing will be wasted, and the best of everything used will be had.

This book will be found to be simpler than many, if not all, other cook books. It contains more receipts, and is in accordance with the advancements of the present age.

CONTENTS.

	Page
COOKING,	7
DIRECTIONS AND EXPLANATIONS,	11
SOUPS,	29
SAUCES,	45
FARCES AND GARNITURES,	58
PUREES,	62
BEEF,	66
FISH,	80
VEAL,	102
MUTTON,	117
LAMB,	126
PORK,	123
POULTRY,	134
GAME,	151
VENISON,	162
SNAILS,	165
VEGETABLES,	169
SALADS,	200
EGGS,	204
OMELETS,	208
PASTRY,	212
CREAM FOR ENTREMETS,	230
DESSERT CREAMS,	232
BILLS OF FARE,	239
NDEX,	250

COOKING.

AFTER a careful study of the art of cooking in all its branches, we have found only ten principal parts on which it is based (the rest is all fancy). These ten parts are: BAKING, BOILING, BROILING, FRYING, MIXING, ROASTING, SAUTÉING, SEASONING, SIMMERING, AND STEWING.

Baking is to bake bread or cakes; to cook eggs, fish, fruit, meat, vegetables, etc., in an oven or furnace, or in any other close place heated.

In baking, see that your oven or furnace be properly heated; some dishes require more heat than others; look at the object in process of baking from time to time, and especially at the beginning; turn the object round if necessary, in case the oven be heated more on one side than on the other, to prevent burning it.

Boiling is to cook eggs, fish, fruit, meat, vegetables, etc., in boiling water or other liquid.

When you boil anything, you must watch it carefully, lest it should boil too fast or too slow; have the same heat all the time. In each of our receipts will be found the necessary and particular explanations.

Broiling is to cook fish, meat, vegetables, etc., over live coals, and generally by the means of a gridiron. No matter what you broil, begin by greasing the bars of the gridiron; then warm it, and afterward place what you wish to broil on it. (For the remainder, see different receipts.)

Frying is to cook eggs, fish, meat, vegetables, etc., in heated fat or oil.

When the meat, fish, etc., are prepared as directed in our different receipts, put in a deep frying pan or in a saucepan, grease, lard or oil enough to cover entirely the object you intend to fry. When you have fried fish, meat or vegetables, let the grease stand five minutes; then strain it into a pot, let it cool and cover it. Repeat the same process every time you use it; also, add once in a while a little grease that has not been used before.

Do the same with oil.

Always fry fish in the grease or oil in which fish has been fried, and do the same for meat, etc.

To ascertain with accuracy when the grease, lard or oil is warm enough to lay the things in the pan, dip a fork in cold water, the prongs only, so as to retain but one or two drops of water, which drops you let fall in the grease, and if it crackles, it is hot enough.

Mixing is to prepare different dishes which are composed of several things, such as cakes, omelets, sauces, pies, etc.

We recommend our readers to pay due attention to the quantities we give in our receipts; but as everybody has not the same taste, it would be very easy to augment or diminish the quantity of salt, pepper, sugar, butter, etc., so as to suit one's own taste.

Roasting is to cook fish, meat, etc., by exposing the object to heat, and generally done by the means of a spit, or in a bake-pan or the like, in an oven. When you have placed an object on the spit and according to our directions, bear in mind that you cannot baste it too often, even if you were attempting to imitate a waterspout. Remember also that the time necessary for roasting a piece of meat, or anything else, depends as much upon the fire as the nature of the meat.

Meat, especially, requires to be put near the fire at first, and then put back by degrees.

Sautéing is to cook meat, vegetables, etc., in a pan, with grease or oil enough to prevent the object which is being cooked from scorching; chickens, chops, cutlets, omelets, and steaks are cooked under this name.

Sautéing differs from frying in two ways. 1st. To fry any object requires grease enough to cover that object entirely, while to sauté it requires just enough of it to prevent it from scorching. 2d. In frying, the object remains as it is laid in the pan, while in sautéing it has to be turned over several times.

Seasoning is, we think, the most difficult part in the art of cooking; to season is not difficult, but to season properly is quite another thing. It is not only necessary to know well how to stew or roast a piece of meat or anything else, but to know well how to season it; to be able to judge what quantity, what kind of spices can be used to season such or such a dish; to what extent all the spices used agree together, and what taste and flavor they will give to the object with which they are cooked; for, if not properly used, they may just as likely destroy the taste and flavor of the object as improve it.

Some dishes require high and much seasonings, others just the contrary. With a good fire and a good spit, it is not necessary to be a cook to roast a piece well, but the cook is indispensable to mix the gravy or sauce with the proper seasonings. Next comes tasting, the most difficult and delicate part of seasoning; it is by tasting that we ascertain if we have seasoned properly.

In this only two of the senses are engaged, and one

1*

principally more than the other. A person may have a good feeling, hearing and sight, and for all that would not be fit for preparing the simplest dish; the senses of smelling and tasting are the ones most required, and without which no one can be a cook.

To taste a sauce, as well as to know if a thing is good to eat, we cannot trust our eyes or fingers nor our ears; we then have recourse, first, to our smelling, and then to our tasting: so do all animals.

We always commence by smelling, and when that sense is satisfied as far as it is concerned, we then apply our tasting qualities; and if that last one is, in its turn, satisfied also, we proceed, that is, we masticate, if mastication is necessary, and then swallow.

Simmering is to cook meat or anything else in hot water or other liquid; most of the soups, sauces, etc., are made by simmering.

Simmering differs from boiling only in the amount of heat allowed under the boiler, kettle, or pan. To simmer, is to boil as gently and slowly as possible.

Stewing is to cook fish, fruit, meat, vegetables, etc., with water or other liquid, in a tightly covered vessel; seething slowly in a moderate manner, or with a simmering heat.

DIRECTIONS AND EXPLANATIONS.

BAIN-MARIE.

A BAIN-MARIE is a large vessel of hot water, in which saucepans, moulds, etc., are placed to prepare or warm food. There are things that are much more delicate when prepared or warmed in hot water. If you have not one made for that purpose, use a large boiler or kettle in its stead.

Be careful not to allow the water to rise too much in bubbles, lest it should upset your saucepans, moulds, &c., or get into them.

BRAISING.

Braising, in cookery, means to cook anything with fire under and upon the pan, kettle, or other utensil.

A good oven is by far more easy, and answers perfectly the purpose. An oven not only warms the under and upper parts of the utensil, but all around it also.

CURRY.

We are of opinion that curry is too strong to be used in this country. They use a good deal of it in Java.

We cannot describe it better than by giving here the answer of a gentleman, who has lived a few years on the borders of the Ganges river, to a question on the properties and qualities of curry; he said that he thought it good, and even necessary, to use some there (in Java), on account of the climate, but **every** time he had eaten it he thought he was swallowing **boiling** alcohol or live coals.

DRAINING.

To drain, **is to** put **in** a drainer anything that has been soaked, **washed,** or boiled, etc., in water or any other liquid, **in** order **to dry it, or** at least to let drop from it the water or other liquid that may be in it.

Salads **of greens, as a general thing,** are drained after **being** washed, before putting them **in the salad dish; they** must **be drained as** dry as **possible, but without** pressing on them, as it would wilt the leaves, **and** give the salad **an** unsightly appearance.

GLAZING.

To glaze meat is to give it a coat by the **means of a** feather, or a small **pencil, which you** dip in reduced sauce, or *coulis*, and where **directed.** To glaze pastry is to sift fine white sugar **on the cake, and** put **it** back in the oven for **a short** time; that **is, the time necessary** to melt the sugar, **and give the** cake a beautiful **appearance.**

LARDING.

Take good fat bacon, **cut it in slices, then** fillet them so as **to** make square fillets; cut **them** the length you want, and according to the **size of the** piece you wish to lard; then lard the piece by the means of a larding pin.

OSMAZOME.

Osmazome is found in beef, mutton, venison, and **game;** in the latter, when the bird or animal is adult. In soup meat, the osmazome is the soluble part of the meat that dissolves in boiling, and makes nutritious broth. In broiled or roasted pieces, it **is that** part which makes a kind of brown crust on the surface of the meat, and also the brownish part of the gravy. Chicken, lamb, sucking pig, veal, etc., do not contain any osmazome.

STRAINING.

To strain, is to pass sauce or anything else through a sieve, or through a piece of cloth, in order to have it freed from particles of every kind. You strain broth to make soup, so as to remove the small pieces of bones that may be in it, etc.

WINE IN SAUCES.

Put at first half the quantity you are to use, and when nearly done put the other half in; boil or simmer for a while longer, and use.

KITCHEN UTENSILS.

Gastronomers use, in preference to anything else, earthen pans, or, for want of these, tin pans. Copper requires to be examined every day, and to prevent any accident, it is necessary to have the inside of the pans lined very often; in the end, crockery or tin is as cheap, if not cheaper, than copper, and besides, quite harmless.

Many indispositions are caused by food prepared in copper not properly lined; even food prepared in a well lined pan would be dangerous if allowed to cool in it.

TIME TO LEAVE MEAT ON OR BEFORE THE FIRE.

The time to cook meat depends as much on the quality of the meat as on the fire. Some persons like meat more done than others; in many cases you must consult your own taste or that of your guests. Beef, lamb, mutton, fowls, and game may be eaten rather underdone, according to taste; but veal must be at least a little overdone, or else it is very unwholesome.

DIRECTIONS AND EXPLANATIONS.

The following table may be used as a guide:

Bear and Buffalo,	a five pound piece,	5 to 7 hours.
Wild Boar and Woodchuck,	Do. do.	3 to 4 hours.
Beef,	Do. do.	1 hour 30 min.
Do.	a ten pound piece,	2 hrs. 30 min.
Capon,	a large one,	1 hour.
Chicken,	a middling sized one.	45 min.
Duck,	a large one,	45 min.
Do.	a small one,	30 min.
Goose,	a large one,	2 hours.
Do.	a small one,	1 hour 30 min.
Grouse, Heathcock, Snipe, and Woodcock,	a fat one,	30 min.
Do. do. do. do.	a lean one,	20 min.
Guinea Fowl,	a middling sized one.	1 hour.
Hare,	an old one,	1 hour 30 min.
Do.	a young one,	about 1 hour.
Lamb and Kid,	a large quarter.	1 hour.
Do. do.	a small one,	45 min.
Mutton,	a four pound piece,	1 hour.
Do.	a six " "	1 hour 30 min.
Partridge, Pheasant, and Prairie Hen,	a middling sized one.	30 to 45 min.
Pigeon,	one,	30 min.
Pork,	a two pound piece	1 hour 15 min.
Do.	a four " "	2 hours.
Quail,	one,	20 min.
Sucking Pig,	a large one,	2 hrs. 30 min.
Do. do.	a small one,	2 hours.
Rabbit,	a middling sized one.	30 to 45 min.
Robin, Blackbird, Fig-pecker, High-holder, Lapwing, Meadow Lark, Plover, Reed Bird, Thrush, Yellow Bird, and other small birds,		15 to 20 min.
Turkey,	a large one,	1 hour 30 min.
Do.	a small one,	about 1 hour.
Veal,	a two pound piece,	1 hour 15 min.
Venison,	a four " "	about 1 hour.

The time meats may be kept, in a cool, dry, and dark place, and protected from flies or other insects is—

	In Summer.	In Winter.
Bear and Buffalo,	3 to 4 days.	10 to 15 days.
Wild Boar and Woodchuck	3 to 4 "	8 to 10 "
Beef and Pork,	2 to 4 "	6 to 10 "
Capon,	2 to 3 "	4 to 8 "
Chicken, old one,	3 to 4 "	4 to 10 "
Do. young one,	1 to 2 "	2 to 6 "

DIRECTIONS AND EXPLANATIONS.

	In Summer.	In Winter.
Deer, Partridge, Pheasant, Prairie Hen, Quail, Guinea Fowl, and Turkey,	2 to 3 days.	6 to 10 days.
Duck and Goose,	3 to 4 "	4 to 8 "
Hare and Rabbit,	2 to 3 "	4 to 8 "
Grouse, Heathcock, Snipe, and Woodcock,	3 to 4 "	8 to 15 "
Lamb, Kid, Sucking Pig, and Veal,	2 to 3 "	3 to 6 "
Mutton,	2 to 3 "	6 to 10 "
Pigeons, Blackbirds, Fig-peckers, High-holders, Lapwings, Meadow Larks, Plovers, Reed Birds, Robins, Thrushes, Yellow Birds, and other small birds,	2 to 3 "	6 to 10

The time must be reduced one half in summer, in stormy or damp weather, and one third in winter, in thawing or rainy weather.

Fish—when cleaned and prepared as directed, place it in a crockery stewpan, cover it with cold water, add a little salt, two or three sprigs of thyme, and one or two bay leaves. It will keep thus for some time.

FANCY WORDS AND EXPRESSIONS.

As some persons might think that we have omitted some important receipts, because we have not made use of fancy expressions, we give here the meaning of some of those found in cook books or in bills of fare.

Chaud-froid de poulet, ...A roasted chicken served cold.
Filet de bœuf en Bellevue, ...A fillet of beef served cold the next day.
Galantine de chasse en Bellevue, ...Galantine of partridge served cold.
Langue en Bellevue, ...A beef tongue prepared by pork butchers, and served cold.
Perruque de veau à la millionnaire, **Peruke** of veal, served millioniare-like.
Saumon au beurre de Montpellier, ..Salmon served cold.
Ciboules, ...Cives, or green onions.
Beurre noir, ...Brown butter

COFFEE.

It is very simple to make **good coffee;** but to do this it is necessary to take good Java, or any **other** good coffee, to have a good coffeepot, and to keep it clean (be it a French filter or an Old Dominion coffeepot).

How to roast it.—Although it is very easy to roast coffee in an apparatus for that purpose, after having seen it done once or twice, still it is difficult, if not impossible, to explain well the whole process; we will, however, try to give some directions.

Put coffee in your apparatus, the quantity to be according to the size of the cylinder; have a slow fire at first; when the coffee has swollen, augment the fire, turning the cylinder all the time, and take from the fire before it is roasted enough; the roasting will be finished before the coffee gets cold, and before taking it from the cylinder; continue turning the latter as if it were yet on the fire. It is well roasted when it evaporates a pleasing odor, and when of a brownish color. Take it from the apparatus then, spread it on a matting or on a piece of cloth, and put it in a tin box as soon as cold; cover the box well, air-tight if possible, and grind it when you want it. It might be ground some days before using it, if kept in an air-tight box.

How to make it.—Take a French filter, or an Old Dominion coffee-pot, and put the coffee into it; have water in a clean kettle and on a good fire (the water must not have been boiled or warmed before); at the first boiling, pour on the coffee from half to a pint of it, put back on the fire, and again at the first boiling pour another half or a pint on it, etc., till you have poured the quantity you desire.

The quantity of coffee must be according to the strength you wish it, and also according to the quantity wanted.

Four tablespoonfuls make a quart of very good coffee for breakfast for grown persons. It would be rather too strong for children.

For coffee after dinner, it is different; some persons like it very strong and others weak, but eight tablespoonfuls for a quart, make what may be called very strong coffee. For the quantity of coffee necessary, you cannot be guided by anything but by your own taste or that of your guests.

No matter what quantity of coffee you put in your filter, the liquid must be clear; the more you use, the blacker the substance is, but it must never be muddy. If muddy at all, you may be sure that you have not used good coffee. One pound of good coffee to a quart of water, should make black but clear coffee.

TEA.

There are a thousand ways to make tea; we might say that every one makes it in every one's way; but, after many experiments and much information, we have found the following to be the best:

Put good tea in your teapot (the quantity to be according to the strength and also to the quantity you want); place the teapot on the corner of the range, and when warm, pour boiling water on the tea, just enough to wet it. Leave it thus about one minute, then pour all the water you want, and about three minutes after it is ready for use.

CHOCOLATE.

Break the chocolate in pieces, put it in a tin stewpan, with milk or water (with milk it is better and more nourishing), set it on a moderate fire, stir with a wooden spoon till done, and serve.

COCOA.

Put in a tea or coffee cup, one or two tablespoonfuls of ground cocoa, pour boiling water or boiling milk on it while stirring with a spoon, and sweeten it to your liking. A few drops of essence of vanilla may be added, according to taste.

CHOCA.

Choca is nothing more nor less than one cup of coffee

and milk mixed with a cup of chocolate, and for breakfast. Let every one try how it tastes, and let those who may like it use it if they choose.

LEMONADE OR ORANGEADE.

Put two ounces of loaf sugar in a quart of water, also the rind of an orange or one of lemon. Half an hour after strain the whole, and press into it the juice of the orange, and a few drops of lemon juice. If found too strong, add water and sugar. It is a very good drink in summer, or for evening parties. A little currant jelly may be added to make a variety.

LEMONADE WITH BARLEY.

To the above lemonade or orangeade you add, instead of water and sugar, some barley water and sugar; it is very good and very refreshing.

Barley water is made by soaking in lukewarm water a pint of barley, drain it two or three minutes after; put the barley in a crockery pan, cover it with cold water (about three quarts), set it on the fire, and boil till the barley is perfectly cooked; skim off the scum during the cooking, drain, let cool, and use the water.

BARLEY SUGAR FOR CHILDREN.

Soak a quart of barley in lukewarm water for two or three minutes, and drain. Put the barley in a crockery stewpan, with four or five quarts of water, and set it on a good fire, boil till the barley is overdone, and then take from the fire, mash it as well as possible and strain, throwing away what there is in the strainer, and if the remainder does not make a kind of jelly when cool, the barley has not been boiled enough.

Mix that jelly with sugar and fry it; it is better than

any other candy, barley being refreshing, and the principal substance of it.

PUNCH.

Put a saltspoonful of black tea in a crockery pot, with one clove, a little cinnamon, and the rind of a lemon cut in pieces, pour on the whole half a pint of boiling water; let it remain thus five minutes, and strain. Put a bottle of rum or brandy in a crockery vessel, with twelve ounces of loaf sugar, set the rum or brandy on fire, and let burn till it stops. Then mix tea and rum together, and it is ready for use. It is drunk cold or warm, according to taste. When wanted warm, if made previously, set it on a moderate fire, in a tin or crockery kettle.

It keeps very well if carefully bottled and corked when cold.

Another way to make it is to mix the rum or brandy with the tea without burning it. It is warmed, used, and kept like the above. The quantity of water may be reduced or augmented, according to taste, and so also the sugar.

MINT.

Put four sprigs of mint into a quart of brandy, cork well, or cover air-tight if in a pot, and leave thus forty-eight hours; then strain through a cloth. Put half a pound of loaf sugar in a stewpan, with a pint of water, set it on the fire, and, at the first boiling, pour it into the quart of brandy; cover with a cloth, let it cool, and again strain the whole through a fine cloth. Bottle and cork carefully, and use when wanted.

A small liquor glass of it is very good against stomach-ache; it is also very good after having eaten something difficult of digestion.

CARAMEL.

Set on a slow fire a tin kettle with fine white sugar

in it, stir with a tin spoon and let boil gently till brown, and use where directed. It keeps very well.

CROUTONS.

Cut slices of the soft part of bread, either round, square, oblong, star-like shape, or any other fancy shape, and about one quarter of an inch in thickness. Have hot butter in a frying pan, on a sharp fire; place the slices of bread in it, turn over when fried on one side, and take off when both sides are of a fine color; drain them as dry as possible, and they are then ready for use.

CRUMBS AND EGGS FOR FRYING.

Have in a vessel eggs well beaten, with chopped parsley, salt, and pepper. Have in another vessel fine bread crumbs. Dip the fish, or whatever else you wish to fry, in the beaten eggs, and roll it over in bread crumbs, and lay it immediately in hot grease or oil.

BATTER FOR FRYING.

Put in a bowl two tablespoonfuls of flour, with one beaten egg, a tablespoonful of vinegar, salt, and pepper: mix well together; then add the quantity of milk necessary to make a paste thin enough to dip into it either fish, vegetables, or other objects, so that a thin coat only sticks to it.

GREASE FOR FRYING.

Take beef suet, the part around the kidneys, or any kind of fat, raw or cooked, and free of fibres, nerves, thin skin, or bones; chop it fine, add to it, if you have any, the fat skimmed off the top of meat soup; put it in a cast iron or crockery kettle. Set it on a moderate fire, boil gently for fifteen minutes, skim it well during the process; take from the fire, leave thus five minutes, and strain it;

after which, put it in pots, and keep them in a dry and cool place; cover the pots well every time you use some, but never cover them while the grease is warm. This grease is as good, if not better, than any other to fry fish, fritters, and other similar things, which require to be entirely covered with grease

LARD.

Never buy lard ready made if you can help it, but take hog's fat, the part enveloping the kidneys, or the part called hog's caul, or leaf lard, and chop it fine; put it in a cast iron or crockery kettle, with a bay leaf to every two pounds of fat; set on a moderate fire, and as soon as it begins to melt, take the melted part out with a ladle, and put it in a pot or vessel; be careful not to take some pieces of fat not melted yet. Continue that process till it is all melted. The dry or hard part that remains at the bottom of the kettle when done, is not good, and must be thrown away.

Lard made thus is as white as snow, and may be kept a long time.

BUTTERED PAPER.

Dip in lukewarm butter a piece of white paper of the size you want, and envelop the piece to broil or roast with it. Tie the paper around with fine white twine or coarse thread.

OILED PAPER.

The only difference between oiled and buttered paper is that you dip it in sweet oil instead of lukewarm butter.

DRIED PARSLEY, THYME, CELERY, SAGE, &c., FOR WINTER USE.

Hang in the shade, under a shed, or in a garret, and in a clean and dry place, some small bunches of parsley, celery, &c., the roots upward; leave them thus till perfectly dry, then place them in your spice box for winter use.

The best time for drying them is at the end of October or the beginning of November; dig them up in fine and dry weather, so as to have them clean without washing.

Soak in cold water half an hour before using.

FRIED PARSLEY.

Have grease enough in a pan, over a good fire, to cover the parsley entirely without pressing on it at all; when the grease is hot enough (see direction for frying), lay the sprigs of parsley in, and take them off with a skimmer when fried, which is done at once; drain and use.

WHITE PARSLEY.

Throw sprigs of parsley in boiling water, and a little salt; take it out with a skimmer almost immediately and drain it.

WHITE PEPPER.

Put peppercorns in a bowl, cover with cold water, and leave thus till the skin is tender; then drain. Take the skin off, let it dry, grind it; place with your other spices and use where directed. It takes many days for the skin to become tender.

TOASTS.

Cut slices of bread about one quarter of an inch in thickness, dry it before the fire, or in an oven; put in a dry place, and use when wanted.

BAVAROISE WITH CHOCOLATE.

Put in a tin pan a pint of milk, with one ounce of chocolate, and two of sugar; set it over the fire, but do not allow it to boil; stir well with a wooden spoon during the process, and when the whole is well mixed, serve warm in cups.

It is an excellent and wholesome drink in the evening.

The same with Coffee or Tea.—Proceed as above in every particular, except that you put in the pan a small cup of coffee or tea instead of chocolate, and a little more sugar.

BICHOF.

Put in a crockery tureen two bottles of white wine, with an orange and a lemon, both cut in slices; cover, and place it in a warm place for about ten hours; then strain into a vessel, and mix well with the liquor about a pound of loaf sugar, and a little grated cinnamon.

It may be served warm or cold.

Another way.—Melt a pound of loaf sugar in half a pint of cold water, and then mix with it two bottles of white wine, a pinch of grated cinnamon, the juice of an orange, and that of a lemon, and use.

It takes only a few minutes to make it.

If found too strong, add water and sugar.

TO PRESERVE BIRDS.

Broil or roast, according to our directions, chickens, ducks, geese, turkeys, partridges, pheasants, prairie hens, quails, &c.; then carve them; take the bones off the pieces, which you place in a crockery pot, and which you fill with melted butter or lard, and cover well when cold. Place it in a cool and dry place and it will keep for months.

When you wish to eat them, take out the quantity you want, and place it in a frying pan, with the butter or lard that is around; fry till warm, and serve.

INDIGESTION.

A cup of tea and chamomile, half of each, with a few drops of orange flower water, and the whole well sweetened, and taken warm, is very good after having eaten something difficult to digest.

Many cases of dyspepsia may be avoided by taking it after dinner.

PAP.

French babies eat nothing else till twelve or fifteen months old; after that, and till they are about three years of age, they eat every kind of soup, principally milk soup, and then they eat the same kind of food as their parents.

Pap is very easily made. Put a little butter in a pan over the fire; when melted, turn in it a thin batter of milk and flour; stir with a wooden spoon, and boil gently from ten to fifteen minutes, according to the quantity you make; then put it in a crockery vessel, add salt and sugar, and use.

An egg may be mixed in the batter, when the infant is over three months old.

PICKLED CUCUMBERS.

The small green ones are the best.

Clean them well in cold water with a brush. Put cold water in a vessel, with some gray salt in it; move to dissolve the salt, and soak the cucumbers in it for three days, after which take them out; put them in pots with small onions, a few cloves of garlic, peppercorns, gray salt, cloves, and a bunch tied with twine, composed of bay leaves, tarragon, and burnet; pour boiling vinegar on them, and enough to cover the whole; cover the pots air tight when perfectly cold.

Look at the cucumbers every two or three days for the first three weeks, and after that, only once in a while.

for, if you have not used good vinegar, it will turn white; in that case, throw away vinegar and spices, put new spices in, cover again with boiling vinegar, and cover when cold as before. If you have not left them too long in bad vinegar, they will be just as good after that second process.

The quantity of spices must depend upon the quantity of cucumbers.

BACON.

Never use smoked bacon or ham except when especially directed. The smoky taste would spoil every dish; follow the same rule with, old stale butter.

BREAD.

It is next to an impossibility to make good bread in a small family range or stove; four times out of five the bread is too much or not enough baked. Good baker's bread, besides saving a great deal of time and labor, is as cheap as you can make it at home.

BROTH.

Broth that has been used to warm meat in it, may be used for the same purpose another time, or for soup after having been strained.

CATSUPS AND PICKLES.

Beware of what is sold under the names of catsups and pickles; many cases of debility and consumption come from eating such stuff.

DIET. (*See also Breakfast and Supper.*)

Take a hearty but by no means heavy dinner.
Eat and drink moderately, under any circumstances.

See that everything you eat or drink is of a good quality and wholesome.

Eat slowly and masticate well, but do not bolt your food.

Drink slowly also, and taste before swallowing.

Vary your food as much as possible.

Have at least two dishes of vegetables, and one kind of fruit for dinner, besides meat.

FINES HERBES.

Parsley and cives chopped fine, and used for omelets, or with cold meat, sauces, &c., are called thus.

FISH.

Avoid the contact of fish with meat, or anything else in the shape of edibles, in the kitchen as well as in the service of the table.

GARLICS.

No one need be afraid of using garlics in cooking. When cooked they have nothing left of their bad odor when in a raw state, and really give a fine flavor to any thing they are cooked with. If we were in an age or country of ignorance and superstition, we would not speak of them, but here we will tell to all the incredulous, try garlics and judge them afterward.

MEAT.

Avoid washing meat as much as you can; i. e., never do it when you can wipe it clean.

SAVORY.

French cooks never use savory; they are of opinion that it destroys instead of improving the taste of dishes so think many gastronomers we have consulted.

e eschew savory in our **receipts**, all dishes prepared according to them will be savory dishes.

SOUPS.

To make good broth, and therefore good soup, you must have an even fire all the time; you spoil the soup by boiling it fast for some time, and then setting the soup kettle on the corner of the range where there is not enough heat.

SOUP PLATES

Must be warmed before putting them on the table, especially in winter.

STIRRING.

Never use any spoon but a wooden one to stir anything on the fire or in a warm state.

QUALITY OF MEAT, FISH, VEGETABLES, AND FRUIT.

The quality of meat depends entirely on the quality of food with which the animal has been fed.

For fish, the taste or quality is according to the kind of water in which they have lived; fish from a muddy pond smells of mud, while fish from a clear brook is delicious.

The same difference exists in vegetables and fruit; their quality is according to the quality or nature of the ground in which they have been grown.

Why is this book smaller than many other cook books, though it contains more receipts?

The reason is this: we could have written some forty or fifty pages of receipts for pies or *vol-au-vent*, but, since all pies are prepared in the same way, there is no necessity for doing it. With a receipt for a currant pie, you can prepare a blackberry pie; the only difference is that you use blackberries instead of currants, &c.

In fishes, a great many having the same kind of food are cooked alike, and do not require different or separate receipts.

Ducks and geese, ducklings and goslings, wild and tame, are cooked alike.

Partridges, pheasants, prairie hens, quails, &c., are also cooked alike, and it would be quite useless to make a separate receipt for each.

We are of opinion that the shortest and simplest way is as good and advantageous in cooking as in anything else.

To simplify a thing is to render it more easy to be understood; that has been our aim in writing this book

BAY LEAF.

The leaf of the sauce laurel tree; it is used in Italy instead of straw or hay for packing bottles of oil, &c., and is imported into this country with the oil; it is very cheap and gives a very good flavor to sauces, soups, &c.

SOUPS.

Soups are made with meat or vegetables, and grease or bacon.

Beef, mutton, veal and chicken are used to make soup or broth. The best pieces of beef to make soup or broth are the ribs, shin or knuckle, and loin; the bones make a fat broth, but not as nutritious as good lean meat. One pound of meat for three persons is enough.

Always use fresh meat; meat with a venison taste would spoil, if not entirely destroy the broth.

The proportion, to make good broth, is about five pints of water for three pounds of meat.

POT-AU-FEU.

Take six pounds of fresh beef (ribs, knuckle or loin), which put in a crockery kettle with five quarts of cold water, salt, and a little pepper, set on a slow fire; take the scum off carefully as soon as it comes to the surface; then add two white onions with one clove stuck in each, a small parsnip, a carrot, two middling sized turnips, half a head of celery, two leeks or four small ones, two sprigs of parsley, one of thyme, a clove of garlic, a bay leaf, and a little caramel to color it. Simmer five or six hours; dish the meat with the parsnips, turnips and leeks around, to be served warm after the soup, or kept for the next day. (See boiled beef.) Strain the broth, skim off the fat at the top, put back on a good fire, and at the first boiling, pour on croutons in the soup dish and serve. This broth may be kept till the next day, even in summer.

CONSOMMÉ.

Take a chicken, at least two years old, clean and prepare it as directed, place it on the spit before a good fire for about ten minutes, and take it off; put it in a crockery kettle, with about two pounds of beef, two quarts and a half of cold water, salt and a little pepper; set the kettle on a slow fire, and skim carefully; season with one white onion and one clove stuck in it, a piece of parsnip, same of carrot, a small turnip, two stalks of celery, a leak, a sprig of parsley, one of thyme, a clove of garlic, half a bay-leaf, and a little caramel to color it. Simmer gently from seven to eight hours, then strain the broth and serve it hot, either with or without croutons, according to taste.

BROTH FOR SAUCES.

When the sauces are to be kept a few days, or when you have no other broth, chop fine about half a pound of good fresh beef, which put in a stewpan with about one pint of water, a small white onion with a clove stuck in it, one clove of garlic, half a sprig of parsley, same of thyme, half a bay leaf, salt and pepper; set on a moderate fire, skim carefully, simmer till the meat is properly cooked, strain and use.

This broth may be kept eight days in winter, and four days in summer.

BROTH FOR SOUP POTAGE OR PURÉE.

Put in a crockery kettle two pounds of beef (ribs, knuckle or loin), three quarts of cold water, an old lean chicken, or an old duck, or half of a goose or turkey, or two partridges, prairie hens, or pheasants, either of them half roasted, also salt and pepper, set on a slow fire, skim it carefully; then add a white onion with a clove stuck in it; a piece of parsnip, a piece of carrot, a small turnip, a stalk of celery, a leek, half a sprig of parsley, same of thyme, a small clove of garlic, half a bay leaf, and a little caramel to color it. Simmer five or six hours, and finish and use as pot-au-feu.

Another.—Put two pounds of beef with nearly two quarts of water in a crockery kettle; add all the remains you may have from roasted pieces of beef, veal, mutton, fowls, or even game; add also two quarts of water for three pounds of remains; season, cook and serve as the preceding one.

BEEF AND MUTTON SOUP.

Take three pounds of beef (ribs, knuckle or loin), and two pounds of breast of mutton, put both pieces in a crockery kettle with four quarts of cold water, salt, and pepper, set on a slow fire; skim carefully, then add half a carrot, two turnips, one parsnip, two onions with one clove stuck in each, two stalks of celery, two leeks, one sprig of parsley, same of thyme, a bay leaf, and one clove of garlic. Simmer four or five hours; dish the meat with carrots, turnips, parsnips and leeks around, to be served after the soup if you choose; strain the broth, skim the fat off, put back on the fire and use at first boiling.

This broth is better in summer than if made with beef only.

BROTH MADE QUICKLY.

Cut about a pound of beef in small pieces, put it in a stewpan with half a pint of cold water, a piece of carrot, one onion, and a quarter of a pound of bacon, also cut in small pieces; set on the fire and simmer twenty minutes, then add a pint of boiling water, salt, and pepper; boil forty-five minutes, strain and use the broth. The meat is not very good.

RICE SOUP.

Soak the rice in lukewarm water, one tablespoonful for two persons; put it in a stewpan with half a pint of cold water for every two tablespoonfuls of rice; set on a moderate fire, stir gently with a wooden spoon till dry, then add as many pints of broth as you have tablespoonfuls of rice; simmer about two hours, stirring now and then, and serve.

Another.—Soak the rice in lukewarm water; put broth in a stewpan, set on a moderate fire, and when boiling, throw the rice in; subdue the fire, simmer till thoroughly cooked, stir now and then, and serve.

The quantities are the same as for the preceding one.

POTAGES.

Potage with Beans, or à la Condé.—Take half a pint of kidney beans, soak them in lukewarm water, put them in a stewpan with three small onions, cover with three pints of water, set on the fire, and when thoroughly cooked, throw away the onions, mash and strain the beans, then put them back in the stewpan with the water in which they were cooked, set again on the fire, add butter, salt, pepper, and a little chopped parsley; boil a few minutes, pour on croutons in the soup dish, and serve.

Potage with Carrots, or à la Crécy.—Peel, wash, cut in pieces and put in a stewpan, half a pint of carrots, two middling sized onions with a clove stuck in each, a leek, two ounces of butter, and a teaspoonful of sugar, wet with a quart of broth; set on the fire, and when well cooked throw away the onions and leek; then mash and strain the carrots, put them back on the fire, add salt, pepper, and a little chopped parsley; simmer gently about fifteen minutes, during which time skim it if necessary; pour on croutons in the soup dish, and serve.

Another, with Carrots, Celery, and Potatoes.—Peel, wash, cut in pieces and put in a stewpan, half a pint of carrots, two heads of celery, and a quarter of a pint of potatoes, also two sprigs of parsley, one leek, salt, and pepper; add also, but do not cut them, a bay leaf, two middling sized onions with a clove stuck in each; cover with boiling water, set on the fire, and leave till well cooked; when, take from the fire, throw away bay leaf and onions, mash and strain the remainder, put it back in the stewpan with three ounces of butter; should it be found too thick, add a little boiling water, set on the fire again, simmer five minutes, and serve as it is or with croutons.

Potage with Celery.—Clean, wash, drain and cut in small pieces about half a pint of soup celery; throw it in boiling water with a little salt, boil three minutes and drain, then mash as well as possible, strain and put back in the stewpan, cover with a quart of cold water, add two ounces of butter, a pinch of grated nutmeg, salt, pepper, and a little chopped parsley; boil gently half an hour, pour on croutons in the soup dish and serve.

Potage with Chestnuts.—Cook in boiling water a quart of chestnuts, then shell them, mash and wet them with warm broth so as to make a thin paste, put them in a crockery kettle, cover with broth, simmer about one hour, add two tablespoonfuls of fine white sugar; simmer five minutes longer, stirring with a wooden spoon the while; pour on croutons and serve.

Potage with Frogs.—Take the hind legs of fifty well-skinned green frogs, put them in cold water and a little salt for half an hour—drain them; then put them in a crockery kettle, with a leek, half a carrot, two stalks of celery, a middling sized parsnip, a turnip, two onions, one clove of garlic, two ounces of fat bacon, a little salt, and white pepper; cover the whole well with cold water, set on the fire, simmer gently about four hours; strain, pour on croutons and serve.

These **hind legs of frogs** are taken from the strainer, and **placed** on a dish and served at breakfast the next day, with a white sauce, or **in a** fricassee, as a chicken.

Potage with Lettuce.—Clean, wash, and drain dry two heads of cabbage lettuce, throw them in boiling water and a little salt for two minutes, take off and drain; then tie them with thread or twine, put them in a stewpan, cover with broth, set on the fire, and simmer gently till well cooked; then pour the broth on croutons, place the heads of lettuce at the top and serve.

Potage with Macaroni.—Put three pints of broth in an earthen kettle, and set it on a good fire; at the first boiling put some macaroni, in with a little salt and white pepper; boil gently till cooked, stirring now and then with a wooden spoon, and serve.

If liked, very dry cheese might be grated and put in the kettle a few minutes before taking from the fire. This adding of cheese is an Italian fashion.

Potage à la Monaco.—Roast till they have a pale yellow color, thin slices of bread with sugar sprinkled on; put them in a crockery vessel, pour boiling milk on, enough to cover them entirely; have ready to pour on them also, and immediately after, two yolks of eggs well beaten with lukewarm water for every quart of milk, and serve.

Potage Printanier.—Chop fine twelve leaves of sorrel, six sprigs of chervil, a cabbage lettuce, two leeks, a middling sized parsnip, a like carrot, one turnip, a head of soup celery, two onions, a tablespoonful of green beans, same of green peas, same of tops of asparagus, and half a dozen small spring radishes; throw the whole in boiling water and a little salt for one minute; drain, put in a stewpan with four ounces of butter, salt, and pepper, set on the fire, stir now and then till about half cooked, when, cover with broth, simmer till well cooked and serve.

Potage with Pumpkins.—Peel, take away the seed and cut the pumpkin in small pieces; put them in a stewpan with water just enough to cover them, a little salt and white pepper, set on the fire and take off when cooked; throw away the water, mash and strain the pumpkin, put it back in the stewpan, cover with milk, add a little sugar, set it again on the fire, and take off at the first boiling; pour a little of it on croutons in the soup dish, and keep covered in a warm place for ten minutes; then pour also the remainder in, and serve.

Another.—Prepare as above, throw the pieces in boiling water with a little salt for five minutes, mash and drain; put butter in a stewpan, set it on the fire; when melted put the pumpkin in, stir about five minutes; have ready in your soup dish some slices of bread fried in butter, and dusted with sugar, pour on them some boiling milk, keep covered in a warm place two or three minutes; then turn the pumpkin on, at the same time mixing the whole gently, and serve.

Potage with Rice.—Soak half a pint of rice in lukewarm water, put it in a stewpan with two quarts of cold water, salt, pepper, and a little chopped parsley; set it on the fire, boil till cooked, stirring now and then, and take from the fire; melt two ounces of butter in, stirring the whole; then mix well with the whole two well beaten yolks of eggs, and serve.

Another.—Soak half a pint of rice in lukewarm water, put it in a stewpan, with a pint of milk and a tablespoonful of sugar; set it on the fire, stir till nearly dry; then add two quarts of milk, simmer gently two hours, and serve.

Potage with Semoulina.—Put in a stewpan a quart of broth; when boiling, sprinkle semoulina in it, little by little, stirring with a wooden spoon; stop when it begins to thicken, add salt and a little white pepper; take from the fire after twelve minutes' boiling, and serve.

Potage with Fecula.—Proceed as for semoulina in every particular, except that you leave it on the fire only ten minutes, and serve.

Potage with Sago.—Proceed as for semoulina in every particular, except that you leave it on the fire about one hour, and serve. Being coarser, it takes a longer time to cook.

Potage with Tapioca.—Proceed as for semoulina in every particular, except that you leave it on the fire about forty-five minutes, and serve.

All other Italian pastes are prepared in the same way.

The same with Milk.—Semoulina, fecula, sago, tapioca, &c., may also be prepared with milk, instead of broth, and sugar instead of salt and pepper, and proceed as with broth in every other particular.

Potage with Sorrel and Potatoes.—Wash, drain dry, and chop fine a handful of sorrel, which put in a stewpan with four ounces of butter and a little salt; when cooked add a pint of potatoes cut in small pieces, also pepper, a teaspoonful of chopped parsley, and a leek; cover with warm water, boil gently till cooked, then strain; pour on two or three croutons and serve.

Potage with Tomatoes.—Soak in water, wipe dry with a towel, and throw in boiling water about a quart of tomatoes, add a little salt, and leave thus till cooked; it takes about fifteen minutes; then take from the fire, drain and mash the tomatoes, and strain them into a stewpan, in which you have previously melted four ounces of butter; do it as soon as the butter is well melted; add also, immediately, a teaspoonful of chopped parsley, a bay leaf, and a little pepper, cover with warm broth; boil five minutes, take the bay leaf out, pour on croutons, and serve.

Potage with Vermicelli.—Put a quart of broth in a crockery kettle, set it on the fire, and as soon as it boils put in it, little by little, and breaking it at the same time, two handfuls of vermicelli; keep stirring with a wooden spoon, add salt and white pepper; boil gently about half an hour, take from the fire and mix in it two well beaten yolks of eggs, turn in the soup dish, and serve.

The same with Milk.—Put about three pints of milk in a crockery kettle, set it on the fire, and as soon as it begins to rise, put in it, little by little, and breaking it at the same time, two handfuls of vermicelli, stirring the while; add two tablespoonfuls of sugar, simmer gently about forty minutes; take from the fire, mix in it two yolks of eggs, well beaten, turn in the soup dish and serve.

Prepare and serve any other similar paste in the same way.

Potage Purée with Dry Beans, Lentils, or Peas.—Soak in lukewarm water a quart of dry beans, lentils, or peas, drain and put them in a crockery kettle, with two leeks, half a head of celery, two middling sized onions, one carrot, two cloves, salt, and pepper, half a pound of bacon, or four ounces of butter; cover entirely with cold broth, set on the fire and boil gently till the whole is well cooked; then take from the fire, throw away the cloves, put the bacon aside, mash the beans and seasonings, strain them, and put back in the kettle with the broth in which they have been cooked; in case there should not be enough to cover the whole, add a little to it, set again on the fire, stir, give one boil, pour on croutons and serve.

Potage Purée with Green Beans, Lentils, Peas, or any

other green vegetables.—Put two quarts of broth in a stewpan, set it on the fire, and at the first boiling, throw in it a quart of green beans, peas, &c.; add the same seasonings as in the preceding one, and cook and serve also in the same way.

For a potage purée with carrots, parsnips, potatoes, turnips, &c., proceed as directed in the preceding receipt, except that you cut in small pieces carrots, parsnips, &c.

JULIENNE.

Chop fine a dozen leaves of sorrel, four or five sprigs of chervil, half a head of cabbage lettuce; peel and cut in small fillets, as square as possible, not over an inch long, and an eighth of an inch thick, two leeks, two parsnips, one carrot, one turnip, a head of soup celery, and two middling sized onions, and, if handy, a gill of green peas or beans, salt and pepper. Put the whole in a stewpan, in which you have previously put two ounces of butter, set on the fire, stir now and then till half cooked, then cover with broth, simmer till well cooked, and serve.

Some purée may be mixed with it just before serving.

Another way.—When the Julienne is ready to be served drain it, mash all the vegetables well, then mix them with the broth in which they have been cooked, and strain the whole in a stewpan; set on the fire again, pour on croutons at the first boiling, and serve.

Another, with Rice.—When the Julienne is ready to be served, drain it, to separate the broth from the vegetables; put the broth back in the stewpan; soak in lukewarm water two or three tablespoonfuls of rice, put it in the pan and add about a pint of broth, boil gently till cooked; stir now and then; then put also back in the pan all the cooked vegetables, give one boil only, and serve.

Another, with Eggs.—When the Julienne is ready to

be served, poach in it as many eggs as there are persons at table, and serve. One egg is thus served to each person, with the soup.

CABBAGE SOUP.

Put in a kettle with two quarts and a half of water a pound of salted pork, same of breast of mutton; also, if handy, the remains of a roasted piece; set on a slow fire, skim before it boils, and then boil for about an hour and a half; strain, to remove the small bones, if any; put back in the kettle broth and meat, also one middling sized cabbage, which you must have previously thrown in boiling water, and boiled ten minutes; add then, two carrots, one turnip, two leeks, half a head of celery, one onion, with a clove stuck in it, a little salt and pepper, and about half a pound of sausage (not smoked); then boil gently about two hours, strain the broth, pour it on croutons in the soup dish, and serve.

The pork, mutton, and sausage, with the cabbage around, may be served on a dish after the soup at a family dinner, or kept for breakfast the next day.

CAULIFLOWER SOUP.

Clean and cut in small pieces three middling sized cauliflowers. Put in a stewpan two ounces of butter, and set it on a moderate fire; when hot put the cauliflowers in; stir now and then till it turns brown, then add a sprig of thyme, same of parsley, a bay leaf, one onion with a clove stuck in it, salt and white pepper; simmer gently till the whole is well cooked, throw away the onion, clove, thyme, and bay leaf; mash well the cauliflowers, strain and put back on the fire with the broth; give one boil, pour on croutons, and serve.

SOUP WITH CHEESE.

Put four ounces of butter in a soup kettle, with an

onion chopped fine; set on a brisk fire, stir now and then till it has a yellow color, then sprinkle on it half a tablespoonful of flour, keep stirring till it turns brown; then add two quarts of water, salt, and pepper; boil about five minutes. Have prepared in the soup dish the following: a thin layer of grated cheese (Gruyère or Parmesan), on it a layer of thin slices of bread, then another of cheese, and again another of bread, &c., three or four of each; strain and pour your broth on the whole; keep in a warm place five minutes, and serve.

MILK SOUP.

Put the quantity of milk you want in a tin kettle, and set it on a good fire (a quart for three persons), when on the point of boiling, sugar it according to taste, and at the first boiling pour it on roasted bread, and serve.

Another.—Put in a tin kettle the milk you want, with four beaten eggs to every quart of milk; set the kettle on a slow fire, simmer gently, and keep it stirred with a wooden spoon till it adheres to the spoon; then pour it on fried croutons in the soup dish; set it in a warm place for ten minutes, and serve.

MOCK-TURTLE SOUP.

Throw a piece of calf's head (upper part) in boiling water for five minutes, drain it; place it in a crockery pot with cold water, salt, and white pepper, and set it on the fire; take it off when half cooked, cut it in dice, then put it back on the fire in a stewpan, with two sprigs of thyme, a bay leaf, a pinch of grated nutmeg, three onions with a clove stuck in each, butter, and a quarter of a pound of lean ham (not smoked), and cut in dice; when the whole has taken a yellow color, take from the fire, then make a sauce by putting butter in a pan on the fire; when the butter is melted, add a little flour, gradually, stirring all the time till brown; then put the whole in a crockery pot, cover with cold water, add two sprigs of parsley, boil about two hours and a half, when your broth must be rather thick; strain it; add, if you like it, a little of **lemon juice, half a wine** glass of Madeira wine, also Cayenne pepper, salt, and two yolks of eggs boiled hard; serve warm in bowls.

The whole is **served except thyme,** bay leaf, parsley and onions.

ONION SOUP.

Peel, cut in slices and again crosswise, so as to make square pieces, a dozen small **onions;** throw them in boiling **water for five** minutes, drain, put them in a stewpan with butter, salt and pepper, cover with broth; let simmer till well cooked, pour on croutons, and serve.

The same with Milk.—Proceed as in the preceding one in every particular, except that you cover with milk instead of broth, and add sugar to your taste.

The same with Rice.—Prepare the onions and cook them in broth, as above; then soak rice in lukewarm water, put it with the onions, boil gently two hours, and serve as above, with or without croutons.

The same with Vermicelli.—Proceed as with rice in every particular, except that you boil only twenty-five minutes after having put the vermicelli in the pan.

OX TAIL SOUP.

Cut one or two ox tails in small pieces, or at every other joint; put in a crockery stewpan two ounces of butter for each tail. When the butter is melted, put the tail or tails in, and let the pieces take a yellow color, when, cover with about three pints of water for each tail, season with four sprigs of parsley, one of thyme, a bay leaf, a small carrot, a turnip, four small onions, a leek, two stalks of celery, a clove of garlic, two cloves, salt and pepper; set on a slow fire for twenty minutes, then augment the fire, and when on the point of boiling, skim carefully; boil gently till well cooked, which you will know by seeing that the meat comes off the bones; then strain the broth, pour it on croutons and serve.

The meat is good, and may be served with the carrot, turnip and leek, and a little green parsley or horse radish, or both, after the soup. It may also be kept for breakfast the next day.

HERB BROTH.

Wash, drain and chop fine a handful of sorrel, a dozen sprigs of chervil and half a head of lettuce; put an ounce of butter in a stewpan, set it on a good fire; when melted, put the sorrel, chervil and lettuce in, add salt and pepper and cook well, then cover with lukewarm water; boil three minutes, beat well three yolks of eggs, take from the fire and put the eggs in while stirring; pour immediately on croutons, and serve.

CHICKEN BROTH FOR THE SICK OR INVALID.

Put a rather lean chicken in a crockery pan with three pints of cold water, set it on a moderate fire, add half a head of lettuce, a leek, a stalk of celery, four sorrel leaves, four sprigs of chervil, and salt; skim before boiling; let boil gently about an hour, and strain; serve on toasted slices of bread, or according to the physician's prescription.

The chicken may be served cold the next day with an oil sauce.

VEAL BROTH, ALSO FOR THE SICK OR INVALID.

Put one pound of fillet or knuckle of veal in a crockery pan with three pints of cold water, set on a moderate fire, add half a head of lettuce, a leek, a stalk of celery, four sorrel leaves, four sprigs of chervil and some salt; skim before boiling; let boil gently about an hour, strain and serve either as it is or with slices of toasted bread.

PANADO.

Put in a stewpan about one pound of good wheat bread, the soft part only, cover with cold water, add one ounce of butter, salt and pepper; let simmer about an hour, stir now and then, and strain. Beat three yolks of eggs with cream in a bowl and put it in a warm place, but not on the fire, as it must not boil; let it remain thus five or six minutes, when, pour the eggs over the bread in the stewpan, stirring and mixing the whole well with a wooden spoon; take from the fire and serve.

LAIT DE POULE. (*To soothe cold or sore throat.*)

Beat one or two yolks of eggs with about a teaspoonful of fine white sugar, then pour on slowly, and stirring at the same time, half a glass of warm water for one yolk of egg, add a few drops of rose or orange water, according to taste, and drink warm.

This is very good to take just before going to bed, for a person having a sore throat or a cold; it cannot do any harm to a person in good health, and it is sufficient for the supper of a person of difficult digestion.

TURTLE BROTH.

Cut the turtle in dice, throw it in boiling water for two or three minutes, and drain; put it in a stewpan with onions and ham, also cut in dice; season with thyme, parsley, bay leaf, salt, pepper, and a wine glass of Madeira wine or of good brandy; wet with Espagnole sauce or with consommé, set on a good fire, boil about half an hour. Ten minutes before taking from the fire, chop the eggs of the turtle, after having boiled them, and put them in a stewpan; if the turtle has none, chop and use hard boiled eggs instead. When done, throw away parsley, thyme, and bay leaf, turn in bowls, add a little chopped chervil, and a quarter of a rind of lemon, also chopped; the latter is enough for six persons. Serve warm.

It may be strained before putting it in bowls, according to taste.

Turtle steaks are prepared like beefsteaks.

SAUCES.

HOW TO MAKE A SAUCE THICKER WHEN IT IS TOO THIN.

Take two fresh eggs, break them gently, and separate the white part from the yolk; be careful to have the yolk free from any white (there is in every yolk a little white spot which you cannot detach without using a fork, knife, or spoon); mix well the two yolks with two or three tablespoonfuls of the sauce that is too thin, and a piece of butter the size of a pigeon's egg; then take the sauce from the fire, pour the mixture in it, little by little, stirring all the time; when the whole is in, put back on the fire for three or four minutes, but do not allow it to boil; take away and use.

ALLEMANDE.

Chop fine and fry in butter four or five mushrooms; then add four or five tablespoonfuls of broth, reduce it to a sauce; put a piece of butter the size of an egg in it, also a sprig of white parsley chopped fine, one of thyme, a clove, a bay leaf, a clove of garlic, a little nutmeg grated fine, the juice of a quarter of a lemon, and three well beaten yolks of eggs; boil two or three minutes and use. If found too thick, add a little broth.

ANCHOVY.

Take out the bones from a dozen of anchovies, saving

the juice; put the juice and flesh in a stewpan, with half a pint of water, set on the fire and simmer till melted; take off, pass through a hair sieve, and use.

This sauce may be preserved, in a bottle well corked and in a cool place, for five or six weeks in winter and two or three in summer.

ANCHOVY BUTTER.

Take out the bones from six anchovies, wash the flesh well, put in a mortar, pound as fine as possible, then strain through a hair sieve; after which work well with the same quantity of butter, in order to make a paste very much resembling ordinary butter.

BREAD.

To make this sauce take the soft part of a two-pound wheat loaf, crumble it into a stewpan, cover with milk, set on a moderate fire and let it simmer about an hour; then strain into a stewpan, add salt, pepper, and a dozen of pepper corns; boil two or three minutes, take from the fire, add also butter of the size of an egg, stir a little, and use after it is strained.

BÉCHAMEL—No. 1.

Take a piece of bacon of about four ounces (not smoked), with the same quantity of veal fat, a small carrot, one turnip, and two onions; cut the whole in dice, put it in a stewpan, set on the fire, and when nearly done, cover with broth; add a piece of nutmeg, two cloves, a sprig of thyme, and one of parsley, salt, white pepper, and a bay leaf; boil about an hour and take from the fire; throw a few drops of cold water in and the fat will separate from the rest, skim it off, and strain the rest through a sieve. Put in another pan a piece of butter the size of a duck's egg, set it on the fire and let it melt; then mix with it two tablespoonfuls of flour, little by little, stirring continually; when turning brown, pour it in the broth you have strained, boil the whole about five minutes, and use.

Double or triple the quantities according to your wants.

This sauce will keep a few days.

BÉCHAMEL—No. 2.

Set a stewpan on the fire, with four ounces of good fresh butter, a little salt, and white pepper; when melted, pour in it gently half a pint of good warm milk; then sprinkle in it a tablespoonful of flour, little by little, stirring the while; do not let it boil, but keep it on a moderate fire till well mixed, and it is ready for use.

BROWN BUTTER.

Put about six ounces of butter in a pan, set it on the fire and leave it till it begins to blacken; throw in it three or four sprigs of parsley, and fry two or three minutes. Have at the same time in another pan, on the fire, half a glass of vinegar, which must be warm but not boiled; use both butter and vinegar at the same time, i. e., as soon as you have poured your butter and parsley on your fish, or anything else, pour your vinegar, and serve.

BUTTER MAÎTRE D'HÔTEL.

Chop fine five or six sprigs of parsley, and two of tarragon; knead them well with about half a pound of fresh butter; then mix well with a little salt, pepper, and a few drops of lemon juice, and use. It will keep a few days, if kept in a cool place or on ice.

CAPER SAUCE.

Set a stewpan on the fire with a quarter of a pound of good fresh butter in it, also salt and white pepper; when the butter is melted, add a glass of warm broth (or warm water if more handy), a tablespoonful of flour, little by little, and stirring the whole; do not let it boil, but keep on a moderate fire till well mixed. Have prepared and mixed together two teaspoonfuls of pounded capers, the yolk of an egg, and a teaspoonful of vinegar, which you mix with the sauce as soon as taken from the fire, and it is ready for use.

COULIS OF FISH.

Boil hard four eggs, and put the yolks in a mortar. Take a pike weighing about two pounds, clean, prepare, and broil it as directed; split it open, take all the bones and skin off, put the flesh in the mortar with the yolks, and pound the whole and knead it with a little butter. Place a piece of butter, of the size of a walnut, in a stewpan, and set it on a good fire; when melted, fry in it till of a golden color, two carrots and two onions cut in slices; after that add also a piece of bay leaf, two sprigs of parsley, one of thyme, a little of isinglass, the eggs and fish, and cover with water; simmer gently about one hour and a half, and strain.

If found too thin after it is strained, set it back on the fire, add a little more isinglass, and simmer fifteen minutes longer.

COULIS OF VEAL.

Place in a stewpan about one pound of veal, fillet or knuckle, with four ounces of bacon, not smoked, and cut fine; also a carrot cut fine, a little pepper, and grated nutmeg; set on a slow fire, cover well; half an hour after augment the fire, and as soon as you see the meat sticking to the pan, subdue it, leave it so ten minutes, then take from the fire, put the bacon, veal and carrot on a dish; put butter about the size of an egg in your stewpan; when melted, sprinkle in it a teaspoonful of flour, stir with a wooden spoon, then put the meat back in, cover with warm broth, and put on a slow fire for about two hours; take away, throw in it a few drops of cold water, skim the fat off, strain, and use.

COULIS OF LOBSTER OR SHRIMPS.

Put the lobster in a kettle (a lobster must be alive or else it is not good); cover well with cold or warm water, set on a good fire, take off when cooked, break the joints a little to let the water out; then take the flesh, mash it well, drain; mix well with two tablespoonfuls of broth, and one of Espagnole sauce; put an ounce of butter in a stewpan, set it on the fire, and when melted, mix the whole together; add a little grated nutmeg and pepper, leave on the fire about five minutes longer, and use.

Follow the same process for coulis of shrimps.

CREAM.

Set a stewpan on the fire with a piece of butter the size of a duck's egg in it, also one teaspoonful of shallots, and one of parsley, both chopped fine, two peppercorns, salt, a little grated nutmeg, and about half a glass of cream, or a glass of very good milk; leave about fifteen minutes, stirring the while, and then use.

CURRANT.

Soak in water, drain and let dry a pint of currants, just as they begin to ripen, throw them in boiling water with a little salt, and cook them—drain; and when cold, put them in an earthen pot, cover with broth, set on a gentle fire, mix with it a little fecula and essence of spinage;

as soon as warm take from the fire, and use where directed.

ESPAGNOLE.

Spread about half a pound of butter in the bottom of a stewpan, lay in it lean ham and veal, partridge, wild rabbit, pheasant or fowl of any kind, about four ounces of each, a small carrot cut in dice, one onion with a clove stuck in it, half a turnip, and a sprig of thyme; cover the pan and set it on the fire; let it simmer till reduced to a jelly, then mix in it two tablespoonfuls of flour, a wine glass of white wine, cover with broth, add salt, pepper, a clove of garlic, a sprig of parsley, one clove, a bay leaf, and two mushrooms cut in pieces; simmer from three to four hours, skim off the scum as soon as it comes on the surface; when done, take it from the fire, throw a few drops of cold water in, and skim off the fat, then strain and use.

It will keep for some time if kept air-tight in a pot or bottle, and in a cool dry place.

ESSENCE OF SPINAGE OR GREEN ESSENCE.

Soak in water, drain, dry and pound well two or three handfuls of spinage, put them in a coarse towel and press the juice out, put it in a pan on a moderate fire, and when nearly boiling, take it off, strain, and add to it a little fine crushed sugar, stir a little, and bottle when cold; it may be kept for months; use it where directed.

CUCUMBER.

Chop fine a handful of parsley and cives, put them in a stewpan with a piece of butter the size of an egg; when half fried, add half a teaspoonful of flour, little by little, keep stirring with a wooden spoon, and when it begins to become thick, add also four or five pickled cucumbers chopped fine, salt, and pepper, cover with broth, let simmer till done, and use.

FISH.

Boil hard two eggs, take the yolks and pound them well, and place them in a bowl. Have boiling water on the fire, and put in it cives, burnet, chervil, tarragon and parsley, four or five sprigs of each; boil five minutes, take off, drain and pound them well, then strain them on the eggs, add two tablespoonfuls of cider vinegar, two of French mustard, salt, pepper, and four tablespoonfuls of sweet oil, which you pour in, little by little, at the same time mixing the whole well with a boxwood spoon, and it is ready for use.

HAZELNUT BUTTER.

Chop very fine two teaspoonfuls of cives, parsley, and tarragon, work them well with the same quantity of butter; then shell half a dozen of good hazelnuts, pound them, and work again the whole into a paste, and use.

INDIAN.

Have a stewpan on a moderate fire, with two ounces of butter in it; when melted, add a teaspoonful of pimento, salt, a pinch of saffron, and one of grated nutmeg, also one and a half tablespoonful of flour—the latter you sprinkle in, little by little, stirring the while; cover with broth, boil twelve minutes and strain; afterward add two ounces of butter, stir a little, and use.

ITALIAN.

Tie together two sprigs of parsley, one of thyme, and a bay leaf; put them in a stewpan with two or three mushrooms cut fine, one shallot, a small onion and a clove stuck in it, a piece of butter the size of a walnut, and half a pint of white wine; set on a gentle fire, and reduce it half then add about one tablespoonful of olive oil, and half a pint of broth, simmer forty minutes, strain, and use.

JUICE.

Butter the bottom of a stewpan with about a quarter of a pound of butter; put on it a layer of thin slices of onions, then four ounces of beef suet cut fine, as much of bacon not smoked, the same quantity of ham also cut in thin slices, one carrot cut fine, a clove of garlic, a sprig of parsley, a bay leaf, salt, pepper, a clove, two or three mushrooms cut fine, wet with a glass of water, cover and set it on a sharp fire; as soon as it begins to stick to the bottom of the pan, subdue the fire, leave it till turning brown, then add about a glass of warm water, skim it off, take from the fire, throw a few drops of cold water in and skim off the fat; put back on the fire, and add warm water enough to make a sauce; simmer till done and of a proper thickness, strain, and use.

Another way is to put half a pound of butter instead of beef suet and bacon (if more handy.)

MAITRE D'HÔTEL.

Chop fine a teaspoonful of parsley, and half that quantity of cives or green onions, a little grated nutmeg, salt, and pepper, knead well the whole with four ounces of fresh butter, mix with it a teaspoonful of cider vinegar, and the juice of half a lemon, and use.

If you like it warm, when you have kneaded it with butter, add a quarter of a pint of water, and set on a slow fire for about ten minutes, sprinkle in it half a teaspoonful of flour, stirring the while; take from the fire, mix in it the juice of a lemon, and serve.

MARINADE, OR SAUCE THAT CAN BE USED INSTEAD OF CATSUP.

Put in a stewpan a piece of butter the size of an egg, set it on the fire, and when melted, fry in it till of a brownish color, one tablespoonful of onions cut in slices, and the same quantity of carrots also cut in slices; then add two sprigs of parsley, and one of sweet basil, one of thyme, a bay leaf, three peppercorns, salt, half a pint of water, and a gill of cider vinegar; simmer till well cooked, strain and bottle when cool, cork well, put in a cool dry place, and use when wanted. It may be kept for months.

MAYONNAISE.

Put one or two yolks of eggs in a bowl, half a teaspoonful of vinegar, salt and pepper, mix the whole well with a boxwood spoon, pour a tablespoonful of olive oil in it, drop by drop, stirring the while, and when the sauce is thick, add a tablespoonful of vinegar; it takes fifteen minutes to make a Mayonnaise sauce, but when carefully made it is one of the best sauces ever used; a brisk stirring must be kept up, from beginning to end. In warm weather, it is necessary to put the bowl on ice while making it.

OIL.

Chop fine a shallot, half a teaspoonful of chervil and cives, or green onion, and half a clove of garlic (this latter if it suits you); put the whole in a saucer, with salt, pepper, and mustard; mix the whole with two tablespoonfuls of vinegar, then pour four or five tablespoonfuls of olive oil in it, little by little, stirring the while, and it is ready for use.

OYSTER.

Open two dozen of oysters and save the water, then throw oysters and water in boiling water; boil about three minutes, take off and drain; then mix the oysters with a white sauce and the juice of a lemon, and use.

PIQUANTE.

Take a bay leaf, a sprig of thyme, a clove of garlic,

one shallot, a peppercorn, about one glass of vinegar, salt, and pepper, and place them in a pan, set it on the fire, and reduce about two thirds; then add a glass of broth, stir and strain, mix then with a little of Roux, and use. You may also add two pickled cucumbers cut in slices.

POIVRADE.

Put a piece of butter the size of an egg in a stewpan, and set it on the fire; when melted, sprinkle in it, little by little, about a tablespoonful of flour, stirring the while; when of a proper thickness, and of a brownish color, take from the fire, add a tablespoonful of vinegar, a wine glass of claret wine, a glass of broth, a shallot cut in two, a middling sized onion also cut in two, with a clove stuck in each piece, a sprig of thyme, one of parsley, a bay leaf, a clove of garlic, a little salt, and two peppercorns; boil about twenty minutes, strain and use.

POULETTE.

Set a stewpan on the fire with a piece of butter the size of an egg in it; when melted, sprinkle in it a tablespoonful of flour, stirring the while; pour gently in it also, and little by little, a glass of warm water, and a wine glass of white wine, salt, pepper, a sprig of parsley, one of thyme, a bay leaf, a chopped shallot, a little nutmeg, four small white onions, and two or three mushrooms (the latter cut fine and fried in butter before using them); simmer till the whole is well cooked, strain and use.

In case it should be found too light, add when done and before taking from the fire, two or three yolks of eggs, and the juice of a lemon.

PROVENÇALE.

Chop fine two or three mushrooms, and two shallots;

put the whole in a stewpan with a clove of garlic, and two tablespoonfuls of olive oil; set on a moderate fire, and leave till half fried; then sprinkle in it half a teaspoonful of flour, stirring the while; add also half a pint of white wine, and as much broth, and two small onions, two sprigs of parsley, one of thyme, half a bay leaf, salt, and pepper; simmer about half an hour, take from the fire, and a few minutes after skim off the fat; take out garlic, onions, parsley, thyme, bay leaf, and it is then ready for immediate use.

RAVIGOTE.

Chop fine, and in equal proportion, two tablespoonfuls of chervil, tarragon, and peppergrass, also, in equal proportion, one teaspoonful of burnet and table celery; place the whole in a stewpan with salt and pepper, cover with broth, set on the fire, and boil twenty minutes; after which take from the fire, and strain. Mix two ounces of butter with flour enough to make a paste, put it with the sauce on the fire, add a tablespoonful of cider vinegar; simmer till of a proper thickness, and use.

ROBERT.

Put about four ounces of butter in a stewpan, set it on a moderate fire; when melted, sprinkle in it about a tablespoonful of flour, stirring the while; when of a brownish color, add three small onions chopped fine, salt and pepper; stir, and leave on the fire till the whole is turning brown, then add a glass of broth, boil about thirty minutes, and strain; mix well in a cup one teaspoonful of vinegar, and one of mustard, which mix again with the sauce, and it is ready to be used.

ROUX.

Set a stewpan on a moderate fire with a piece of butter the size of an egg in it; when melted, sprinkle in it little by little, about a tablespoonful of flour, stirring the while; when of a proper thickness, and of a brownish color, take from the fire, and use where directed.

SUPRÊME.

Make an Allemande sauce, and when done add two ounces of butter, and two tablespoonfuls of broth; set it on a brisk fire to start it boiling at once; take it from the fire as soon as it becomes thick, add then a few drops of lemon juice, and use.

TARTAR OR COLD.

Chop fine three shallots, also about half that quantity of chervil and tarragon, which put in a crockery tureen, with half a teaspoonful of mustard, salt, and pepper, also two or three teaspoonfuls of cider vinegar; pour in, little by little, about two tablespoonfuls of olive oil, stirring the while, and it is done. In case it should become too thick, while stirring, add a little vinegar.

TOMATO.

Take twelve middling sized tomatoes, cut each in two or four pieces, and take out the seeds. Put them in a stewpan with two ounces of butter, a clove of garlic, half a bay leaf, salt, two peppercorns, a sprig of thyme, one of parsley, and an onion; cover with two glasses of broth, set on the fire, keep stirring till cooked, and strain; then put again two ounces of butter in your stewpan; when melted, sprinkle in it a tablespoonful of flour, stirring the while, then pour in, little by little, your tomato juice, and as soon as well mixed, take from the fire, and it is ready for use.

TRUFFLE.

Chop fine one large or two middling sized truffles, two

or three mushrooms, and a sprig of parsley; put them in a stewpan with a piece of butter the size of a walnut; set on the fire for about ten minutes, then add salt, pepper, half a pint of white wine, and as much of broth; keep on a moderate fire till the whole is well cooked, then take from it, sprinkle in it a few drops of cold water, skim off the fat, and use.

WHITE.

Put in a stewpan about a quarter of a pound of good fresh butter, set it on the fire, with a little white pepper, and salt; when melted, add a glass of warm broth, or warm water if more handy; then sprinkle in it a tablespoonful of flour, little by little, stirring the while; do not let it boil, but keep on a moderate fire till well mixed. Have prepared and mixed together the juice of half a lemon, the yolk of an egg, and a teaspoonful of vinegar, which you mix with the sauce as soon as you take it from the fire, and it is ready for use.

3*

FARCES AND GARNITURES.

BREAD FARCE.

Put in a tureen about a pound of the soft part of bread, and cover with broth; when it has absorbed the broth, place it in a stewpan, set it on a slow fire, and leave till it becomes a thick paste; stir now and then, then mix well with it three yolks of eggs, and it is ready for use.

CABBAGE GARNITURE.

Throw in boiling water, a little salt, and a middling sized cabbage; boil it half an hour, take it from the kettle with a skimmer, and throw it in cold water, and drain it, pressing it a little in the drainer to force the water out; cut off the stump, and chop the cabbage fine. Have in a stewpan on the fire, three or four ounces of fresh butter; put the cabbage in when the butter is half melted, sprinkling on while stirring a teaspoonful of flour; pour on it, little by little, some broth, stirring the while, and when it has a fine brownish color, wet with broth enough to boil it; season with salt, a little grated nutmeg, and four peppercorns; boil gently till the sauce is thick enough, take away the peppercorns, and use.

CROUTONS GARNITURE.

Cut a piece of bread, the soft part only, about two eighths of an inch thick, and of different forms, such as stars, half moons, squares, rounds, butterflies, flowers, etc.

Have in a frying pan on the fire good fresh butter; when melted and very warm, put your pieces of bread in it, and when of a yellow or light brown color, turn them over in order to have the two sides alike; take gently from the pan, either with a fork or skimmer, put them on a clean towel for two or three minutes to take some of the grease off, and it is ready for use.

MATELOTE GARNITURE.

Peel a dozen of small onions. Have on the fire in a stewpan, four ounces of butter; when melted, put the onions in with eight or ten mushrooms; season with salt, white pepper, and a little grated nutmeg; sprinkle on it while stirring a tablespoonful of flour; as soon as the onions and mushrooms begin to take color, cover with broth and white wine, half of each; simmer till cooked; then take it from the fire, mix well with the whole the juice of half a lemon, a teaspoonful of cider vinegar, three yolks of eggs, and use.

MUSHROOM FARCE.

Chop fine half a pint of fresh mushrooms, and two tablespoonfuls of parsley. Have in a stewpan on the fire two ounces of grated bacon (not smoked), and as much of butter; when the butter is melted, put the mushrooms and parsley in, season with salt, pepper, a little grated nutmeg, and a quarter of a pint of white wine; let boil gently till reduced to a jelly.

It may be preserved a few days in a refrigerator.

MUSHROOM AND EGG FARCE.

Proceed as for mushroom farce in every particular, till reduced to a jelly; mix well in it three or four yolks of eggs, and use.

It may also be preserved a few days in a refrigerator.

PAPILLOTTE FARCE.

Place in a stewpan four ounces of butter, half a pound of chopped bacon, two tablespoonfuls of chopped mushrooms, two teaspoonfuls of chopped shallots, and four tablespoonfuls of sweet oil; set on a brisk fire for five or six minutes, then add salt, pepper, a little of allspice, and one teaspoonful of chopped parsley; put back on the fire for three minutes, and it is ready for use.

This farce may be kept a few days on ice.

QUENELLES.

Chop fine half a pound of veal. Put in a stewpan about twelve ounces of beef suet; set on the fire, and when melted, drain it. Work well together chopped veal and beef suet, with parsley and thyme chopped fine, salt, pepper, three eggs, a little grated nutmeg, and flour enough to make a kind of paste, which you divide and make quenelles with, giving them the shape of small flat sausages. Have boiling broth in a pan, throw the quenelles in, and leave till well cooked.

SALPICON GARNITURE.

Cut in dice, an equal quantity of each, and to weigh altogether about one pound and a half, calf sweetbread, livers, or flesh of fowls, and ham—three kinds in all; also two mushrooms, and two truffles; all must be nearly cooked in water beforehand. Put them in a stewpan, season with salt, pepper, a bay leaf, a clove of garlic, an onion, a sprig of parsley, and one of thyme; cover with half a pint of broth, and as much of white wine; set on a slow fire; it must not boil, but simmer gently; stir now and then till the whole is well cooked; take out bay leaf, onion, garlic, parsley and thyme; in case the sauce should not be thick enough, add a little fecula, stir, and leave a while longer on the fire, and it is ready for use.

TRUFFLE GARNITURE.

Dry a handful of truffles, cut them in slices or in dice. Put in a stewpan a piece of butter the size of an egg; when melted, place your truffles in, fry fifteen minutes, then wet with a quarter of a pint of broth, and as much of white wine; simmer till cooked, stirring now and then, and use.

Another way is, when the truffles are cut, put them in a stewpan, cover with half a pint of broth, and as much of claret wine; add a little salt, and a teaspoonful of sugar; set on a slow fire, to simmer till cooked, stirring now and then, and it is ready for use.

In case the garniture should not be thick enough, add a little fecula ten minutes before taking from the fire.

VEGETABLE GARNITURE.

Throw in boiling water with a little salt, six small onions, two cabbage-lettuces, two or three mushrooms, a handful of sorrel, half a handful of chervil, and a small turnip cut fine; after three minutes' boiling, drain and chop the whole fine. Have in a stewpan on the fire, four ounces of butter; when melted, put your vegetables in; when these are half fried, sprinkle on them a teaspoonful of flour, stirring the while; then cover with broth, season with a little salt, pepper, and half a teaspoonful of sugar; let simmer till well cooked, and it is ready for use.

Put a little fecula in it fifteen minutes before taking from the fire, if the garniture is not thick enough.

PUREES.

OF BEANS.

SHELL a quart of large horse beans, when full grown, but not yet dry, throw them in boiling water with a little salt for fifteen minutes; drain, and throw them in cold water, leave ten minutes, and drain again. Have in a stewpan on the fire a piece of butter the size of an egg; mix with it a teaspoonful of flour, pepper, and salt, then put the beans in, and cover with broth; add two stalks of cives, two sprigs of parsley; leave on the fire till the whole is well cooked, mash and strain, then mix again with it two ounces of butter, and use.

OF KIDNEY BEANS.

Soak a quart of kidney beans in lukewarm water for ten minutes, and move them well in it, take out and drain them; put them in a kettle with a pound of salted bacon (not smoked), cover with cold water, season with a bay leaf, a sprig of thyme, two of parsley, two middling sized onions, with two cloves stuck in them, and a carrot cut in pieces; when the whole is well cooked, throw away thyme, bay leaf, onions and cloves; mash well, and strain the rest except the bacon; put back in the stewpan, add to it half a pint of broth, salt and pepper, and leave on a moderate fire till well done, and use with or without the bacon.

OF CARROTS.

Clean well, and cut in slices, a dozen of middling sized carrots; put them in a stewpan with four ounces of butter, and set on the fire; when about half fried, cover with broth, season with half a bay leaf, a small sprig of thyme, one of parsley, a small onion, and a clove stuck in it; when the whole is well cooked, throw away onion, clove, bay leaf, and thyme, mash and strain the rest, and put it back in the pan, with half a pint of broth; set it on the fire again, simmer about three hours, and it is ready for use.

OF CHESTNUTS.

Put chestnuts in a kettle, enough to make a quart when shelled; cover with cold water and set on the fire; take them out when cooked, shell them, put them in a kettle, cover with broth, boil twenty minutes and drain; then pound the chestnuts well, put them with the broth in a stewpan, add a glass of warm broth, boil gently three hours, take from the fire, mix in a tablespoonful of crushed sugar, and use.

In case it should be found too fat, throw in a few drops of cold water when you take from the fire, and skim off the fat.

OF CELERY.

Clean, wash, and peel well, about a quart of soup celery, which cut in small pieces; throw them in boiling water, with a little salt and pepper; when well cooked, drain. Put in a stewpan on a moderate fire, four ounces of butter; mix with it when melted, a tablespoonful of flour, then add the celery; cover with broth, simmer two hours, take from the fire, mix in a teaspoonful of crushed sugar, and use.

OF LENTILS.

Soak a quart of lentils in lukewarm water for ten minutes, and drain; put them in a kettle, cover with broth, boil till cooked, mash and strain into a stew pan; put back on the fire, add half a pint of broth, salt and pepper, simmer four hours, stirring now and then; in case it should become too thick, while on the fire wet with broth; it is then ready for use.

OF MUSHROOMS.

Clean well and cut in pieces, a quart of fresh mushrooms; soak them in cold water, in which you have put the juice of a lemon; drain, and chop them fine. Put a stewpan on the fire, with a piece of butter the size of a duck's egg; when melted, put your mushrooms in; when half fried, add the juice of a lemon, finish frying, then cover with some roux sauce, let simmer till it becomes rather thick, strain and use.

OF GREEN PEAS.

Throw a quart of green peas and a little salt in boiling water, boil five minutes, and drain. Put two or three ounces of butter in a stewpan; when melted, put the peas in, with salt, pepper, and a sprig of parsley; cover with broth, and stir till cooked; mash, strain, and use.

OF CRACKED OR DRY PEAS.

Proceed as for lentils in every particular.

OF SORREL.

Wash and chop fine a peck of sorrel. Put two ounces of butter in a stewpan, and set it on the fire; when melted, put the sorrel in, and leave till cooked, stirring now and then with a wooden spoon, and strain it, in doing which you must press on it in the strainer, otherwise it would not go through; then put it back on the fire, wet moderately with Espagnole sauce, simmer half an hour, salt, and use it.

OF POTATOES.

Soak in water a quart of potatoes, and cook them in water with a little salt; then peel and mash them well, place them in a tureen, and mix with milk; at the same time, have two ounces of butter in a stewpan and on the fire, and when melted, put the potatoes in; keep stirring all the time, and after about twenty-five minutes, it will be thick enough; take from the fire, and use.

Another way is to mix them with broth instead of milk, and proceed as above in every other particular.

OF TURNIPS.

Wash, clean, and cut in slices a quart of turnips; throw them in boiling water for three minutes, and drain; put them in a stewpan, cover with broth, season with half a bay leaf, a small sprig of thyme, and one of parsley, a small onion with a clove stuck in it; put on the fire and boil gently till the whole is well cooked, then throw away bay leaf, thyme, onion and clove, mash and strain the rest, and put it back on the fire, adding then about half a pint of warm broth; simmer about two hours, and use.

BEEF.

HOW TO SELECT.

SEE if the meat is fine, of a clear red color, with white yellowish fat.

COW BEEF.

Cow beef must also be of a clear red color, but more pale than other beef; the fat is white.

BULL BEEF.

Bull beef is never good; you recognize it when you see hard and yellow fat, the lean part is of a dirty reddish color.

Beef must be put upon or before a very sharp fire, which you subdue after a while, *i. e.*, after the surface of the piece looks nearly like well roasted meat.

In roasting or broiling it, baste often with the gravy, and at first with a little lukewarm butter.

Beef, if not tender, may be beaten for half a minute with a round stick before being put upon or before the fire.

A LA MODE.

Take from six to twelve pounds of rump or fillet of beef, and take the bones out; lard the piece through with bacon (not smoked), half a pound of it for six pounds of beef. Put in a crockery stewpan half a calf's foot, half a handful of parsley and cives, a bay leaf, a clove of garlic, a sprig of thyme, two onions, with one clove stuck in each, salt, pepper, half a carrot cut in pieces, a quarter of a pound of bacon (not smoked) cut in dice, two shallots chopped fine, wet with half a glass of white wine and a glass of water (the above quantities are for six pounds of beef); place the beef upon the whole, cover the pan as air-tight as possible; set it on a moderate fire, or in a moderately heated oven, and simmer gently for about five hours; then dish the meat, strain the sauce on it, and serve warm; in case there should be too much fat, skim it off before straining.

To eat it cold is very good; in that case, after you have strained the sauce on the meat, let it cool till it looks like a jelly, and serve.

BRAISED.

Take about six pounds of a rump piece of beef, the nearest to the knuckle, lard it with half a pound of bacon (not smoked), and tie the piece with twine. Put in a stew-pan two ounces of bacon cut in dice, four sprigs of parsley, two of thyme, two bay leaves, a clove of garlic, a sprig of sweet basil, two cloves, three carrots cut in pieces, salt, and pepper; put the piece of beef on the whole, wet with a glass of broth, and one of white wine (a liquor glass of French brandy may also be added); season with six or eight small onions; place in a moderately heated oven, put paste around the cover to keep it air-tight; simmer about six hours; dish the meat with the onions and carrots around it, strain the gravy on the whole, and serve.

Almost any piece of beef may be cooked in the same way, and will be found good, wholesome, and economical.

FILLET.

How to improve it.—Put the fillet in a tureen, with four tablespoonsfuls of sweet oil, salt, pepper, two tablespoonfuls of chopped parsley, four onions cut in slices, two bay leaves, and the juice of half a lemon; put half of all the above under the fillet, and half on it; cover, and leave thus two days in winter, and about eighteen hours in summer.

BROILED OR ROASTED.

Take three pounds of fillet, cut off part of the fat and the thin skin on the top, lard it with about half a pound of bacon, improve it if you choose, envelop it with buttered paper, and place upon the spit before a sharp fire; take the paper off five minutes before taking from the fire; baste often during the process, and serve with the gravy, to which you add salt, pepper, a teaspoonful of vinegar, a saltspoonful of chopped shallots, and two or three pickled cucumbers, cut in slices.

It may also be served with a tomato sauce.

Instead of roasting, the same may be put on a gridiron, and on a sharp fire, and broiled, and served in the same way as above.

If any of it is left, it may be served the next day, after having enveloped it in buttered paper and warmed it on the spit or on the gridiron, and also with the gravy.

WITH CUCUMBERS, OR A PURÉE, OR GREEN PARSLEY.

You may improve the fillet as directed, if it suits you.

Put in a stewpan a quarter of a pound of bacon, cut in slices, three or four sprigs of parsley, salt, pepper, two carrots, four onions cut in slices, and a glass of white wine, then three pounds of fillet on the whole; cover with broth, set it in a quick oven or on a sharp fire, with live coals on the cover of the pan, and leave thus half an hour; then subdue the fire and finish the cooking; after which put the meat on a dish, strain the sauce on it, and surround it with cucumbers cooked in water, or with green parsley.

It may also be surrounded with a purée or tomato sauce instead of cucumbers or parsley.

The same with Mushrooms.—Cut the fillet in slices half an inch thick, place them in a crockery vessel, with salt and pepper sprinkled on, leave them thus three or four hours. Put in a stewpan a piece of butter the size of an egg, set it on a good fire, and, when warm, lay the meat in; when the under side is of a golden color, turn over and do the same for the other side; then sprinkle on it a teaspoonful of flour, and four mushrooms cut in slices, cover with broth, and leave thus till done; then put the slices of meat on a dish; after that, pour into the stewpan, where you have left the sauce, half a wine glass of good white wine; simmer half an hour; add the juice of half a lemon, pour the whole on the fillet, which you have kept in a warm place during this last process, and serve it, taking care to have the slices of meat surrounded by the slices of mushrooms.

The same, Sauté.—Cut the fillet in slices nearly one inch in thickness, and sprinkle salt and pepper on them; then put a piece of butter in a frying pan, and set it on a good fire; when warm, lay the slices in, turning them over two or three times while cooking; serve with fried parsley around, or with anchovy butter on them.

FILLET THE NEXT DAY.

In case you have a piece of fillet left, and large enough to be served a second time, put broth enough in a stewpan to cover the slices of fillet, set it on the fire, and when warm, lay the slices in the stewpan; simmer, but not boil, till they are warm, dish them, and on each layer of slices spread a little chopped parsley and butter kneaded together, add a few drops of lemon juice, and serve.

This makes a good dish for a family.

The broth that is left may be used for **any other** purpose.

LOIN.

A loin of beef may be improved the same as a fillet.

Trim off the fat, the greasy end, and the thin skin; **envelop it with buttered** paper, place on the spit and set before a **good fire, basting** often; it takes about two hours to cook it; dish the fillet and set it in a warm place, then put in a stewpan on the fire the gravy, four pickled cucumbers **cut in slices, a** teaspoonful of chopped parsley, salt, pepper, two teaspoonfuls of cider vinegar, and half a pint of broth; boil the **whole twenty minutes;** serve after it is strained into **a saucer, to be used with the** loin.

A loin may also **be prepared** like a fillet.

RIBS.

How to prepare.—Cut the ribs in slices of from one to one and a half inch in thickness; trim off bones, nerves, and fibres as much as possible, beat and flatten them gently with a chopper, and they are ready to be cooked.

BROILED.

Prepare about six pounds of ribs, sprinkle salt and pepper on them, lay them on a gridiron and on a sharp fire; spread a little butter on, turn over three or four times, and when done serve them with a cucumber, oil, piquante or poivrade sauce, or with a maitre-d'hôtel sauce, and fried potatoes.

ROASTED.

Place the piece of ribs on **the spit** before a sharp fire, baste often with a little melted butter and the drippings, at the **same time** dredging some flour on it; after ten or fifteen minutes remove it a little further from the fire or subdue it a little. When done, serve with the gravy, to which you add salt, pepper, a teaspoonful of vinegar, **and two or three pickled cucumbers** cut in slices

STEWED.

Prepare **five or six pounds of** ribs as directed. Put in a stewpan about **a quarter of a pound of** bacon (not smoked) cut in dice, lay the **meat on,** set on a good fire **for** fifteen minutes, **and take off;** place the slices of meat on a dish with the **bacon;** then add to the juice in the stewpan a piece **of butter the size of** a walnut; as soon as melted, sprinkle **in, little by little, about** a tablespoonful **of** flour, stirring with a wooden spoon; **when of a proper thickness, and of a brownish color,** put back in the stewpan **meat and bacon, add half a wine glass** of French brandy, two small **carrots cut in** slices, four small onions, **salt, and** a pinch **of** allspice; also, tied together **in** a bunch, two sprigs of parsley, **two of** thyme, a bay leaf, a clove of garlic, **and** a dozen stalks **of cives;** simmer about five hours, take **out** the bunch of **parsley, etc.,** skim off the fat, **if too** much of **it,** and serve.

Ribs may also **be prepared** and served like braised beef, fillet with cucumbers, and fillet with mushrooms.

STEAKS.

Always put the steaks on or before a sharp **fire.**

Procure a good **fillet** or rump of beef, cut it **in slices about one inch thick, trim off the** thin skin around, **also the fibres as well as possible, but do not** cut off the **fat; beat and flatten with** a chopper, dip **the slices in** lukewarm butter, or spread a little butter **on both sides; lay** them **on a** warmed gridiron, **set** it on **a sharp fire** (if cooked with a range, place before and not on the fire), turn over two or three times, and take off when rather underdone;

have on a dish some butter kneaded with chopped parsley, lay the steaks on, sprinkle salt and pepper on them, also a few drops of lemon juice if you choose, and serve.

Cooks and epicures differ about the turning over of steaks; some say that they must not be turned over twice, others are of opinion that they must be turned over two or three, and even more times; we have tried the two ways many times, and did not find much difference; we think the difference exists (if there is any at all) in the person's taste or in the cook's care. Hunters generally prefer game to butcher's meat.

A steak or steaks look better when surrounded with watercress or fried potatoes; with watercress a little vinegar is necessary.

Instead of butter and parsley on the dish and on the steaks, anchovy butter may be used.

Another way, generally used in families.—Cut the steaks as above, and trim and flatten them. Put butter in a pan and set it on a sharp fire; when hot lay the steaks in, sprinkle a little salt and pepper on them, and when the under side is cooked, turn over to cook the other, and then serve with watercress or fried potatoes.

FANCY STEAK.

Take a good piece of rump steak, about two inches thick, butter both sides slightly, lay it on a gridiron well greased and warmed, set it on a moderate fire, and broil it well; in order to cook it through, you must turn it over many times on account of its thickness; serve it like another steak, that is, surrounded with watercress or fried potatoes.

It requires a great deal of care while cooking, but it is good when properly done.

BOILED BEEF.

By boiled beef is understood all the pieces that have been used to make soup or broth; it is very often called minced beef.

Boiled beef is very seldom put on the table for a dinner of ceremony, but always for a family dinner. It may be served in the following ways:

AFTER THE SOUP, AND WHEN STILL WARM.

Place it on a dish, surrounded with sprigs of green parsley, or spring radishes, or horseradish well grated, or with fried slices of bread. The latter are prepared thus: cut round or square slices of bread, dip them in well beaten eggs, place them in a pan on the fire with hot butter, and fry both sides; then drain and use them.

BROILED.

Cut the boiled beef in slices one inch thick, spread a little butter on both sides, and lay on the gridiron; broil gently both sides, and serve with an oil sauce.

FRIED.

Cut in dice four ounces of bacon, which put in a frying pan, with four ounces of sausages; when half fried, put the boiled beef in, after having cut it in slices; wet with about half a wine glass of broth, and two or three minutes before it is done add a teaspoonful of vinegar, and serve.

IN GRATIN.

Set a crockery pan on the fire, with a piece of butter the size of an egg in it; when melted, sprinkle in two or three tablespoonfuls of fine bread crumbs, add two or three mushrooms cut in slices, a teaspoonful of chopped onions, half a one of chopped parsley, a pinch of allspice, same of pepper and salt; put the boiled beef, cut in slices, on the whole; wet with half a glass of white wine, and as much of broth; simmer from twenty to thirty minutes, and serve.

IN MAITRE-D'-HÔTEL, PIQUANTE, ROBERT, OR TOMATO SAUCE.

Cut it in slices, place them on a dish, spread on them some chopped parsley and slices of pickled cucumbers, and send thus to the table, with either of the above sauces in a saucer, to be used with it.

IN MIROTON.

Put a piece of butter the size of an egg in a stewpan (this is for about two pounds), and set it on the fire; when melted, put in it four middling sized onions, cut in slices; when nearly cooked, sprinkle on them a pinch of flour, and stir till it takes a golden color; then add half a glass of white wine, and as much of broth, also, salt, pepper, and a little grated nutmeg; boil until well cooked, and till the sauce is reduced; then add the boiled beef, cut in slices, and leave it fifteen minutes; dish it, pour on a few drops of vinegar, and serve.

IN SALAD.

Cut it in very thin and short slices, and place them on a dish with chopped parsley; put in a saucer sweet oil and vinegar, according to the quantity of beef you have, two tablespoonfuls of oil to one of vinegar, salt, pepper, and some mustard; beat the whole a little, pour on the slices, and serve.

OX BRAIN.

Soak it in lukewarm water and clean well, so as to have it free from blood, fibres, and thin skin; then soak it again in cold water for twelve hours in winter and six in summer. Put in a crockery stewpan one ounce of bacon cut in slices, one carrot cut in pieces, two sprigs of parsley, one of thyme, a bay leaf, a clove, four small onions cut in slices, a teaspoonful of chopped cives, salt, pepper, a pint of white wine, as much of broth, and then the brain; set on a moderate fire for half an hour and take it off; dish the brain and place it in a warm place; then strain the sauce, put it back on the fire with the brain in it, add two or three mushrooms cut in pieces, leave on the fire from ten to fifteen minutes, and serve it, parted in two, with fried parsley around.

Another way.—When the brain is cleaned and prepared as above, cut it in eight pieces. Mix well together a little flour, chopped parsley and cives, also a pinch of allspice; roll the pieces of brain in it, so as to allow the mixture to adhere to them; have some butter in a frying pan on the fire, and when hot put the pieces of brain in it; fry gently, and serve with fried parsley around.

OX HEART.

Soak it in lukewarm water for two hours, free it from blood and skin, drain and wipe it dry; then stuff it with minced meat, to which you have added three or four onions chopped fine, salt, and pepper; put it in a rather quick oven, or on the spit before a good fire (if on the spit, envelop it with buttered paper), basting from time to time; it takes about an hour and a half to cook a middling sized one; serve it with an oil, piquante, poivrade, or ravigote sauce.

It may also be fried with butter and cut in slices, but it is not as good as in the above way; it generally becomes hard in frying.

OX KIDNEYS.

First split the kidneys in two or four pieces, trim off

as carefully as possible the sinews that are inside, then cut in fillets and throw them in boiling water, with a little salt; boil three minutes, and drain dry. Put a piece of butter in a frying pan, set it on the fire, and when melted, sprinkle in it two teaspoonfuls of flour, stirring the while; then add a wine glass of white wine, two tablespoonfuls of broth, a teaspoonful of chopped parsley, salt, and pepper, and boil about ten minutes; then put the fillets in, have a quick fire, and as soon as cooked, dish; add a few drops of lemon juice, and serve.

OX LIVER.

Cut the liver in slices a quarter of an inch in thickness, sprinkle on them salt and pepper, place them on a gridiron, and set on a sharp fire; turn over only once and serve rather underdone, with butter and chopped parsley kneaded together and spread between the slices.

Another way.—When the liver is cut in slices as above, put a piece of butter in a frying pan on the fire, and when melted lay the slices in; turn over only once, and serve with chopped parsley on.

OX TAIL.

Cut the tail at the joints, so as to make as many pieces as there are joints; throw the pieces in boiling water for fifteen minutes, and drain them; when cold and dry, put them in a stewpan with a bay leaf, two onions with a clove stuck in each, two sprigs of parsley and one of thyme, a clove of garlic, salt, pepper, half a wine glass of white wine, and a few thin slices of fat bacon; cover with broth, and set on a moderate fire for two hours; dish the pieces of tail, strain the sauce on them, and serve with a garniture of cabbage or with a purée.

OX TAIL THAT HAS BEEN COOKED TO MAKE SOUP.

Dip each piece in lukewarm butter, and then roll them in fine dry bread crumbs, put them on the gridiron, set on a good fire, and when well broiled, serve them with an oil, piquante, poivrade, or tartar sauce.

BEEF TONGUE.

How to prepare.—Soak it in cold water for twenty-four hours in winter, and twelve in summer; change the water four times, that is, every three or six hours; take off, throw it in boiling water for ten minutes, take out, and skim it well.

STEWED.

Cut square fillets of bacon, which dredge in a mixture of chopped parsley, cives, salt, pepper, and a little allspice; lard the tongue with the fillets. Put in a crockery stew-pan two ounces of bacon cut in dice, four sprigs of parsley, two of thyme, one of sweet basil, two bay leaves, a clove of garlic, two cloves, two carrots cut in pieces, four small onions, salt, and pepper; lay the tongue on the whole, wet with half a glass of white wine, and a glass of broth; set on a moderate fire, and simmer about five hours—keep it well covered; then put the tongue on a dish, strain the sauce on it, and serve. It is a delicious dish.

It may also be served with vegetables around, or with tomato sauce.

Another way.—When prepared as above directed, put it on the fire with the same seasonings as the preceding one; simmer four hours and take from the fire; put the tongue on a dish and let it cool, then place it on the spit before a good fire, and finish the cooking; serve it warm with an oil, or piquante sauce.

If any is left of either of the two, put in a pan the next

day, wet with a little broth, set on the fire, and when warm, serve it on a purée; do not allow it to boil.

WHEN SMOKED.

Soak the smoked tongue in cold water for three hours, change the water twice during the process; take the tripe off, if there is any around, then put the tongue in a crockery pan with two sprigs of thyme, two of dried parsley, a bay leaf, two cloves, six small onions, a clove of garlic, a little salt, and pepper; fill the pan with cold water, and let simmer six hours on a slow fire. Take from the fire, let cool as it is, then take the tongue out, and clean it; let dry, and serve it when cold with a cucumber, oil, piquante, poivrade, or tomato sauce.

DOUBLE TRIPE.

How to clean and prepare.—Scrape and wash it well several times in boiling water, changing the water every time; then put it in very cold water for twelve hours, change the water two or three times, place it in a pan, cover it with cold water, season with cives, parsley, onions, one or two cloves of garlic, cloves, salt and pepper; boil gently five hours, take out and drain.

In case the water should boil away, add some.

You may save all the trouble of cleaning and preparring, by buying it ready prepared, as it is generally sold in cities.

BROILED.

When prepared dip it in lukewarm butter, roll each piece in fine dry bread crumbs, place on a gridiron, and set it on a moderate fire; turn over as many times as is necessary to broil it well, and serve with an oil, piquante, or tartar sauce.

STEWED.

Put in a crockery stewpan two ounces of bacon cut in

dice, three carrots cut in slices, eight small onions, four cloves, two bay leaves, two cloves of garlic, a piece of nutmeg, four sprigs of parsley, two of thyme, a dozen stalks of cives, six peppercorns, the fourth part of an ox foot cut in four pieces, salt, pepper, about two ounces of ham cut in dice, then three pounds of double tripe on the whole; spread two ounces of fat bacon cut in thin slices on the top; wet with half white wine and half water, or water only if you choose; put the cover on, and if not air-tight, put some paste around; set in a slow oven for six hours, then take the tripe out, strain the sauce, skim off the fat when cool, then put the sauce and tripe again in your pan, warm well, and serve in crockery plates or bowls placed on chafing dishes, as it is necessary to keep it warm while eating it.

It is good with water only, but better with half wine.

FISH.

HOW TO SELECT.

To be good, fish must be fresh; it is fresh when the eyes are clear, the fins stiff, the gills red, hard too pen, and without bad odor.

HOW TO CLEAN AND PREPARE.

The sooner it is done the better. First you scale the fish well, holding it by the head or tail; then cut the belly open and take the inside out; trim off gills, fins, and tail; split the head; wash well, and wipe dry immediately with a clean towel, in and outside.

If you do not cook it at once when cleaned, put it on ice.

Turbot must be well rubbed with lemon before cooking it.

HOW TO CLEAN AND PREPARE EELS, EEL-POUT, CONGER, LAMPREY, AND OTHERS OF THE SAME FAMILY OR KIND.

When skinned, clean, head, and tail them. Then throw them in boiling water, in which you have put a little salt and a teaspoonful of vinegar; leave them in it about five minutes, take out, and drain.

SAME FAMILY OR KIND.

We give only one receipt for all the fishes of the same family, or having the same kind of flesh, as they are cooked alike, and require the same spices.

Almost every kind of fish is boiled, broiled, fried, or stewed. Some are better boiled than broiled, others better fried than stewed, &c. With few exceptions, any eatable fish may be cooked in these four ways. Few are roasted.

HOW TO KNOW WHEN COOKED ENOUGH.

It is very difficult, if not entirely impossible, to tell how long it takes to cook fish, as it depends as much on the size, kind, or quality of the fish as on the fire; but as soon as the flesh comes off the bones easily the fish is cooked; this is very easy to be ascertained with a knife.

HOW TO STUFF.

Soak a piece of bread in water for about an hour, and take it out, press the water out of it with your hands, and then put the bread in a bowl. Peel, chop fine, and fry in butter (half done only) two or three onions, and put them in the bowl also. Chop fine the soft roe of the fish you wish to stuff, mix it well with the bread and onions, add salt and pepper, and then stuff the fish with the mixture.

Pike, shad, salmon, sturgeon, turbot, halibut, sheep's-head, &c., may be stuffed in the above way.

A LA CRÊME.

Halibut, salmon, shad, sheep's-head, sturgeon, tunny, turbot, &c., if they have been broiled or roasted.

If you have a piece of the above worth serving a second time, put it in warm but not boiling water to warm it, drain and dish it; pour on it a cream or white sauce, or a béchamel No. 2, with hard boiled eggs around.

Fish served a second time, if boiled or stewed, should be warmed the next day before being served.

BOILED.

Clean and prepare as directed three pounds of either of the following fishes:—Black or blue fish, porgy, weak fish, black, striped, and sea bass, perch, carp, barbel, tench, pike, pickerel, and bream.

Place the fish entire in a fish kettle, with three sprigs of parsley, two of thyme, a bay leaf, a small carrot cut in four pieces, three cloves, one of garlic, four onions cut in slices, a wine glass of claret wine or a few drops of vinegar, salt, and pepper; cover with water, boil gently till cooked, that is, when the flesh comes off the bones easily; put a napkin on a dish, place the fish on it, and serve with green parsley around.

It may also be served with a caper, oil, piquante, or tomato sauce, but in that case you omit napkin and parsley.

Proceed as above for haddock, turbot, dab fish, and whiting, except that you season with parsley, thyme, onions, and bay leaf only; the other seasonings do not agree with these kinds.

BROILED.

Before broiling bass, dab-fish, salmon, tunny, and turbot, they may be improved in the following way:

After the fish is cleaned and prepared, place it in a crockery vessel, with parsley and onions chopped fine; also salt, pepper, thyme, two bay leaves, and two or three tablespoonfuls of sweet oil, half under and half on it, and leave thus two or three hours.

Carp and tench are improved in the same way, except that a few drops of vinegar are used instead of oil.

For broiling, begin by kneading butter with chopped parsley, salt, and pepper, spread it all over the fish; then envelop it in buttered paper, place it on the gridiron, set it on a good fire, and serve when done with an anchovy, caper, maitre d'hôtel, or white sauce.

Carp, barbel, and tench may be cooked and served like the above. Dab fish, salmon, tunny, turbot, shad, halibut, haddock and trout are broiled in the following way: mix well together, chopped parsley and bay leaf, a pinch of allspice, and oil or butter; put some of the mixture all around the fish, and envelop it with oiled paper, if you have used oil in your mixture, or buttered paper, if you have used butter; place on a gridiron and on a good fire, and serve with an anchovy, caper, maitre d'hôtel, or white sauce, when done.

They are broiled entire or in slices, about half an inch in thickness.

EEL, EEL-POUT, CONGER, AND LAMPREY, BROILED.

Clean and cut two pounds of eel, or of either of the others, in pieces about three inches long. Put in a stew-pan a piece of butter the size of an egg, and set it on the fire; when hot, lay the eels in, fry about three minutes, turning them over the while; then turn the whole in a crockery vessel, add a teaspoonful of chopped parsley and onions, a pinch of grated nutmeg, a tablespoonful of sweet oil, salt, and pepper; set on the fire and simmer two hours; take off, roll the pieces in fine bread crumbs, place them on a gridiron, and on a good fire, and serve when done with piquante sauce.

From the nature of their flesh, eels require to be prepared thus; and when properly done, make really a very good dish.

STURGEON, BROILED WHEN FRESH.

Sturgeon is broiled in slices like salmon, except that the seasonings are only composed of butter, a little grated nutmeg, and chopped parsley kneaded together, and spread all over the fish; envelop it with buttered paper, and serve like salmon.

BROILED SPRATS.

There are none in or near American waters; they are imported under their French name, sardines. Fresh sprats are very good broiled without any grease, and without being cleaned and prepared like other fish; but when on the plate, skin them, which is easily done, as then the flesh is so easily detached from the bones that the inside need not be touched at all; they are eaten with salt and pepper only.

FRIED.

All small fishes are better fried than prepared in any other way.

Clean the fish as directed. Put in a vessel two tablespoonfuls of flour, one beaten egg, a tablespoonful of vinegar, salt, and pepper; mix well together, then add the quantity of milk necessary to make a batter thin enough to dip the fish into, so that a thin coat only sticks to it. Dip the fish in the above mixture, or in flour only, according to taste, and lay it in hot lard, grease, butter or oil, in a pan, and on a sharp fire (see direction for frying); when done, serve it as it is, or with fried parsley around, and sprinkle a little salt on it.

Fry as above, carp, tench, bass, perch, black fish, blue fish, bream, porgy, weak fish, halibut, flounder, pike, pickerel, sole, herring, white fish of the lakes, whiting and barbel, all of them when small; also smelts, and any kind of small fish.

FISH.

ROASTED.

Only large sized fishes are roasted.

The best are: eels, pike, shad, salmon, sea trout, tunny, and sturgeon.

Improve them as for broiling.

EELS, EEL-POUT, AND LAMPREY, ROASTED.

Clean as directed for eels; improve as directed; also put some chopped parsley, salt, and pepper around, and envelop it in buttered or oiled paper; place it upon the spit before a good fire, baste often with melted butter or oil; have slices of roasted bread in the dripping-pan, take the paper off ten minutes before it is done, and serve it on the slices of bread, with a ravigote sauce.

PIKE.

Clean, prepare, and improve the fish as directed, roll it in chopped parsley, grated nutmeg, salt, and pepper; envelop it in buttered paper, put it on the spit before a good fire, baste often with vinegar; twenty minutes after take the paper off, finish the cooking, basting often with melted butter instead of vinegar, and serve with the gravy.

SALMON, SEA TROUT, AND TUNNY.

Prepare and improve as directed; cut in slices about half an inch in thickness, envelop every slice in buttered paper, put on the spit and set before a good fire; baste with the seasonings in which it has been improved; take the paper off five minutes before it is done, and serve with the gravy, after you have taken out the bay leaf. The next day serve it cold, with an oil sauce.

SHAD.

Clean and improve it as directed; spread the seasonings in which it has been improved around the fish, and which you envelop in oiled paper; then place it on the spit before a good fire; baste with vinegar; twenty minutes after take **the paper** off, finish the cooking, basting often the while with the drippings, and serve with the gravy.

It is a very delicate dish; you augment or diminish the seasonings according to the size of the fish.

STURGEON.

Clean, and **cut in** slices half **an inch thick**, or leave entire, as it suits **you; skin** it well **; lay it in a** crockery vessel, **spread over it some chopped parsley,** grated nutmeg, **salt, pepper, and two gills of white wine** (this is for about three pounds), leave thus two hours; then take the fish only, envelop it in buttered paper, **fix it on** the spit before a good fire, baste with the wine and seasonings from the crockery dish, and when **nearly done** take the paper off; finish the cooking, basting the while, and serve with the drippings, to which you may add a little vinegar, sweet oil, and mustard.

If there is any left, you can **serve it cold the next day** with an oil sauce.

STEWED.

Clean and prepare as directed three pounds of fish, cut it in pieces about two inches long. Put in a fish kettle four ounces of butter, kneaded with a teaspoonful of flour, and the same of chopped parsley, add two or three mushrooms cut in pieces, salt and pepper, then the **fish and a** glass of claret wine, or a wine glass of vinegar; cover with water, set on a good fire, boil gently till cooked; dish the pieces of fish, strain the sauce on them, spread the pieces of mushrooms over, and serve.

Stew as above, carp, tench, bass, perch, black fish, blue fish, bream, porgies, weak fish, whiting, and the white fish of the lakes.

FLOUNDERS, HALIBUT, AND FLAT FISH, STEWED.

Clean three pounds of the above fish. Put in a crockery dish four ounces of butter, set it on a good fire, and when melted sprinkle in it a teaspoonful of flour, stirring the while; also, a pinch of grated nutmeg, salt, pepper, a saltspoonful of chopped parsley, two or three mushrooms, also chopped, then the fish; pour on it a glass of white wine, and a liquor glass of French brandy; cover the dish, take it from the fire, and put it in a moderately heated oven, and serve when done just as it is, and in the crockery dish.

SALMON, SHAD, STURGEON, SEA TROUT, AND TUNNY, STEWED.

Clean and prepare as directed three pounds of salmon (fresh), or shad, &c.; place it in a fish kettle with three sprigs of parsley, one of thyme, a bay leaf, four small onions cut in slices, a pinch of allspice, salt, pepper, two or three mushrooms cut in slices, one carrot cut in four pieces, cover with half claret wine and half water, and boil gently till cooked; then take the fish from the kettle, using a dipper or a skimmer, in order not to break it, and place it on a dish; put two ounces of butter in the kettle, and when melted and mixed with the sauce, sprinkle in it a tablespoonful of flour; stir with a wooden spoon till reduced to a proper thickness, strain it on the fish (which you have kept warm), and serve.

If there is any left for the next day, warm it, but do not allow it to boil.

SALMON IN ESCALOPS.

Cut it in round slices, about one eighth of an inch in thickness; fry them with butter, and serve.

The pieces should be tastefully arranged on a dish, imitating a flight of stairs.

SMELTS, STEWED.

Spread on the bottom of a crockery dish some butter, sprinkle on it a pinch of grated nutmeg, then lay in gently the smelts, after having cleaned them; add salt, pepper, and a glass of white wine, cover the dish and put it in the oven; when done, serve as it is, that is in the dish in which they have been cooked; the changing of the dish would spoil them.

The following fishes, after being cleaned and prepared, may be boiled, broiled, and stewed as other fish:

Cat fish, chelmon, coal fish, doree or dory, sea dragon, flying fish, gar fish, gold fish, growler, gurnard fish, great horned hake, hard-head, head fish, king fish, lancelot, sand-launce, ling, loach, sea loche, mullet, gray mullet, red mullet, or surmullet, pilchard, pilot fish, remora, roach, rockling, shiner, stickleback, sucker, sucking fish, sun fish, sword fish, torpedo, torsk, trygon, wolf fish, wrasse, or rock fish.

Crocodile, porpoise, and shark are eaten when young by some persons; we have never cooked any, but they are of species to be boiled or broiled.

MATELOT.

Take bass, black fish, blue fish, barbel, carp, eels, lamprey, perch, pike, pickerel, brook pike, porgies, tench, troutlet, weak fish, and white fish of the lakes, or eels and one of the others, or (if not handy) eels only, say four pounds; clean and prepare as directed; save the eggs and soft roe of the carp only; then cut the fish in pieces about two inches long. Put in a fish kettle large enough to hold the fish easily, a bunch composed of six sprigs of parsley, three of thyme, two bay leaves, four cloves, and two cloves of garlic, tied together with twine; also four ounces of butter, a dozen of small onions, half fried in butter, six or eight mushrooms, a pinch of allspice, salt, and pepper, then the fish; cover with claret wine, and set it on a very brisk fire; at the first boiling throw in it two gills of French brandy, light a small piece of wood and set the brandy and wine on fire; do not take the kettle from the fire for that; it will burn for a while; then put again in the kettle about six ounces of butter, kneaded with two tablespoonfuls of flour; move the kettle now and then so as to prevent the pieces of fish from sticking to the pan; when done, which will be in about half an hour, take the fish from the kettle by the means of a dipper or skimmer, and be careful not to break the pieces; lay it gently on a dish, strain the sauce on it, spread tastefully, and all over it, the onions and mushrooms; surround the dish with croutons, and serve.

Another way.—Clean, prepare, and cut in pieces the same fish and the same quantity as in the above. Put in a fish kettle large enough to hold the fish easily, a bunch composed of six sprigs of parsley, three of thyme, two bay leaves, four cloves, and two of garlic, tied together with twine; also a small carrot, cut in four pieces, four small onions, cut in slices, a piece of nutmeg, salt, five or six peppercorns, and then the fish; cover entirely with white wine and broth, half of each, set on a very sharp fire in order to start it boiling as soon as possible, and for about twenty-five minutes. Put at the same time in a stewpan on a good fire, ten ounces of butter; when melted, add a dozen small onions, six or eight mushrooms, and when of a golden color, sprinkle in it a tablespoonful of flour, stirring with a wooden spoon the while; wet with warm water, then add also the eggs, and soft roe of the carp if any; cook the whole well.

After twenty-five minutes' boiling, take the fish from the kettle by the means of a dipper or skimmer; lay it gently on a dish, then strain on it the sauce in which it has cooked, spread with taste, on the fish and sauce, the dozen of small onions, and the six or eight mushrooms, and lastly, pour on the whole the sauce in the stewpan, and serve.

Some croutons may be put around the dish as an ornament.

This last is no better than the preceding one, only it is **more sightly,** and is generally used for a grand dinner.

ANCHOVY.

Split in two, so as to take the back bone out easily, wash well in and outside, **throw** them in hot lard in a frying pan on a sharp fire, after having rolled them in flour; it **takes a** few minutes to fry them; serve hot with a little **salt.**

How to preserve them.—Split **them** in two, take the back bone out, wash well in and outside, and wipe dry with a clean towel immediately after washing; salt well, and keep them air-tight in a pot or bottle.

ANGEL FISH, RAY, AND SKATE.

Clean as directed for fish, put it in a fish kettle, season with parsley, thyme, onions cut in slices, bay leaf, cloves, salt, and pepper; cover with water and half a pint of vinegar; set on a good fire, boil only three or four minutes, take the fish out, skim and clean it, place on a dish, and put it in a warm place. Put a piece of butter in a frying pan, and on a good fire; when melted, fry some parsley in it; then add a teaspoonful of vinegar, give one boil, pour on the fish, and serve with the fried parsley around.

The same may be **served as soon** as you place it on a **dish** with a caper or white sauce.

FRESH COD, HADDOCK, AND SHEEPSHEAD.

It must be fat and fresh to be good.

Clean it as directed. Put in a fish kettle, on a slow fire, three sprigs of parsley, two of thyme, a bay leaf, a pinch of allspice, four onions cut in slices, pepper, salt, and then the fish (say three pounds); cover with water, simmer till cooked, drain the fish only; dish it, and serve warm with boiled potatoes, and melted butter in a saucer.

It may also be served with a caper, oil, or piquante sauce, but without potatoes.

The same, broiled.—Envelop the fish in buttered paper, place it on the gridiron, and on a sharp fire; turn over two or three times, and when done, take the paper off, and serve with a piquante or poivrade sauce.

The same, fried, or rather sauté.—Prepare two pounds of it. Put a piece of butter the size of an egg in a frying pan, and on a good fire; when hot, roll the fish in flour, and lay it in the pan; add a teaspoonful of chopped parsley when nearly done; dish fish and parsley, and add a few drops of lemon juice just before putting on the table.

SALTED COD, OR, AS IT IS SOMETIMES CALLED, STOCK FISH.

How to prepare.—Soak it in cold water for two days, changing the water twice, then scale it well, and clean; put it in a fish kettle, cover with cold water, set on a slow fire skim off the scum, let it boil about one minute, take the kettle from the fire, cover it well, and leave thus ten minutes; then take off the cod, and drain it.

In béchamel.—When prepared and cooked as above directed, put the cod in a stewpan in which you have a warm but not boiling béchamel No. 1; simmer about five minutes, and serve.

In brown butter.—When prepared as above, place it on a dish, and keep it in a warm place. Put four ounces of butter in a frying pan, and on a good fire; when turning brown, add three sprigs of parsley, fry about two minutes, pour the whole on the fish, and serve.

You may also pour on it a hot caper sauce, and serve.

With croutons.—Prepare and cook as directed, three pounds of cod; take the bones out, break in small pieces, and mash with the hand as much as possible; put it then in a stewpan, beat three yolks of eggs with two tablespoonfuls of cream, and mix with the cod; set on a slow fire, and immediately pour in, little by little, stirring the while, about one gill of sweet oil; simmer ten or twelve minutes, and serve with croutons around.

In maitre d'hôtel.—Lay three pounds of cod on a dish, after being cooked as directed; keep it warm, pour a warm maitre d'hôtel sauce on it, and serve.

With milk.—Put two ounces of butter in a stewpan, set it on a good fire, and when melted, sprinkle in it a tablespoonful of flour; stir the while, add pepper, a little grated nutmeg, and two tablespoonfuls of milk; as soon as mixed, lay three pounds of prepared cod in it; simmer five minutes, and serve.

With potatoes.—Cook and place on a dish three pounds of cod; pour on it a warm piquante sauce, and serve warm with boiled potatoes, in another dish.

With oil and vinegar.—When the cod is cooked as directed, place it on a dish, and serve with oil, vinegar, mustard, and chopped parsley.

It may be served thus, warm or cold.

Salted cod the next day.—If you have any left, serve it cold the next day with an oil or poivrade sauce, or warm, and serve it as it is.

EEL, CONGER, AND LAMPREY.

Fried.—Clean as directed, then cut in pieces about three inches long, roll them in flour, or in paste for frying, lay them in hot grease or oil, serve when done, sprinkling salt and pepper on.

It may be served on a tomato sauce.

In poulette.—Put in a stewpan a piece of butter the size of an egg; set it on a good fire, sprinkle in it a tablespoonful of flour, add a pinch of grated nutmeg, salt, and pepper; when hot, lay the fish in, which must be cut in pieces three inches long; two minutes after, add half a pint of broth, same of white wine, four or five mushrooms, three sprigs of parsley, one of thyme, a bay leaf, three cloves, and four small onions; boil half an hour, dish the pieces of fish, and place the dish in a warm place; let the sauce remain a while on the fire, and then strain it on the fish; spread the mushrooms on the whole, add a few drops of lemon juice, and serve.

FROGS.

The hind legs only are used as food; formerly frogs, were eaten by the French only, but now, frog eating has become general, and the Americans are not behind any other in relishing that kind of food.

Fried.—Skin well, and throw into boiling water with a little salt for five minutes, the hind legs only; take out and throw them in cold water to cool and drain. Have hot grease in a pan on the fire (use grease for fish, see direction for frying); lay the frogs in, and serve when done with fried parsley around.

Stewed.—Skin, boil five minutes, throw in **cold water,** and drain as above. Put in a stewpan two ounces of butter (for two dozen of frogs); set it on the fire, and when **melted, lay the** legs in, fry two minutes, tossing now and **then; then sprinkle on them a** teaspoonful of flour, stir with a wooden spoon, add two sprigs of parsley, one of thyme, a bay leaf, two cloves, one of garlic, salt, white pepper, and half a pint of white wine; **boil** gently till done, dish the legs, reduce the sauce **on the** fire, strain it, mix in it **two** yolks of eggs, pour on **the** legs, and serve them.

FRESH HERRING, BROILED.

Clean as directed; grease well a gridiron, and set it on a good fire; when warm, **lay** the herrings on it, broil gently, turning them over two or three times; place on a dish, sprinkle salt on them, and serve.

A caper, maitre d'hôtel, piquante or tomato sauce, may be spread on them before **serving.** This is a very good dish for breakfast or supper.

SALTED HERRINGS.

Soak them in cold water for twenty-four hours; change the water twice, then scale and clean them, wash and dry them with a **towel, rub them** with butter, set on a gridiron, and on a **good fire,** and when done, serve them with a purée under.

RED HERRINGS.

Wipe clean, **but do not wash them, cut** off head and tail, split the back open, put them on a warm and greased gridiron, set on a slow fire, put a little butter or sweet oil on, and as soon as it is absorbed, turn the herrings over, and do the same for the other side; broil very little, and serve them with an oil sauce, and some mustard.

Another way.—Clean and split them as above, soak them in lukewarm water for two hours; take out, drain, and wipe dry. Mix two or three yolks of eggs with a teaspoonful of chopped **parsley,** salt, **pepper, and** a little melted butter; put some of the mixture around every herring, then roll them in fine bread crumbs, place them on a gridiron on a slow fire, and when lightly broiled, serve **as** the preceding one.

FRESH MACKEREL, AND SPANISH MACKEREL.

Broiled.—Clean as directed for fish; split the back **in** two, so as **to open** them; sprinkle salt and pepper on, also a little chopped parsley; then envelop the fish in buttered paper, place it on **a** gridiron, and **on a** good fire; turn over **two or** three **times, and when** done, take **the paper off, and serve.**

They may be served cold or warm with a caper or tomato sauce.

With butter.—When broiled as above, place them on **a dish, fry** a few sprigs of parsley in butter, turn the whole **on the fish, add a few drops** of **lemon juice, and serve, having the sprigs of** parsley around the fish.

In maitre d'hôtel.—Knead butter and chopped parsley and spread some on the bottom of **a** dish, then lay on some mackerels broiled as above; spread again some butter and parsley on, put the dish in an oven for two or three minutes, sprinkle on **them a few** drops **of** lemon juice, and serve.

Stewed.—Put in a stewpan a piece of butter the size of an egg, set it on **a** good fire; when melted, lay three middling **sized mackerels in;** add a little grated nutmeg, two middling sized onions cut in slices, two sprigs of parsley, a bay leaf, salt, pepper, half a pint of white wine, same of water, and the juice of half a lemon; boil gently till done, place the fish on a dish, strain the sauce on it, and serve.

Salted mackerel is served like salted herring.

SALTED SALMON.

Soak it in cold water for two days; scale and clean it well, place it in a fish kettle, cover with cold water, set on a moderate fire, skim off the scum, boil gently about two minutes, take from the kettle and drain it. Put butter in a frying pan on the fire; when it turns brown, add two sprigs of parsley; one minute after, pour the whole on the fish in a dish, and serve warm.

It may also be served with a caper, or maitre d'hôtel sauce, or cold with an oil sauce.

SMOKED SALMON.

Cut it in thin slices; have very hot butter or oil in a frying pan, and lay the slices in, only long enough to warm them; then take out, drain them, and serve with a few drops of lemon juice or vinegar sprinkled on them.

SOLE, IN MAITRE D'HÔTEL.

Clean as directed for fish, and skin the back part of it (about three pounds). Put in a fish kettle two sprigs of parsley, one of thyme, a bay leaf, two small onions, salt, pepper, and then the fish; cover with water, boil gently till cooked, take the fish out without breaking it, and serve warm with a maitre d'hôtel sauce.

In Normande.—Take about three pounds of sole and clean as the above. Put in a fish kettle four ounces of butter, two sprigs of parsley, a bay leaf, two small onions, a pinch of grated nutmeg, salt, and white pepper, half a pint of broth, same of white wine, and then the fish; cover the kettle, and when done, dish the fish gently, strain the sauce on it, and serve.

If the sauce is not thick enough, boil it a little after the fish is out of the kettle, and during that time keep the fish in a warm place.

Another way.—When cleaned and prepared as above, take the back bone out, and put in its place chopped parsley and butter kneaded together, with a little salt, pepper, **and** grated nutmeg; **then** put it in a crockery dish, **add** half a pint **of white** wime, same of broth; place **in a** moderately heated oven, and when done, serve in the dish in which it has been cooked, and without moving the fish at all.

This is a very delicate dish, and very easily made with a little attention and taste.

CLAMS.

Wash clean with a scrubbing brush and put them in a kettle; set on a good fire, and leave till they are wide open; then take from the kettle, cut each in two or three pieces, put them in a stewpan with all the water they have disgorged in the kettle, and about four ounces of **butter** for **fifty** clams; boil slowly about an hour, take from the fire, and mix with the whole two beaten eggs, and serve warm.

Clams are also eaten raw with vinegar, salt, and pepper.

CRABS.

Soak in water and drain them. **Put four ounces** of butter in a stewpan, set it on a good fire, add four **sprigs** of parsley, two of thyme, a bay leaf, two carrots and four onions cut in slices, also a pinch of allspice, two cloves, salt, pepper, and two cloves of garlic, with a tablespoonful of vinegar, and three quarts of crabs; boil till done, drain, and serve with parsley.

Another way.—Put three quarts of crabs in a stewpan with butter and the same seasoning as above, and also some white wine, just enough to cover half of them, then cover the pan, set it in a hot oven, stir now and then till cooked, when place the crabs on a dish, strain the sauce, and when the crabs and sauce are cold, put them in a stewpan, warm, and then serve them.

LOBSTER.

In salad.—Select heavy ones; never buy a dead lobster; soak in water, and drain. Have a kettle of boiling water on a good fire, and place the lobster in it and alive; for a five pound one, season with four sprigs of parsley, two of thyme, two cloves of garlic, a bay leaf, two cloves, two carrots and four onions cut in slices, salt, pepper, and a teaspoonful of vinegar; boil about half an hour, take the kettle from the fire, and leave the lobster in it till cold, then take off and drain it. Split the back open from head to tail, take out the yellow part, and eggs, if any; mix them with two yolks of eggs, a teaspoonful of mustard, two or three tablespoonfuls of sweet oil, one or two of vinegar, salt, and pepper; put the whole in a bowl or saucer, beat well till mixed, and then it is ready to be used.

Cut the flesh of the lobster in slices, and place them tastefully on a dish; the claws are generally left entire; put a few sprigs of parsley around, and serve either warm or cold, with the sauce above described.

Another way.—When cooked and prepared as above, place the slices on a salad of lettuce, and serve with the same sauce as above.

Three or four eggs boiled hard and cut in two, might be put around the dish as an ornament.

In omelet.—When the lobster is cooked in boiling water, a few thin slices of it may be put in the middle of an omelet, and served as another omelet.

Slices of lobster left from the preceding day are very good in omelet.

Some cooks use lobsters with different sauces, such as curry, etc.; but it is so inferior to the above ways, that we do not recommend them; we think that curry is very good on the borders of the Ganges river, and from that very reason we think too that it ought to be avoided on the borders of the Hudson and thereabout.

MUSCLES.

Bear in mind that muscles are not wholesome between April and September.

Soak them in water, scrape if necessary, wash well, changing the water several times, and then drain. Put them in a pan on a good fire, season with a little chopped parsley; as soon as they are opened, take off the shell to which they are not attached, examining carefully at the same time if there are any small crabs around the muscle and in the shell, and drain them. Put four ounces of butter in a stewpan; when melted, sprinkle on it a teaspoonful of flour, same of chopped parsley, salt, and pepper; then half of the water which they have disgorged while on the fire; stir a little; ten minutes after put the muscles in, boil about eight minutes, and take from the fire; mix two yolks of eggs with a tablespoonful of vinegar, mix again with the muscles, and serve.

The quantities above are for about two quarts of muscles.

FRIED OR SAUTÉ.

When they are opened detach them entirely from the shell, lay them in hot butter in a frying pan, and on a good fire, with chopped parsley, salt, and pepper; fry about two minutes, and serve them.

OYSTERS, RAW.

When well washed, open them, detaching the upper shell, then detach them from the under shell, but leave them on it; place on a dish, and leave the upper shell on every oyster, and serve thus.

To eat them, you remove the upper shell, sprinkle salt, pepper, and lemon juice on, and eat.

BROILED.

When well washed, open and detach from both shells, save the water, and put it on a sharp fire in a kettle; when it boils, throw the oysters in, boil one minute, take off and drain them. Put each oyster on a shell, dust them a little with fine bread crumbs, put on each a little butter and chopped parsley kneaded together, and place them on a gridiron; set it on a good fire, watch carefully, and as soon as you see any of them beginning to boil, take off, and serve.

FRIED.

Wash, open, and boil them one minute as above; take off and drain them. Put an ounce of butter for each dozen of oysters in a frying pan; when the butter is hot, dip the oysters in milk or in paste for frying, and lay in the pan with a little chopped parsley; it hardly takes one minute to fry them; place them on a dish, with or without the shells, sprinkle a few drops of lemon juice on them, and serve.

If you serve them with the shells, put two oysters on a shell; it is a sightly as well as a good dish.

The shells that are to be served must be the largest ones, and well cleaned.

STEWED.

Oysters to stew are generally bought opened, and by the quart. Procure two quarts of good and fresh oysters, put the water coming from them in a stewpan, after having strained it, and set it on a good fire; at the first boiling put the oysters in and boil them one minute, take out and put them in cold water one minute also, and drain them.

Put in a stewpan four ounces of butter, set it on a good fire, and when melted, sprinkle in it a teaspoonful of flour, same of chopped parsley; add half a pint of broth, boil the whole to a sauce, and then put the oysters in, with salt and pepper; place them on a dish, strain the sauce on them, add a few drops of lemon juice or vinegar, and serve.

Do not boil them longer than one minute.

Another way is to put the oysters in the stewpan at the same time as the broth, boil about one minute, dish the oysters, strain the sauce on them, and serve with a few drops of lemon juice or vinegar.

SHRIMPS.

Wash well, put two quarts of them in a stewpan, with four onions cut in slices, two sprigs of parsley, one of thyme, a bay leaf, two cloves, salt, pepper, half a pint of white wine, and two ounces of butter; cover with water, and set on a good fire; when properly cooked, drain, and serve warm with green parsley around.

VEAL.

Never buy too young veal. It is very easy to know it; when too young, the bones are very tender, they are more like nerves than like bones; the meat is glueish, and has little or no taste.

Epicureans say that if a calf is killed before it is two months old, it is not fit for eating. We are of that opinion, although, perhaps, very few are allowed so long a life. We will therefore recommend our readers to beware buying too young veal; many diseases, especially in children, come from eating it.

When you broil or roast a piece of veal, baste often. Veal is better when a little overdone; it is not good, and operates like a physic, if underdone.

BLANQUETTE. (*Also called Poulette.*)

Take two pounds of fillet, or loin, or rump of veal, which cut in square pieces, two inches in size, throw them in boiling water, with a little salt, for five minutes, and drain them. Put in a stewpan a piece of butter the size of an egg, set it on a good fire, and when melted mix in it a tablespoonful of flour, stirring all the time, and when turning yellow pour gently and slowly in the pan, a pint of boiling water; add a teaspoonful of chopped parsley and green onions, salt, pepper, six small white or red onions, two or three mushrooms, then the meat; boil gently about three hours, and **serve**.

BREAST, STEWED.

Cut in dice two **ounces of** bacon, **put it in** a stewpan and set on a good fire; add two ounces of butter, and two onions cut in slices; **when melted, lay the breast in,** turn it over and leave **till of a** golden color on **both sides**; add then two small carrots cut in pieces, one teaspoonful of chopped green onions, three **sprigs of** parsley, half **a turnip,** salt, and pepper; **moisten** with half **a** pint of warm water; leave thus about three hours on a moderate fire. Strain the juice in a dish, put the meat on it, and serve.

The pieces of carrots and of bacon may be served with the meat, if you choose.

The same, with green peas.—Cut **the** breast in square **pieces** about two inches in size. Put in a stewpan a piece **of** butter the size of **an** egg, and **set** it on the fire; when melted, mix **in it a** teaspoonful of **flour, then lay the meat in, and wet with half a glass of** broth, same of warm wa**ter,** also two sprigs of parsley, salt, and pepper; stir now and then. One hour after add green peas, and leave on **the** fire till the whole is cooked, when skim off the fat on **the surface, and serve.**

The same, roasted.—Chop fine a tablespoonful of parsley, a teaspoonful of shallots, same of green onions, a bay **leaf, two sprigs of** thyme, two or three mushrooms; **add** pepper, salt, **a** little grated **nutmeg; cover the bottom** of a tureen with half **of each, put on it a breast** of veal well **larded,** cover with the other half of **the** seasoning, then **pour gently on the whole** two tablespoonfuls of sweet oil; leave it thus four hours in winter, and two in summer. Take the breast **after that** time, place **it on** the spit with the seasoning around, which you fix by the means of sheets of buttered paper. Place before a moderate fire, and when cooked, take off the paper, scrape off the seasoning from the paper and meat, and leave the meat five minutes more before the fire, basting it all the time with melted butter. Put the seasoning which you have scraped from the paper and meat in a stewpan with two ounces of butter, kneaded with a teaspoonful of flour, salt, and pepper, also a little of the juice of the meat, and a tablespoonful of good vinegar; set on the fire, stir now and then, and when of a proper thickness, turn on a dish, lay the breast on it, and serve.

Another way.—Put in a stewpan a piece of butter the size of an egg, and set it on the fire; when melted, lay a breast of veal in, turn over, and when of a golden color on both sides, add salt, pepper, half a bay leaf, half a glass of water, cover the pan well, subdue the fire, and leave thus three hours. Take off the bay leaf, and serve the whole as it is.

Another way, with onions.—Take a breast of veal, which cut in square pieces two inches in size; then put in a stewpan a piece of butter the size of an egg, set it on a good fire; when melted lay the meat in, stir now and then till of a golden color, when take the meat from the pan which you leave on the fire, and in which you add a tablespoonful of flour, little by little, keep stirring about five minutes; add also half a pint of broth, same of warm water, one onion with a clove stuck in it, a bay leaf, two sprigs of thyme, two of parsley, a clove of garlic, a small carrot cut in two or three pieces, salt, and pepper, then the meat, and cover the pan. Half an hour after your meat is in, fry in butter in a frying pan, six small onions, which you also put in the stewpan as soon as fried. When the whole is cooked, place the meat on a dish, strain the sauce on it, surround the whole with the six small onions, and serve.

The same in matelote.—Cut the breast in square pieces about two inches in size; have in a stewpan and on a good fire, a piece of butter the size of an egg; when melted, put the meat in, stir now and then till of a golden color; then take the meat from the stewpan, which you leave on the fire, and in which you put half a pint of warm water, same of claret wine, same of broth, a bay leaf, two cloves, two sprigs of parsley, one of thyme, a clove of garlic, salt, and pepper; when turning brown, put the meat back in the pan, and fifteen minutes before it is cooked, add also ten small onions fried in butter beforehand, and four or five mushrooms; then have a brisk fire to finish the cooking; place the meat on a dish, strain the sauce on the meat, put the ten small onions around it, and serve.

CUTLETS, BROILED.

Butter the cutlets on both sides, place them on a gridiron, the bars of which you have greased and warmed previously; set on a good fire, turn over two or three times, baste slightly while broiling with melted butter; serve with a poivrade or piquante sauce when done, at the same time sprinkling some salt and pepper on them.

Another way.—Flatten the cutlets with a chopper, dip them in lukewarm butter, and roll them in fine bread crumbs, so as to permit the crumbs to adhere to every part; place them on a warm and greased gridiron, set it on a moderate fire, turn over and allow about fifteen minutes to each side for broiling; serve, and at the same time sprinkle salt and pepper on them.

The same in papillotes.—Cut the cutlets rather thin; chop fine one ounce of bacon, a teaspoonful of parsley, same of shallots, or green onions, two or three mushrooms (if handy); knead the whole with bread crumbs, salt, and pepper. Spread that paste on both sides of the cutlets, which envelop in buttered paper; place them on a gridiron, the bars of which must be greased and warmed before, and on which you put a sheet of buttered paper, to prevent the burning of the paper surrounding the cutlets; set on a slow fire for about fifty minutes, during which you turn them over two or three times. Serve them with the paper around, which paper is only taken off when on the plate, and by every guest.

The same, with fines herbes.—Put in a stewpan, which set on a good fire, a piece of butter the size of an egg; when melted, add a pinch of allspice, salt, pepper, and then the cutlets; toss them over five minutes, sprinkling on, little by little, a teaspoonful of chopped parsley and green onions, same of mushrooms; keep tossing all the time. When cooked, take from the fire, add the juice of a lemon, place the cutlets on a dish, spread the sauce on them, and serve.

FRICANDEAU.

Take a good fillet of veal and lard it; then put in a stewpan two ounces of bacon, cut in dice, four onions, two carrots cut in pieces, one sprig of thyme, two of parsley, a clove of garlic, a bay leaf, two cloves, salt, and pepper, then the fillet on the whole; wet with a pint of broth, set on a good fire, and boil about three hours; once in a while you baste the fillet with the sauce at the bottom of the stewpan while cooking, and in case the broth becomes too thick, add a little more of it. After that time take from the fire, place the fillet in a tureen, throw a few drops of cold water in the sauce, skim off the fat, strain the sauce, put it back in the stewpan with the meat, set on a brisk fire, turning over the fillet so as to have it of a nice color all around; then pour the sauce on a dish with the fillet on it, and serve.

The sauce may be mixed with a purée of sorrel, or with a tomato sauce if you choose.

LOIN, STEWED.

Take a good loin of veal and lard it, fasten it with twine or skewers. Have in a stewpan, and on a slow fire, three or four tablespoonfuls of sweet oil; when hot put the loin in, turn it over till of a yellow color all around, then **add a bay leaf, salt, pepper, and a pint of warm water ; simmer four** hours, and serve with the following sauce, which **you** must have prepared at the same time. Fry in butter till of a golden color ten middling sized onions, then add to them half a glass of claret wine, two tablespoonfuls of broth, and two of the juice of the loin, ten mushrooms (if handy), simmer till cooked, **and strain.** Mix that sauce **with the juice of the** loin, **and put it on a dish,** place the **loin upon it, and** serve with **the onions and** mushrooms **around the meat.**

In case the juice of the loin should be found too fat, throw in it (and before mixing it with the sauce) a few drops of cold water, and skim off the fat.

The only **thing** to throw away **before** mixing is the **bay leaf.**

The same, roasted.—Take a loin of **veal,** leave the kidney to it, sprinkle on it salt and pepper, roll **and fix it** with skewers so as to imitate a large sausage ; place it on the spit, surrounded with buttered paper, and when **cooked** take the paper off, leave five minutes more before the fire, **baste** with melted butter **so as to give it a fine** yellow color, **and** serve with an oil, poivrade, or piquante sauce.

The same, with a garniture of cabbages.—Put in a stewpan and **set on** a good fire a piece of butter the size of an egg; when melted, add four onions and two small carrots, cut in slices, fry them two or three minutes, then put the loin in, with half a bay leaf, wet with warm broth; then subdue the fire, let simmer about two hours and a half; strain the sauce on a dish, place the meat on it, and serve with a garniture of cabbages around.

ESCALOPS.

Take a rump of veal and cut it in slices about three eighths of an inch in thickness, and which you cut again in round or square pieces; flatten them with a chopper, glaze them with some yolks of eggs by the means of a pencil, dust them with bread crumbs, and lay them in a pan in which you have hot butter; keep the pan on a good fire, add a little chopped parsley, salt, and pepper. When cooked, place them tastefully on a dish, so as to imitate a flight of stairs, add a few drops of lemon juice, and serve.

They may also be served with a tomato sauce.

RUMP, ROASTED.

Lard it well, envelop it in buttered paper, and place it on the spit before a good fire, baste now and then with melted butter; when properly cooked serve on a purée, or on a tomato sauce.

SHOULDER, ROASTED.

Butter well a shoulder of veal, place it on the spit before a good fire, leave it about two hours, basting it once in a while, and serve with the gravy; it is as good as it is simply done.

Another way.—Take the bones from the shoulder, sprinkle on it chopped parsley, grated nutmeg, salt, and pepper, then tie it with twine, or fix it with skewers, so as to give it the form of a sausage. Have in a stewpan and on a brisk fire a piece of butter the size of an egg, when hot lay the meat in, and when of a golden color all around, add a bay leaf, one sprig of thyme, two of parsley, a clove of garlic, four onions, two carrots cut in pieces, and half a pint of warm water; then subdue the fire and boil gently about three hours; strain the sauce on a dish, place the meat on it, and serve with the onions and carrots around.

VEAL LEFT FOR THE NEXT DAY.

Put a piece of butter the size of an egg in a stewpan and set on a good fire, mix in when melted two teaspoonfuls of flour, stir till of a brownish color, when add a saltspoonful of chopped parsley, four leaves of tarragon, salt, pepper, and half a pint of broth (more or less of the above according to the quantity of meat you have left), boil the whole fifteen minutes, then if what you have left is from an entire piece, cut it in slices, lay them in the pan, and serve when warm enough, as it is.

If what you have left is in pieces or slices, you merely place them in the pan and serve with the sauce when warm.

Another way.—All that is left from roasted pieces may be cut in slices and served cold with an *oil* or piquante sauce.

CALF'S BRAIN.

How to prepare.—Soak it in lukewarm water and clean it well, so as to have it free from blood, fibres, and thin skin, then put it in cold water for twelve hours in winter and six in summer, and drain it.

How to cook.—Put in a stewpan a piece of butter the size of two walnuts, one teaspoonful of chopped parsley, one glass of broth, half a one of white wine, set on the fire and put two brains in the pan as soon as the butter is melted, boil gently till cooked, and serve.

Another way.—Prepare the brain as above directed, then boil it gently ten or fifteen minutes in brown butter sauce, after which time serve it with fried parsley around.

Another way.—Have butter in a stewpan and set it on the fire; when hot, sprinkle in and mix with a wooden spoon a tablespoonful of flour, add half a glass of claret wine, a glass of broth, salt, pepper, a little piece of nutmeg, eight small onions, and four or five mushrooms; boil the whole an hour and ten minutes. Put two or three brains in the pan (after having prepared them as directed above), boil again ten or twelve minutes, take the brains off and lay them on a dish, strain the sauce in the pan on them, place the onions and mushrooms around, add then the juice of half a lemon beaten with two yolks of eggs, and serve.

CALF'S EARS.

Put them in cold water for one day in winter and eight hours in summer, changing the water twice; place them in a stewpan and set it on the fire; cover them with cold water and boil about ten minutes; drain and clean them. Put in a stewpan two ounces of bacon cut in slices, two sprigs of parsley, a small green onion cut in slices, the quarter of a lemon cut in slices, two or three tarragon leaves, lay the ears on the whole, cover with half white wine and half broth, set on a good fire, boil gently nearly two hours; take the ears off, drain, and serve them on a *piquante* or *ravigote* sauce.

CALF'S FEET.

Throw them in boiling water for five minutes, split them in the middle and lengthwise after having taken off the large bone and hair, and tie them with a string. Put a piece of butter the size of two walnuts in a stewpan and set it on the fire, when melted add a teaspoonful of chopped parsley and green onions, half of each, a quarter of a lemon cut in slices, salt, and pepper, then the feet; wet with a glass of warm water; boil gently two or three hours, take from the fire and when nearly cold dip them in bread crumbs, place them on a gridiron and set on a good fire, baste slightly with the juice in which they have cooked, and serve with fried parsley around.

The same, in poulette.—Prepare and cook them as above. When you take them from the fire, instead of dipping them in bread crumbs, put them in a *poulette* sauce, simmer ten minutes, and serve.

CALF'S HEAD.

How to prepare.—When the hair is off and the whole head well cleaned (this is generally done by butchers, but if not, throw the head in boiling water for five minutes and scrape the hair off with a knife immediately after taking it from the water), put it in water for twenty-four hours in winter and ten in summer, changing the water three times; then take the bones out, cut it in pieces about two inches in size, leave the ears and brain entire, clean well, so as to have it free from blood, hair or bones, place it in a stewpan, cover with cold water and set on a good fire, boil ten minutes, and take from the fire, throw the pieces in cold water for about ten minutes, and drain them.

How to cook.—After it is cleaned and prepared as directed above, you put in a stewpan four ounces of lard, as much of bacon cut in dice, four onions, two parsnips, one carrot cut in pieces, three cloves, four sprigs of parsley, two of thyme, two cloves of garlic, two bay leaves, the juice of half a lemon, and set on a brisk fire. Five minutes after, add two tablespoonfuls of flour, sprinkling it little by little and stirring continually; when it turns yellow, add also a pint of warm water and a tablespoonful of vinegar. Then rub the pieces of head with a lemon, tie them in a towel and put them in the stewpan; twenty minutes after subdue the fire, let simmer about three hours, and serve on a dish with the following sauce in a saucer: sweet oil three or four tablespoonfuls, vinegar two tablespoonfuls, salt, pepper, three sprigs of chervils, three of parsley, and five or six leaves of tarragon, these last three chopped fine.

It may also be cooked in the same way entire, after having taken out the jaw bones only.

The same, in poulette.—When prepared and cooked as above directed, you cut it in pieces and put them in a poulette sauce and set on the fire; simmer for ten minutes, and serve.

If any is left for the next day, if in poulette, you merely warm and serve it; if in another way, serve it cold with the sauce described above.

CALF'S KIDNEYS.

Cut the kidneys in fillets after having split them in two and having cut off the nerves which are inside. Put a piece of butter the size of half an egg in a frying pan and set on the fire; when melted, sprinkle in a teaspoonful of flour, stirring with a wooden spoon the while, add half a wine glass of white wine, a tablespoonful of broth, a pinch of chopped parsley, salt and pepper, boil ten minutes and lay the fillets in; have a quick fire and as soon as cooked dish them, spread the sauce over, sprinkle on a few drops of lemon juice, and serve.

CALF'S LIGHTS.

Cut them in four pieces, soak and wash them three or

four times in lukewarm water, changing the water each time; press them with the hands to extract all the blood. Place the lights in a stewpan, cover them with cold water, and set on a good fire; boil two minutes, take them off, throw them in cold water, and drain them; cut the lights in dice. Have butter in a stewpan on the fire, and when melted, lay the lights in, fry five minutes, keeping them tossed the while, then sprinkle on a tablespoonful of flour, stirring all the time with a wooden spoon; pour on, little by little, about a pint of warm broth, also a saltspoonful of chopped parsley, a pinch of allspice, salt, pepper, a bay leaf, and a sprig of thyme; have a brisk fire, and when about half done, add four or five mushrooms, and eight small onions. When the whole is cooked, take off bay leaf and thyme, then take from the fire, beat two yolks of eggs with a tablespoonful of vinegar, and mix with the whole, turn on a dish, and serve.

CALF'S LIVER.

How to prepare.—Have water, with a little salt, on the fire, and at the first boiling, throw the liver in for about five minutes, and drain it.

How to improve the liver before cooking it.—Put in a tureen two tablespoonfuls of sweet oil, a bay leaf broken in four pieces, two sprigs of thyme, four of parsley chopped fine, a green onion also chopped fine, salt, and pepper; lay the liver on the whole, and leave it from four to six hours, turning it over two or three times.

How to cook, roasted.—Envelop the liver with buttered paper, place it on the spit before a good fire, baste often with the oil from the tureen, after having taken off bay leaf and thyme. A few minutes before it is done, take the paper off, baste continually with the drippings till well cooked, and serve it with the gravy.

It may also be served with a piquante or poivrade sauce.

It takes from thirty-five to forty-five minutes to roast it.

The same, sauté.—Put two ounces of butter in a frying pan, and set it on a sharp fire; when melted, add a teaspoonful of chopped parsley and green onions, then the liver cut in slices (after having been prepared as above); sprinkle on a saltspoonful of flour, then half a wine glass of warm broth, same of claret wine, salt, pepper, and a pinch of allspice; serve when done.

It takes only from ten to twelve minutes for the whole process.

The same, in the oven.—Put two ounces of butter in a frying pan on a sharp fire; when hot, put the liver in (after having been boiled as directed above, and after having cut it in pieces); fry it five minutes, turning over once only; then take from the fire, salt both sides of the slices, place them on a warm dish, putting on each slice a little butter kneaded with chopped parsley, salt, and pepper; put two or three minutes in a warm oven, take off, sprinkle on the whole the juice of half a lemon, and serve in the dish in which it has cooked.

The same, stewed.—Boil the liver as directed above, and when drained and cold, lard it well. Have butter in a frying pan on a brisk fire; when hot, put the liver in for about five minutes, turning it over on every side. Have in a stewpan four ounces of bacon cut in dice; set it on a good fire, and when hot, lay the liver in; then add a glass of warm broth, same of white wine, a bay leaf, a sprig of thyme, two of parsley, a clove of garlic, two cloves, and a small carrot cut in two; cover the stewpan, subdue the fire, and let simmer three hours; stir now and then, place the liver on a dish, strain the sauce on it, and serve.

CALF'S PLUCK.

Put the pluck in cold water for twelve hours in winter and four in summer; change the water once, drain, and throw it in boiling water for ten or fifteen minutes; take off and throw in cold water to cool, and drain it. Cut the pluck in pieces, and cook it like calf's head, and serve with the same sauce.

SWEETBREADS.

Soak the sweetbreads in lukewarm water for an hour, changing the water once; then throw in boiling water for five minutes, take off, throw it in cold water to cool, and then drain it. Lard and cook the sweetbreads like a fricandeau, and serve it on a tomato sauce.

Another way.—Prepare as above directed; then, instead of larding it, you knead well together two ounces of butter, a teaspoonful of shallots and parsley well chopped, half a clove of garlic, salt, and pepper; place the whole in a stewpan, with the sweetbreads on it, and thin slices of bacon on the sweetbreads; set the pan on a good fire, and add then half a glass of broth, same of white wine; simmer till cooked; dish the sweetbreads, throw a few drops of cold water in the sauce, skim off the fat, strain the sauce on the sweetbreads, and serve.

CALF'S TAIL, WITH CABBAGE.

Take two tails, cut each in two, throw them in boiling water for three minutes, and drain. Cut a cabbage in two, trim off the stump, throw the two halves in boiling water, with a little salt, for fifteen minutes, and drain it. Put in a tureen the tails, cabbage, six ounces of lean bacon, two sprigs of parsley chopped fine, same quantity of green onions, two cloves, a little piece of nutmeg, a clove of garlic, salt, **and** pepper; cover the whole with half broth and half water, and boil gently till cooked. Then take off cloves, **nutmeg, and** garlic, turn the remainder on a dish, and serve.

CALF'S TONGUE.

Prepare, cook, and serve it **as ox** tongue.

MUTTON.

HOW TO SELECT.

You may be sure that it is good when the flesh is rather black, and the fat white; if the fat breaks easily it is young.

The wether is much superior to the ewe.

You will know if a leg of mutton comes from a wether, if there is a large and hard piece of fat on one side at the larger and upper end; if from a ewe, that part is merely a kind of skin, with a little fat on it.

BREAST OF MUTTON IN THE OVEN.

Put in a stewpan two ounces of bacon, cut in slices; cut the breast in square pieces, two inches in size, and lay them over the bacon; cover again with slices of bacon (two ounces); add a bay leaf, a sprig of thyme, two of parsley, six small onions, one carrot cut in four pieces, salt, and pepper; wet with a glass of broth, place the pan in a moderately heated oven, simmer about three hours, and serve, after you have taken off bay leaf, thyme, and parsley.

The same, broiled.—Put the breast entire in a stewpan, with a sprig of thyme, two of parsley, a bay leaf, a clove, salt, and pepper; cover with water, set on the fire, and **boil** gently till cooked, and then drain. Put in a frying pan three tablespoonfuls of sweet oil, **a** teaspoonful of chopped parsley, salt, and pepper; when hot lay the breast in and fry it all around for five minutes; then take it off, **roll it in bread crumbs**, place it **on** a gridiron, **and set on a good fire for** five minutes, turn it over once only, **then serve it with a piquante,** poivrade, or tomato sauce.

It may also be served on a purée of sorrel.

The same, roasted.—Prepare **the breast as in** the receipt above; instead of frying **it, you rub it with** butter all around, and place **it on** the spit, **before a** good fire; baste often with lukewarm **butter** at first, and **with the** drippings afterward; leave thus from ten to fifteen minutes, and serve with a **piquante** or poivrade sauce.

CHOPS, BROILED.

Flatten the chops with a chopper, sprinkle salt and **pepper on** both sides, dip them in melted butter, place **them on** the gridiron, and set on **a sharp** fire (have the **bars of** the gridiron greased and warmed before putting **the** chops on it), turn **over** two **or** three times, **and** when done, serve them tastefully arranged **on** a dish.

It takes from twelve to fifteen minutes to cook.

Another way.—Flatten them with **a** chopper, sprinkle salt and pepper on both sides, dip **in melted** butter, and roll them **in bread crumb**s; place on the gridiron, set on a sharp fire, **turn over two** or three times, and when done, serve them with a maitre-d'-hôtel sauce, or with a little of melted butter and chopped parsley.

It takes about twelve minutes **to cook them.**

The same, sautées.—**After you** have flattened the chops with **a** chopper, put in a stewpan a piece of butter and set it on a slow fire; lay the chops in as soon as it begins to melt; leave them thus till cooked, turning them over two or three times. Take the chops from the pan and put them in a warm place. Leave in the pan only a tablespoonful of grease, add to it three times as much of broth, a teaspoonful of parsley and green onions, two shallots, and two pickled cucumbers, all chopped fine, and a pinch of allspice; give one boil, pour the whole on the chops, also the juice of half a lemon, and serve.

The same, with vegetables.—Put in a frying pan a piece of butter the size of two walnuts for four chops, set on a good fire, and when hot lay the chops in, after having flattened them with a chopper, and having sprinkled salt and pepper on both sides; add a clove, and a teaspoonful of chopped parsley and green onions; leave thus five minutes, turn over once or twice; then add also half a wine glass of broth, same of white wine, and finish the cooking. Take the chops off the pan and put them in a warm place. Boil the sauce in the pan ten minutes, turn it on the chops, put a garniture of vegetables around, and serve.

Throw away the clove just before serving.

Another way.—Have a piece of butter the size of an egg for eight chops in a crockery vessel, and set it on a good fire; when melted take from the fire, lay the chops in, after having flattened them; then cover them with a sheet of buttered paper; place the vessel in a rather hot oven, and when cooked serve them on a maitre-d'hôtel, provençale, or tomato sauce. They may also be served on a purée of sorrel, or one of potatoes.

The same, in papillote.—Cut the chops rather thin, beat them gently and flatten them; then proceed as for veal cutlets in papillotes in every particular.

FILLET, ROASTED.

Lard well a good fillet of mutton, place it on the spit before a good fire, baste often, and when cooked, serve it on a garniture of vegetables, or one of cabbage, or on a purée of potatoes.

LEG OF MUTTON. (*See above how to select.*)

How to prepare and improve it.—To be tender and exquisite, keep it from four to eight days in winter, and from two to four in summer, according to the heat; then place it in a tureen, with one saltspoonful of pepper, one teaspoonful of chopped parsley, and two tablespoonfuls of sweet oil, the whole spread all over; leave thus one day in winter, and from six to twelve hours in summer.

This process improves it very much.

BOILED.

Take the leg of mutton and dust it with flour all around (after having been prepared as directed above, if you have chosen so to do), envelop it in a clean towel after having bent the smaller bone, throw it thus in boiling water, with a little salt, pepper, a bay leaf, two sprigs of thyme, two of sweet basil, and a pinch of scraped nutmeg; move it gently now and then with a wooden spoon, and when properly cooked, serve it on a white or caper sauce.

The same, roasted.—Improve it as above directed, if you choose.

Place it on the spit before a sharp fire, baste often with sweet oil or melted butter at first, and afterward with the drippings, and when cooked, serve it with the gravy only, or with white kidney beans cooked in water, and fried five minutes in butter.

It will take about one hour and a half to cook it well.

Many persons lard the leg of mutton with fillets of garlic. (See what we say about garlics.)

The same, stewed.—Prepare and improve it if it suits you.

Take the large bone out, leaving the bone at the smaller end as a handle; cut off also the bone below the knuckle, and fix it with skewers; then put it in a stewpan with a pinch of allspice, four onions, two cloves, two carrots cut in four pieces each, a small bunch of parsley, two bay leaves, three sprigs of thyme, salt, pepper, two ounces of bacon cut in slices, a quarter of a pint of broth, and water enough just to cover it; set on a good fire, and after one hour of boiling add a liquor glass of French brandy. Let simmer then for about five hours, in all about six hours; then dish it, strain the sauce on it, and serve.

We would advise those who have never tasted of a leg of mutton cooked as above, to try it.

It may be served also with white beans cooked in water and fried in butter, or on fried potatoes.

The next day.—If you have a piece left for the next day, cut it in thin slices after dinner, place the slices on a dish, with parsley under, in the middle, and above, and keep in a cold place.

A while before dinner you put in a stewpan a piece of butter (the quantity to be according to the quantity of meat), and set it on a good fire; when melted, sprinkle in, gradually, a little flour, stirring with a wooden spoon; when of a proper thickness, and of a brownish color, add a glass of broth, salt, pepper, a few pickled cucumbers cut in slices, and two or three mushrooms; boil ten minutes; lay the slices of meat in, subdue the fire, simmer twenty minutes, and serve.

The same, in another way.—Chop fine the slices of leg of mutton, put a piece of butter in a stewpan, and set it on the fire; when melted, place the chopped meat in, keep stirring with a wooden spoon for about ten minutes; then add two or three tablespoonfuls of broth, salt, pepper, and a pinch of allspice; simmer fifteen minutes, and serve with fried eggs all around the dish.

SADDLE OF MUTTON.

Prepare, cook, and serve the saddle in the same ways as the leg, only you keep it two days instead of four.

SHOULDER OF MUTTON.

Proceed as for leg of mutton in every particular.

SHEEP'S BRAIN.

Prepare, cook, and serve as calf's brain.

SHEEP'S FEET, BROILED.

Throw them in boiling water for ten minutes, clean them and scrape off the hair, and take the large bone out. Put in a stewpan a bay leaf, one clove, a tablespoonful of vinegar, a clove of garlic, two sprigs of parsley, two green onions, salt, pepper, a piece of butter the size of two walnuts, half a pint of broth, then a dozen of feet on the whole; set on a slow fire, simmer one hour, stir now and then, take from the fire and let cool. Then dip every foot in well beaten eggs, roll them in bread crumbs afterward, place them on a gridiron, and when properly broiled serve them with the sauce in which they have been cooked, after having strained it. They may also be served on a piquante sauce.

The same, in poulette.—Prepare and clean as directed above. Put in a stewpan four ounces of lard, same of bacon cut in dice, salt, and white pepper; when warm, add three sprigs of parsley, two of thyme, a bay leaf, one clove, four onions, and one carrot cut in slices, a quarter of a lemon also cut in slices, and free from rind and seed, two tablespoonfuls of flour; this last must be added by sprinkling it little by little, and stirring the while with a wooden spoon; five minutes after, **place the feet in,** cover the whole with warm water, and let **simmer gently for five** or six hours. After that time **see if the meat can be** easily detached from the bones, and if so, **they are cooked;** if not, leave them a little longer, and take from the **fire as soon as** it is easily detached, but do **not detach it.** Put in a stewpan a piece of butter the size of two walnuts; when melted, sprinkle in it a tablespoonful of flour, stir with a wooden spoon, then put **the feet in,** add a teaspoonful of chopped parsley and green onions, a little piece of nutmeg, salt, pepper, and two or three mushrooms cut in slices or pieces; wet with broth; simmer half an hour, take from the fire, and throw away **the piece of nutmeg;** mix with the whole two yolks of eggs **well beaten with a** tablespoonful of vinegar, and serve.

SHEEP'S KIDNEYS, BROILED.

Split them in two, and put them in cold water for five minutes; trim off the pellicle or thin skin, run a skewer through, sprinkle salt and pepper on, place them on the gridiron and set on a good fire; turn over, and when broiled, serve them with a piece of butter and chopped parsley kneaded together, and placed on each kidney; add also a few drops of lemon juice.

You may also, when broiled, serve them on a maitre-d'hôtel sauce.

The same, in brochette.—Proceed as above in every particular, except that you place the kidneys on the spit instead of on the gridiron. Serve them in the same way.

The same, with champagne.—Cut the kidneys in slices, each in ten or twelve pieces. Put in a stewpan a piece of butter the size of two walnuts, and set it on the fire; when melted, add a teaspoonful of chopped parsley, same of mushrooms, a pinch of grated nutmeg, salt, pepper, and the kidneys; keep tossing till they become stiff, then sprinkle on them a saltspoonful of flour, stirring with a wooden spoon the while; add also a wine glass of champagne, or of good white wine; subdue the fire, and let simmer till cooked; take from the fire, add about one ounce of fresh butter, and the juice of half a lemon, and serve.

This is a very delicate dish.

SHEEP'S TAILS.

Put in a stewpan two ounces of bacon cut in slices, with a bay leaf, two sprigs of parsley, one of thyme, one clove, six small onions, one carrot cut in four pieces, then about six tails; cover the whole with broth and white wine, half of each; add salt and pepper. Place the pan in a moderately heated oven; it will take about four hours to cook them. After that time, take the tails from the pan, and put them in a warm place, then strain the sauce in which they have cooked, skim off the fat if too much of it, put the sauce back in the pan, and set on the fire; let it reduce till rather thick, place the tails on a purée, turn the sauce on them, and serve.

SHEEP'S TONGUES.

Soak the tongues in cold water for two hours in winter, and one in summer, and drain. Throw them in boiling water, and leave till you can easily take the skin off; then skin and clean well, split in two lengthwise, and let cool. Put in a stewpan two ounces of bacon cut in thin slices, a bay leaf, two sprigs of thyme, four of parsley, two cloves, three green onions and six small red or white ones, one carrot cut in four pieces, salt and pepper, then the tongues;

add also half a pint of broth, same of water, same of white wine; set in a moderately heated oven, and simmer about four hours; have the stewpan covered as nearly air-tight as possible. Then take the tongues from the pan and drain them; knead well together two ounces of fresh butter, with two teaspoonfuls of chopped parsley, a little salt and allspice; spread some on each of the tongues as soon as they are cold; envelop each in oiled paper, broil them gently on a slow fire, and serve with the paper.

You may also when prepared and cooked as above directed, and instead of broiling them, place a purée on a dish, and serve them on a purée, pouring on the whole the sauce in which they have cooked, and straining it at the same time.

They are really more delicate when broiled.

LAMB.

CHOPS.

PREPARE, cook, and serve them in the same ways as mutton chops.

FORE QUARTER.

According to many epicureans' opinions the fore quarter is the best part of the lamb, but, as we have said previously, every one to his liking.

Lard it slightly, and envelop it with buttered paper, place it upon the spit before a good fire; when done take from the fire, and take the paper off, sprinkle on it salt, pepper, and chopped parsley; put back on the spit before a sharp fire, just long enough to allow it to take a fine color; when take off, run a knife under the shoulder to make a small hole, pour some maitre-d'hôtel sauce in it, and serve either as it is, with its gravy, or on a purée of sorrel.

HIND QUARTER.

Throw it in boiling water for five minutes, and drain. Put in a stewpan a piece of butter the size of an egg, and set on the fire; when melted, mix in it a tablespoonful of flour; after which, pour in, little by little, a pint and a half of boiling water, stirring with a wooden spoon all the time; then put the meat in the pan, add four onions, a bay leaf, two cloves, three sprigs of parsley, two of thyme, salt, and pepper; about fifteen minutes before it is done, add two or three mushrooms cut in slices, take from the fire when cooked, place the meat on a dish with the mushrooms and onions around, or if preferred, without either; strain the sauce on the meat, and serve.

If the sauce is not thick enough, mix the yolk of an egg in it just before serving.

ROASTED ENTIRE.

Skewer a lamb properly on the spit, envelop it with buttered paper, place before a good fire, baste often with melted butter first, and then with the drippings, and when nearly done take the paper off, let the lamb take a fine color all around, and serve it with the gravy.

Left for the next day.—If you have any left from the dinner, be it either from the fore quarter, hind quarter, or from an entire piece, cut the meat in slices, place them in a béchamel sauce, and in a stewpan, set on the fire, let simmer fifteen minutes, and serve.

LAMB'S FEET.

Prepare, cook, and serve like sheep's feet.

LAMB'S HEAD.

Prepare, cook, and serve like calf's head.

KID.

Prepare, cook, and serve kid like lamb.

PORK.

HOW TO SELECT.

When the rind of the bacon is tender and thin, the pork is young; when thick and hard, it is old.

To be good, the meat must be soft and have a fresh and good appearance.

We do not think it necessary to indicate here how to make black puddings, chitterlings, headcheese, Bologna, or other sausages. It is nearly, if not quite impossible, for a person having no practice in it to make them edible; it is better to buy them ready made at pork butchers' shops, or to hire an experienced person to make them.

CHINE.

Take a good chine of pork, place it on the spit before a sharp fire, baste often with a little melted butter first, and then with the drippings; when properly cooked, serve it with an oil, piquante, or poivrade sauce. It will take from two to three or four hours to roast, according to the size of the chine.

HOW TO IMPROVE THE CHINE OF PORK.

Place it in a crockery vessel, pour on it two tablespoonfuls of sweet oil, then sprinkle on two teaspoonfuls of chopped parsley, also salt and pepper, two onions chopped fine, four cloves, and two bay leaves; leave thus twenty-four hours in winter, and ten in summer, turning over two or three times. The taste of the meat is much improved by that process. The oil may be used for basting instead of butter.

CUTLETS.

Flatten the cutlets with a chopper (they may be improved in the same way as the chine), place them on the gridiron and set on a sharp fire; turn over two or three times, and when properly done, serve them with a piquante, Robert, or tomato sauce, adding to them some slices of pickled cucumbers just before serving.

The same, sautées.—Instead of broiling them, when prepared as above, place them in a frying pan with a little butter, turn over two or three times during the cooking, and serve as the above.

LEG, ROASTED.

How to improve it.—Take the skin gently off, put the leg in a crockery vessel, pour on it the following mixture: a pint of white wine, two tablespoonfuls of sweet oil, a bunch of sage, salt, pepper, and a pinch of grated nutmeg. Leave it thus two days in winter and one in summer, turning it over two or three times during the process.

Place the leg on the spit and put before a very sharp fire, baste often with the mixture from the crockery vessel, or with melted butter, and serve when cooked, with the gravy strained.

It will take about two or two and a half hours to roast it.

OTHER PARTS.

Any other piece of pork may be cooked and served like the chine.

HAM.

How to prepare.—Sugar-cured are preferred to others. Scrape off the outside gently, soak in cold water for two days in winter and about one in summer, changing the water twice; then take it off, and hang it in a cool and dry place, to allow the water in or around it to drop.

Boiled.—Envelop the ham in a towel and sew or tie it; place it in a kettle large enough to hold it without bending it; add eight small onions, two carrots, four cloves, two bay leaves, a small bunch of thyme, two cloves of garlic, a bunch of parsley, a pint of white wine and a handful of hay; cover with water, boil gently for about four or five hours, according to the size (pay no regard to the old saying that "it takes half an hour to every pound"); take the kettle from the fire, and when nearly cold take the ham off, and hang it for a while to allow the water to drop.

Just before serving the ham, you skin it nicely within two inches of the smaller end, so as to give the fat a nice appearance, sift on it some fine raspings of bread, and serve with jelly around; it is as wholesome as it is sightly.

In case you would serve it warm, skin it as soon as cooked, and immediately after serve it on a garniture of vegetables or of cabbage.

The bone at the larger end may be taken off.

The same, roasted.—Prepare the ham as above directed, and when nearly dry, place it in a crockery vessel; place on and all around it four onions chopped fine, two bay leaves, two sprigs of thyme, a piece of nutmeg, and pour on the whole a bottle of white wine; cover the vessel air-tight, leave it thus twenty-four hours, turning it over two or three times, so as to let every side take the **seasonings.** Place the ham on the spit before a good fire, baste often with the seasonings from **the** crockery **vessel,** and when done take it off, dust it with fine raspings of bread, place it fifteen minutes **in a slow oven, strain** the drippings, boil them till reduced to a proper thickness, dish the ham, pour the drippings on it, and serve.

SALTED PORK.

The best and only proper way to cook salted pork, **is,** to put **it in a kettle, entirely cover it with cold water,** boil gently till cooked, and serve it with a purée or with a **garniture of cabbage.** Anything else that you might put with it would rather spoil than better it.

PIG'S EARS.

How to prepare.—Soak them in warm water for a few minutes, then wash and **clean them well, and** scrape the hair off, if any.

Boiled.—When prepared, **you throw** them in boiling water for two minutes and take **from the** fire; add four onions for four ears, one carrot, salt **and pepper;** leave just water enough to cover the whole, and when cooked, drain. Serve them on a purée of beans or of lentils.

The same, broiled.—When cleaned, prepared, and cooked as above, just dip them in beaten eggs, roll them in bread crumbs, **place on the** gridiron and on the fire, and broil **for about two or three** minutes; then serve **them with a maitre-d'hôtel sauce.**

PIG'S FEET.

Split **in two** lengthwise **and soak** in lukewarm water **for a** few minutes, six **feet;** envelop each in a piece of **linen well tied** or sewed, place them **in a** kettle or stew**pan, with** four small onions, four sprigs of parsley, two of thyme, two of sweet basil, two bay leaves, two cloves of garlic, two cloves, two small carrots cut in pieces, salt, pepper, and half a pint of white wine; cover with cold water, simmer about six hours, skim them properly, fill with boiling water so as to have them covered all the time; take from the fire when cooked, and when nearly cool, take the feet from the kettle, untie them, throw away the linen, and let them cool. Dip each in melted butter or in sweet oil, roll in bread crumbs, and place on a gridiron and on a good fire; serve them as they are, when properly broiled.

PIG'S HEAD.

Soak in water and clean it well; take all the bones out, put inside of it a little fresh bacon and pork, salt, pepper, six chopped onions, two teaspoonfuls of chopped parsley, half a saltspoonful of allspice, two bay leaves, two sprigs of thyme, a little sage and the juice of half a lemon; lay it in a crockery vessel for from four to six days. Envelop the head in a towel, place it in a kettle with eight small onions, two carrots cut in pieces, salt, pepper, four sprigs of parsley, four of thyme, four bay leaves, two cloves, and a pint of white wine, cover with water, set on the fire, and simmer from six to eight hours; take from the fire and drain, take the towel off and drain again till dry and cold. Serve it with sprigs of green parsley around.

The broth in which it has cooked makes a good soup.

PIG'S KIDNEYS.

Prepare, cook, and serve like sheep's kidneys.

PIG'S TAIL.

Prepare, cook, and serve like pig's ears.

PIG'S TONGUE.

Prepare, cook, and serve like ox tongue.

SUCKING PIG (*also Hedgehog*).

A sucking pig, to be good, must be fat.

When properly cleaned, **hoofs off, clean the** inside, leaving the kidneys; skewer it, **put** in it half a pound **of** butter **kneaded with chopped** parsley and green onions, four or five mushrooms, **and two white** onions with **a** clove stuck in each; place **it on the spit before a** good fire, baste often with melted butter first, and then **with the** drippings, and when done, **serve on an** oil sauce.

Some **truffles may be added to** the seasoning if handy; it gives **it a good taste.**

WILD BOAR.

Prepare, cook, and serve every part of the wild boar as the same parts of pork; also the same for the ears, *i. e.*, like pig's ears, etc.

POULTRY.

Chickens, ducks, and turkeys must be killed not less than twenty-four hours, and not more than three days, in summer, and not less than two days, and not more than six days in winter, before cooking them.

Chickens, ducks, geese, and turkeys, when placed on the spit, must be put very near the fire first, and removed a little from it after a while.

HOW TO CLEAN AND PREPARE.

When well picked, have live charcoal, or, if more handy, light some fine shavings or some paper under a chimney; pass the bird over the flame without stopping, so as to burn the fine feathers or down left after being picked, and without burning the skin. Cut the neck off as near the body as possible, leaving skin enough to cover the place where the neck has been cut; after which cut a hole right under the rump, and large enough to run two fingers inside, and with which you detach the inside, gizzard etc. (everything except the lungs); be very careful not to break the gall-bladder; pull the whole out; wash the inside with lukewarm water, and wipe dry with a clean towel. If there should be anything unclean on the outside, wipe it off with a towel, but do not wash it, except if very necessary, and trim off the ends of the wings.

CAPON, BOILED.

Clean and prepare as directed above; rub the fleshy part with lemon, envelop it with slices of bacon, place it in a stewpan with one sprig of parsley, one of thyme, a bay leaf, one clove, a small carrot, two onions, salt and pepper; cover with half water and half broth, and set on a moderate fire. When cooked, take the capon off, place it on a dish, and set it in a warm place; then boil the sauce till it is rather thick, when strain it on the capon and serve.

The same, with rice.—When cleaned and prepared as above, you place the capon in a stewpan, cover it with water, add one glass of broth, a bay leaf, one clove, a sprig of parsley, one of thyme, a small carrot, two onions, salt, and pepper; boil ten minutes, then add also about four ounces of rice, soaked in lukewarm water before using it, and let simmer for two hours. Take the capon off, and in case the rice should not be found to be cooked enough, finish the cooking of it; then take off clove, parsley, thyme, bay leaf, carrot and onions, pour the remainder on the capon, and serve.

ROASTED.

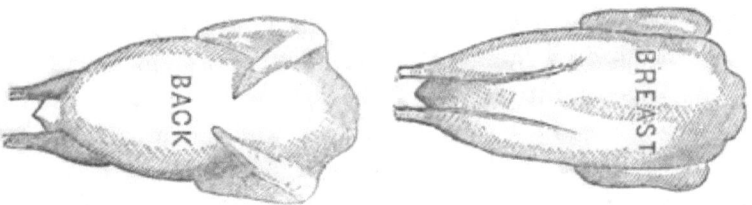

When trussed as seen above, and after you have cleaned and prepared it as we have directed, you envelop it with thin slices of bacon; place it on the spit before a good fire, baste often with the drippings, and after about thirty minutes, take the slices of bacon off, leave five minutes longer, basting all the time, then take off and serve with the gravy; you may also add a little watercresses and vinegar.

CHICKENS.

How to select.—Take a chicken with white flesh and pale yellow **fat**.

You know if young: the cock by his small spurs, the hen by the lower part of the leg and paws, which must be rather soft and smooth; these parts are rough in old ones.

If **the rump is hard** and stiff, they are fresh enough, but if soft, it is necessary to examine the bird carefully; it might be tainted.

SPRING CHICKENS, AND OTHERS UNDER TWO YEARS OF AGE.

Broiled.—Clean and prepare as directed for poultry. Put in a bowl two tablespoonfuls of sweet oil, two onions cut in slices, two sprigs of parsley chopped fine, three cloves, salt, pepper, and a pinch of allspice; mix well together, spread the whole around the chicken, and fasten it with buttered paper, which you fix with twine. Place the chicken on the gridiron, set it on a moderate fire, turn over so as to have every part well cooked, then take the paper off, also the seasoning, such as onions, cloves, etc., and serve it on a ravigote sauce. It takes from twenty to twenty-five minutes to broil properly.

Another way.—(See directions for cleaning and preparing.) Split the back of the chicken open, sprinkle salt, pepper, and a little chopped parsley all over; envelop it with oiled paper, broil as the above, and serve with an oil, piquante or poivrade sauce.

The same, in fricassee.—When cleaned and prepared as directed, cut each leg and wing in two, just at the joint; cut the back in two, the stomach makes one piece, and all, with the gizzard and neck, make thirteen pieces. Throw the pieces and a pinch of salt in boiling water, for one or two minutes, **take off** and drain them. **Put in a stewpan** a piece **of butter** the size of an egg, **and set on the fire;** when melted, sprinkle in little by little, a tablespoonful of flour, keep stirring with a wooden spoon, and when of a proper thickness, and of a brownish color, add a gill of broth, same of water, two sprigs of parsley, a pinch of grated nutmeg, four small onions, salt, pepper, and then the chicken; half an hour after add also two or three mushrooms cut in pieces. It will take from one hour to one hour and a half to cook it. Dish the pieces in the following order: the neck and gizzard with the fore part of the back, and the low part of the legs in the middle; then one leg on each side of the dish, with **one wing** beside each, then the stomach and hind part **of the** back, and lastly the ends of the wings at the top; strain the sauce on the whole after having mixed in it two well beaten yolks of eggs, and a few drops of lemon juice; spread **on** the whole the pieces of mushrooms, and **serve.**

Another way.—After having cleaned and prepared the chicken, cut it in thirteen pieces as the above. **Put a** piece of butter the size of an egg in a stewpan, and **set on** a good fire; when melted, put the chicken in and fry **it** well; it takes six or eight minutes; then take the pieces out, sprinkle a teaspoonful of flour in the pan, stirring the while, and immediately add half **a** teaspoonful of **chopped** parsley, two or three mushrooms cut in slices, salt, **pepper;** two or three minutes after add also two gills of **white wine;** then have a brisk fire, and boil **till reduced;** subdue the fire, put the chicken back in the pan, simmer two or three minutes, and serve the pieces placed on the dish as in the **above, but do not strain the sauce.**

It takes about twenty minutes for the whole process.

This last way is very good for a chicken eight months old or less, but for one older, the first way is preferable.

CHICKEN MARENGO.

Clean, prepare, and cut up the chicken as for fricassee. Put in a stewpan five teaspoonfuls of sweet oil, and set on a good fire; when hot, put the chicken in with salt and pepper; turn over once in a while, till every piece is of a golden color, and nearly cooked; when, add two sprigs of parsley, one of thyme, a bay leaf and one clove tied together with twine; add also three or four mushrooms cut in slices, and if handy, three or four truffles also cut in slices; when the whole is cooked, dish the pieces of chicken thus: the neck and gizzard, with the fore part of the back, and the low part of the legs in the middle, one leg on each side of the dish with one wing beside each, then the stomach and hind part of the back, and the ends of the wings at the top. Have an Italian sauce ready, pour it on the chicken, place on the whole the pieces of mushrooms and truffles, also some croutons fried in butter, and serve.

The same, roasted.—Proceed as for a roasted capon, and serve like it also.

The same, sauté.—When the chicken is cleaned, prepared, and cut up in thirteen pieces, as for fricassee, put in a frying pan a piece of butter the size of a small egg, and set on the fire; when melted, put the pieces of chicken in, turn over till every piece is of a golden color, then sprinkle on a teaspoonful of flour, salt, pepper, and a pinch of allspice, stirring the while; six minutes after add a teaspoonful of chopped parsley, two or three mushrooms cut in pieces, two gills of white wine, same of broth, same of warm water; subdue the fire, simmer till done, when give one boil, and serve hot.

The same, stuffed with chestnuts or truffles.—Clean and

prepare the chicken as directed for poultry in general. Roast a pound or so of chestnuts and shell them, stuff the chicken with them or with about six ounces of truffles fried in butter, sew the chicken up, place it on the spit properly enveloped in buttered paper, before a good fire, baste with melted butter, and leave thus about half an hour; take the paper off, leave five minutes more, basting continually, and serve with the gravy.

The same, in Tartar.—Prepare a chicken as directed; cut the neck off, also the legs at the first joint, split the stomach in two so as to open the chicken, and flatten it with a chopper. Put in a stewpan a piece of butter the size of a small egg and set it on the fire; when hot, add a teaspoonful of chopped parsley, salt, pepper, and a piece of allspice, then the chicken; turn it over once in a while till cooked, then take it from the pan, roll it in fine bread crumbs, place it on a well warmed and greased gridiron, set it on a slow fire, turn over once or twice, so as to have both sides of a fine color, and serve it on a Tartar sauce.

CHICKENS OVER TWO YEARS OF AGE.

With onions.—You prepare the chicken as directed for poultry, and cut it up as for fricassee. Put in a stewpan a piece of butter the size of two walnuts, and set it on a moderate fire; when melted, add two sprigs of parsley, one of thyme, a clove and a bay leaf tied together, then the chicken and about a dozen of small onions; after having fried them about five minutes in butter, turn over now and then with a wooden spoon, and after about ten minutes' time, add a pint of warm broth; simmer till well cooked, take off the bunch of seasonings and serve.

The same, with peas.—Proceed as for the above with onions, in every particular, except that you put with it about a quart of peas instead of onions.

How to prepare when left from the preceding day's dinner, either entire or a part of it.—If not a roasted or broiled chicken, or part of either, you merely warm it in the bain-marie if possible, or on the fire, and serve as it is.

If roasted or broiled, it is served in blanquette, thus:

Cut up the meat in slices, have in a stewpan and on a good fire, a piece of butter the size of two walnuts; when melted, sprinkle in it a pinch of flour, stirring with a wooden spoon the while, then pour in also, little by little, two gills of warm broth, same of boiling water, half a teaspoonful of chopped parsley, salt, pepper, and two or three small onions fried in butter; boil fifteen minutes. After that time subdue the fire, place the slices of chicken in the pan, and serve as it is when well warmed.

Instead of onions, slices of pickled cucumbers may be used.

Another way.—Cut up the chicken or part of it as for fricassee. Put a little butter in a stewpan and set on the fire; when melted, sprinkle in it a little flour, half a teaspoonful of chopped parsley, same of chopped mushrooms, stir with a wooden spoon the while, two or three minutes after add also two gills of white wine, boil the whole fifteen minutes, then subdue the fire, put the pieces of chicken in the pan and serve as it is when warm.

It may also after it is cut up be served cold, with an oil, piquante or poivrade sauce.

The same, in fricassee.—An old chicken that has been used to make broth, either alone or with beef, when cool, or the next day, may be prepared just as a spring chicken in fricassee.

CROQUETTES OF FOWL.

Take the bones off the chicken, or the part of it which you have left from the day before, and cut the meat in very small pieces. Put about four ounces of butter for a whole chicken, in a stewpan, set it on the fire, when melted, sprinkle in one tablespoonful of flour, stirring the while, add two sprigs of parsley chopped fine, salt, pepper, and a little grated nutmeg; five minutes after, add also, if handy, two or three mushrooms cut in pieces; after another five minutes, pour in a gill of warm broth, boil gently till rather thick, then put the meat in the pan for two or three minutes and take from the fire. When cool, work the whole in small balls, dust them with bread crumbs, dip them in beaten eggs and fry them with butter; serve hot.

Fried parsley or fried mushrooms may be put around.

DUCKS AND DUCKLINGS—TAME AND WILD.

How to select.—A young duck has the lower part of the legs soft, and the skin between the claws soft also; you will also know if it is young by taking hold of it by the bill (the under bill only), if it breaks or bends, the duck is young.

If the breast of the duck is hard and thick, it is fresh enough.

To be good, a duck must be fat, be it a Canvas-back, Black-duck, Wood-duck, Shelldrake, Teal, or any other.

How to prepare.—A duck is cleaned and prepared as directed for poultry.

Roasted.—Clean, prepare, and truss the duck as the chicken, to roast it. Put inside of the duck two sage leaves and two sprigs of thyme, and leave it thus in a cool place for two or three hours, then take sage and thyme off, stuff the duck with cooked sausages, or with chestnuts previously cooked in water and properly shelled, fix with small skewers some thin slices of bacon on the fleshy parts, place it on the spit before a sharp fire, or in a quick oven, baste often and serve with the gravy when cooked.

It takes from thirty to forty minutes to roast.

The same, in salmis.—Take a piece of butter the size of an egg, knead it with flour so as to make a paste, put it in a stewpan and set on a slow fire; when melted, add one gill of claret wine, same of broth, two shallots, salt, pepper, three sprigs of parsley, one of thyme and a bay leaf, boil half an hour, then take a roasted duck, cut all the flesh in fillets, place them in the stewpan, simmer five or ten minutes, take from the fire, throw away shallots, parsley, thyme and bay leaf, then dish the remainder, add to it the juice of half a lemon, and send to the table.

This may be done as soon as a roasted duck is cool, or the following day. If a duck is old, it will be better to serve it in salmis than roasted.

The same (cold) for dinner or breakfast.—Take a duck roasted from the day before, cut up the limbs, fillet the stomach, and place the whole on a dish. Mix with the gravy that you have saved in roasting it two tablespoonfuls of sweet oil, salt, pepper, and the juice of half a lemon, a little vinegar may be added; serve in a saucer to be eaten with the duck.

The same, with turnips.—Cut the duck in pieces. Put a piece of butter the size of two walnuts in a stewpan, and set it on a good fire; when melted, sprinkle in it a teaspoonful of sugar, then put in also six or eight small turnips well cleaned and washed, and when of a golden color take them off, then put in the duck and fry it also till of a golden color, and take it from the pan, put again in the pan a little butter, and when hot, sprinkle in it little by little, two teaspoonfuls of flour, stirring with a wooden spoon the while; when of a proper thickness and of a brownish color, add half a glass of broth, two sprigs of parsley, one of thyme, a bay leaf, salt, pepper, then the duck and turnips, boil gently till cooked, take out parsley, thyme, and bay leaf, dish the remainder, and serve it.

POULTRY.

An old hen has red and rough legs; the cock also, besides, has long spurs.

The fatter they are the better; they cannot be too fat. The broader the breast the better; the skin must be white.

It is fresh enough as long as the legs are not stiff.

BOILED.

Clean and prepare a turkey as directed for poultry.

Put in a stewpan, large enough to hold a turkey, a piece of butter the size of a duck's egg, also a teaspoonful of chopped parsley, same of green onions, and four or five mushrooms; set it on a good fire, and as soon as the butter is hot, lay the turkey in; turn over now and then till of a fine golden color, then take it from the pan, cover the breast with slices of bacon tied with twine, and put it back in the pan; add a pinch of allspice, six small onions, salt, pepper, a glass of white wine, and a pint of broth; simmer till cooked, dish it, strain the sauce on it, and serve. It takes about two hours to cook a turkey of middling size.

A little warm broth should be added in case the sauce were boiled away during the cooking.

The same, roasted.—Take a turkey, and if not fat, lard the fleshy parts, envelop it with buttered paper tied with twine; place it on the spit before a sharp fire, basting often with the drippings. About an hour and a quarter after, take the paper off, leave ten or fifteen minutes longer, basting continually, and serve with the gravy.

A few watercresses may be added with a little vinegar.

The same, stuffed.—Stuff the turkey with minced meat nearly cooked, or with roasted chestnuts, and proceed as for roasted turkey in every particular, except that you leave it one hour and a half on the spit before taking the paper off; serve it in the same way also, but without watercress.

The same, stuffed with truffles.—Chop fine about four ounces of truffles, and put them in a stewpan with a pound of bacon cut in dice; set it on a moderate fire, add salt, pepper, a little grated nutmeg, a bay leaf, a pinch of allspice, and a pinch of dried thyme; when hot, add also a pound and a half or two pounds of truffles; boil twenty or twenty-five minutes, tossing now and then, and take from the fire. When nearly cool, put the whole in the turkey, and sew it up; leave it thus, if fresh, four days in winter, and one or two in summer: if not very fresh, leave it a short time. Envelop the turkey in buttered paper tied with twine, place it on the spit before a sharp fire, baste often, and two hours after remove the paper; leave five or ten minutes longer, and serve with the gravy.

This dish is considered exquisite by epicureans.

The same, stewed.—An old turkey is better stewed than cooked in any other way.

Lard all the fleshy parts of the turkey well. Put in a large stew-kettle half a pound of bacon cut in slices, four ounces of knuckle of veal, three sprigs of parsley, two of thyme, a bay leaf, six small onions, one carrot cut in four pieces, three cloves, one clove of garlic, salt, pepper, and then the turkey; wet with a pint of white wine, same of broth, cover as nearly air-tight as you can, place in a moderately heated oven or on a moderate fire, let simmer (not boil) about two hours and a half, then turn it over, put back on the fire or in the oven for another two hours and a half, after which, dish the turkey; strain the sauce and put it back on the fire to reduce it to a jelly, which you spread on it and serve.

Many connoisseurs prefer the turkey served thus when

cold; it does not cost anything to try it, and it is very handy for a grand dinner, as it may be prepared one or two days in advance, and is just as good, if kept in a refrigerator.

The same, the next day.—If you have any turkey left from the day before worth serving again, prepare and serve it as chicken left for the next day.

GALANTINE OF TURKEY.

It is very difficult, if not impossible, for a person who has never seen the whole process of making a galantine, to make one; we will, however, describe it as clearly as possible. It is cheaper to buy one ready made from a restaurant, and besides, it saves a great deal of trouble.

Chop very fine about a pound of fresh pork, same of bacon, two pounds of round of veal, a dozen sprigs of parsley, six of thyme, three or four green onions, and two bay leaves, the latter especially as fine as powder, and work the whole well together, adding salt and pepper, and then your mixture is ready for use.

Take a fat turkey, and when cleaned and prepared as directed, cut off neck, wings at the first pinion and legs at the first joint; then with a carving knife you cut the skin on the back, from the neck to the rump, and very carefully and gingerly take the flesh off the bones, taking good care not to cut the skin; then stretch out the turkey, minus the bones, the skin underneath, and spread on it a layer of the above mixture, about three quarters of an inch in thickness; then place on that about a pound of bacon, same of boiled ham, same of round of veal, and a cooked beef's tongue, the whole cut in fillets about half an inch in thickness; add also a few truffles cut in slices; put again some of the mixture on this to fill the turkey, sew it up, giving it its original form as much as possible, and then envelop it tightly in a towel, which you sew or tie, and place in a stewpan with the bones, after having broken them in two or three pieces each; season with four ounces of bacon cut in dice, two calf's feet split in two, one carrot, four small onions, three cloves, eight sprigs of parsley, four of thyme, salt, pepper, two bay leaves, and two gills of white wine; then cover the whole with water, and set on a moderate fire; simmer about four hours. Take the pan from the fire, allow it to cool, and when the whole has fallen to a milk warmth, take the turkey out of it, press it gently, to force out any liquid that might be in it, and when cold, remove the towel and place the turkey on a dish.

Put the stewpan with what is left in it back on the fire, and just before it boils, skim it well; then take from the fire and strain; when cold, skim off the fat.

Put in a crockery stewpan the white of three eggs, and whip them well with a little water; then pour the sauce in, whipping the while; place the pan on the fire, and continue whipping till on the point of boiling; then take off, place it on a warm, but not hot place; put a large sheet iron cover on the pan, place live coals on it for three or four minutes, and take off the pan; then mix in it the juice of half a lemon, pass this sauce through a fine cloth, and let it cool; decorate the turkey with it according to your fancy, and you have a sightly dish.

Make galantine of capon, chicken, duck, geese, guinea fowl, partridge, pheasant, and of breast of lamb or veal, in the same way, only reducing or augmenting the quantities of meats and seasonings according to the size of the bird or breast.

GIBLETS.

By giblets are understood the gizzards, heads, legs, livers, necks, and ends of the wings of chickens, ducks, geese, turkeys, and other birds, tame or wild.

You begin by cleaning them well, cut off the bills, take the eyes out, warming the legs on live coals, so that you can take off the outer skin and spurs; place the giblets in a tureen, turn boiling water and a little salt on them, leave them thus five or six minutes, then wash well and drain them.

IN FRICASSEE.

Put a piece of butter in a stewpan (the size to be according to the quantity of giblets you have), set it on a good fire; when melted, sprinkle in it, little by little, a teaspoonful of flour; stir the whole with a wooden spoon; when of a proper thickness, and of a brownish color, add half a gill of warm broth, same of warm water, a sprig of parsley, a small pinch of grated nutmeg, two small onions, salt, and pepper; then the giblets. About half an hour after add also two mushrooms, cut in pieces. It takes about two hours to cook them properly. Dish the pieces, strain the sauce, mix in it one well beaten yolk of an egg, and a few drops of lemon juice; pour it on the giblets, place the pieces of mushrooms over the whole, and serve.

The same, stewed.—Put the giblets in a stewpan with butter, and set it on a good fire; when they are of a fine yellow color, add one or two sprigs of parsley, a clove of garlic, a sprig of thyme, one clove, half a bay leaf, two mushrooms cut in pieces, two small onions, and a pinch of flour; wet with broth, let simmer gently for half an hour, and add also two parsnips cut in slices, and previously half fried in butter; simmer again for about an hour; dish the pieces of meat, strain the sauce, put it back on the fire to reduce it a little, pour it on the giblets, place the pieces of mushrooms at the top, and serve hot.

GAME.

HOW TO PRESERVE GAME FOR SOME TIME.

OPEN the animal or bird under the rump, just enough to take the inside out, comprising the stomach and gall bladder (be very careful, especially of the latter; if it bursts, it is better not to try to preserve the piece, but to clean, wash, and use it as soon as possible). Birds must be left in their feathers, and animals in their skins. Fill the inside with dry and clean oats, and put the piece in a heap or barrel of oats. It will keep thus for many days.

Another way is to envelop the piece well in a towel, and bury it in charcoal dust in a cool or dry place.

HOW TO CLEAN AND PREPARE.

Clean and prepare the birds as directed for poultry in general.

After having carefully skinned, take out the inside, and cut the legs off at the first joint of animals; you wash the inside with lukewarm water, and wipe it dry with a clean towel immediately after; wipe also the outside, but do not wash it if possible; that is, if you can clean it well by wiping only.

Wild ducks, geese, pigeons, and turkeys are cooked and served like tame ones.

GROUSE OR HEATHCOCK.

They are good as long as the legs are flexible; if **not,** examine **them** carefully, they might be rotten inside.

Lard them well, envelop each in buttered paper, and place on the spit before a good fire; **baste often,** remove the paper after twenty or twenty-five **minutes; leave** two or three minutes **more,** basting continually with the drippings; dish **the birds; mix** with the drippings a few drops of lemon juice, and a little salt and pepper, **and** serve with the birds.

Grouse may **also be served in salmis like a** duck.

HARE.

How to select.—When **young** it has rather soft paws, ad not much **opened,** and also soft ears; but **if old** the aws are hard and worn out, and the ears stiff and hard.

If fresh, the body is stiff; it is soft, and the flesh is nearly black, if tainted.

Save the blood **as much as possible;** it improves the sauce very much.

IN CIVET.

When the hare is cleaned as directed for game, **cut it** in pieces. **Have** in a stewpan and on a good fire two **ounces** of butter and **one** of **bacon, cut in dice;** when hot, take the bacon off, and put the pieces of hare in the **pan**; stir with a wooden spoon now and then, and till of a fine golden color; then sprinkle on it a teaspoonful of flour, add **ten** small onions, four sprigs of parsley, two of thyme, two cloves of garlic, a bay leaf, salt, pepper, three quarters of a pint of claret wine, same of water, half a pint of broth, three or four mushrooms, and a little grated nutmeg; boil gently till done, when dish the pieces of hare; throw away parsley, thyme, bay leaf, and garlic, mix the blood of the hare in the sauce, boil it about ten minutes, turn it on the hare, and serve.

Many epicures like a civet better when prepared one or two days in advance, and only warmed before serving. When the civet is done, and ready to serve, place the dish in a cool and dry place, and when you want to eat the civet, place the dish in a bain-marie, or in an oven, and serve when warm.

The same, roasted.—Lard the hare well; place it on the spit before a good fire; baste often with the drippings, and when properly cooked, serve it with the following sauce: put in a stewpan a piece of butter the size of a walnut, and set it on a good fire; when melted, put in it the hare's liver well pounded, then the blood, the drippings from the roasted hare, salt, pepper, a tablespoonful of white wine, same of broth, and one teaspoonful of vinegar; when of a proper thickness, serve with the hare.

It takes about an hour to roast it well.

In a small family, the hind part is roasted, and the fore part of the hare is dressed in civet.

It may be roasted in an oven, if more convenient.

The same, the next day.—If any is left from the day before, warm it and serve, if in civet; cut it in slices and serve cold, with an oil sauce, if roasted.

LEVERET.

Cook and serve like a hare.

A leveret may also be sauté like a chicken.

OSTRICH AND CRANE.

Cook and serve like a stuffed turkey.

PARTRIDGE AND PRAIRIE HEN.

An old partridge has a white bill and bluish legs; when young, the bill is of a rather dark gray color, and the legs are yellowish.

As long as the rump does not turn bluish, it is fresh enough.

Clean and prepare a partridge or a prairie hen as directed for poultry in general.

Broiled.—Split the back of the partridge so as to open it, butter it, or grease it well with sweet oil, place it on the gridiron, having previously warmed and greased it, set on a good fire, turn over three or four times, and just before taking from the fire, sprinkle on it salt, pepper, a little allspice, and chopped parsley; serve it when done, on a maitre-d'hôtel, oil, or poivrade sauce.

Another way.—Split the partridge in two lengthwise so as to make two equal pieces. Put a piece of butter, the size of a small egg (for two partridges), in a stewpan; set it on a good fire, and when hot, lay the partridges in; leave them till a little more than half cooked, turning them over three or four times, and then take them off. Envelop them in buttered paper, place them on the gridiron, and on a good fire for about fifteen minutes, and serve with the following sauce: put with the butter in the pan in which were the partridges, a teaspoonful of chopped parsley, same of chopped mushrooms, salt, pepper, and a pinch of allspice; sprinkle in and stir at the same time a teaspoonful of flour, also a gill of white wine, same of broth; boil gently till of a proper thickness, and serve the partridges on it.

Broiled in this way, they might be served also on a Mayonnaise sauce.

The same, with cabbages.—Lard two partridges. Put in a stewpan half a pound of bacon cut in slices, with four onions, two carrots cut in pieces, a small dried or **Bologna sausage**, two sprigs of parsley, one of thyme, two cloves, a bay leaf, a little grated nutmeg, and a cabbage cut rather fine, and which you have previously thrown in boiling water and boiled ten minutes; then the two partridges or prairie hens; place over the whole four ounces of bacon cut in thin slices, cover with broth, set the pan on a sharp fire, and when it has boiled about fifteen minutes, subdue the fire, or put the pan in a moderately heated oven, simmer about two hours if the partridges are old, and one hour if they are young; then take from the fire, place the partridges on a dish with the sausage cut in pieces around them, drain the cabbage and put it on another dish with the bacon, strain the sauce on both dishes, and serve.

Another way.—They may be prepared, cooked and served as above, omitting the sausage and the cabbages. In that case, they may be served with a purée of lentils, or of green peas.

The same, roasted.—Rub the stomach and legs of the birds with lemon, then envelop those parts with slices of bacon tied with twine, or fixed with small skewers; after which envelop the whole bird in buttered paper tied with twine; place them on a spit before a good fire, take the paper off after twenty or thirty minutes, according to the age of the bird; leave two or three minutes longer, baste often during the process of roasting, with the drippings; dish the birds without removing the slices of bacon; mix in the gravy the juice of half a lemon, or half an orange, a little salt and pepper, and serve it with the birds.

The same, in salmis.—Cook and serve partridges or prairie hens like ducks in salmis, except that you put a wine glass of champagne, or good sauterne wine, instead of one gill of claret.

The same, in fricassee.—Proceed as for a fricassee of chicken in every particular.

They may also be sauté, like a chicken.

PEACOCK, PEA HEN, AND PELICAN, OR OTHER LARGE BIRDS.

Prepare, cook, and serve these birds like a stuffed turkey.

PHEASANTS.

How to select.—When young, their claws are short and round at the end, while they are long and sharp when old.

They are not fresh when the rump is of a bluish color, but some amateurs like them then; they say that they have a venison taste.

They are very seldom or never cooked when very fresh, as they have not as delicate a taste as when rather tainted.

Pheasants are cooked and served like partridges in every way.

QUAILS.

You know if quails are young and fresh by the same signs as the partridges.

Roasted.—Quails are just the contrary of pheasants; they must be cooked as fresh as possible. Envelop each with grape vine leaves if handy, or in buttered paper; then again envelop in very thin slices of bacon, tie the whole with twine, place them on the spit, and before a moderate fire; have slices of roasted bread in the dripping pan, baste often with the drippings, and when done, serve them on the slices of bread, and you have one of the most *recherchés* dishes.

The liver may be pounded and mixed with the drippings while basting.

The same, with cabbages.—Quails may also be prepared like partridges, with cabbages, but they are not so much praised as when roasted.

RABBIT.

What we have said of the hare may be applied to the rabbit, to know if young and fresh.

Tame rabbits are very seldom fit to eat; we would not advise any one to eat them, unless they have been kept in a large place, free from any manure or dirt, and having also plenty room to burrow, and in a dry soil.

In gibelotte.—Clean the rabbit as directed for game, and cut it up. Put in a stewpan a piece of butter the size of an egg, with one ounce of bacon cut in dice; set it on a good fire, and when hot, take the bacon from the pan, sprinkle in it a tablespoonful of flour, stirring the while; then lay the pieces of rabbit in, with also a pint of broth, same of white wine, salt, pepper, ten small onions, four sprigs of parsley, two of thyme, a bay leaf, a little grated nutmeg, and three or four mushrooms cut in pieces, then the pieces of bacon; boil gently till cooked. Throw away parsley, thyme, and bay leaf, and serve the rest hot.

The same, with green peas.—Proceed as above as far as putting the pieces of rabbit in the pan, then have ready a quart of green peas, which you have boiled five minutes in water, and a little salt, before, and put them in the pan also; stir a little, and ten minutes after, add as above, broth, wine, etc., and cook and serve as above also.

The same, roasted.—Roast and serve a rabbit as a roasted hare.

The same, stewed, or in civet.—Proceed as for hare in civet, in every particular.

A rabbit may also be served in fricandeau, the same as a piece of veal.

ROBINS, BLACKBIRDS, FIGPECKERS, HIGH-HOLDERS, LAPWINGS, MEADOW LARKS, PLOVERS, REED BIRDS, THRUSHES, YELLOW BIRDS, AND ANY AND EVERY OTHER SMALL BIRD.

All these birds, and any others of the same size, or smaller—the fatter they are the better.

When young, there is no stiffness in the legs. To be good they must be fresh; if the rump is hard, they are fresh and good; if soft, they may be tainted and not good.

Pick, clean, and prepare them as directed for poultry.

Envelop each in grapevine leaves if handy, or if not, in buttered paper; then envelop again in thin slices of bacon, and tie the whole with twine; fix then on the spit by means of skewers, and set before a rather slow fire; baste often with the drippings. It takes from ten to fifteen minutes to roast, according to the size of the birds. Have ready and warm, as many slices of bread fried in butter as you have birds, place them on a dish, and a bird on each slice; mix a few drops of lemon juice with the gravy, and pour it over the whole, and serve as hot as possible. Do not remove leaves, or paper, or bacon, before serving.

This is a very delicate dish, and is as delightful for the eye, as for the palate and stomach.

The livers of the birds may be pounded and mixed with the gravy while basting, according to taste.

Another way.—Put butter in a stewpan, a piece the size of a walnut for two robins, and set it on a moderate fire; when hot, fry the birds in it till they are of a fine yellow color, and take them off; sprinkle in the pan a pinch of flour while stirring, and when of a brownish color, add salt, pepper, a pinch of allspice, a pinch of chopped parsley, a gill of white wine, then the birds; simmer gently till cooked, and serve hot.

You augment the quantity of the seasoning according to the quantity of birds you have.

SNIPE.

Snipes are like pheasants; they are not as good when very fresh as they are when they have been killed four days or more, according to the temperature.

They are good as long as the legs are flexible, but when stiff, you must examine them carefully, as they might be tainted. Some persons like them when rather tainted; but every one to his color and taste.

Pound well the liver, heart and lights, with about the same quantity of bacon; then add to that a teaspoonful of parsley chopped very fine, and the yolk of an egg to every four snipes; make a paste with the whole, stuff the snipes with it, and sew them up; line the bottom of a stewpan with slices of bacon, and lay the birds on them; set on a slow fire for ten minutes, add then two gills of white wine, same of broth; simmer till cooked, dish the birds, strain the gravy on them after having mixed in it a few drops of lemon juice, and serve.

Snipes may also be prepared as robins.

WOODCOCKS.

Cook and serve them as snipes.

OPOSSUM, OTTER, RACCOON, SKUNK, WOODCHUCK, FOX, ETC.

We cannot say that we have had much experience in cooking the above, but all these animals are eaten by many persons in different parts of this and other countries. We have eaten of all of them except the raccoon, and we must say that we found them good.

It is well known that when our soldiers retook possession of Ship Island, they found plenty of raccoons on it, and ate all they could catch. One day we happened to meet a sub-officer who was there at the time, and enquired of him about it. He said he had never eaten any raccoons before, and did not know that they were eatable; but now he would eat them as readily as rabbits, as they were quite as good.

The best time to eat either of the animals enumerated above is from Christmas to the 15th of February; squirrels also are not good in warm weather.

How to prepare them.—As soon as the animal is killed skin it, take the inside out, save the liver and heart, and wash well with lukewarm water, and a little salt, in and outside; then wipe dry with a towel, put inside of it a few leaves of sage, bay leaves, mint and thyme, and sew it up. Hang it outside in a place sheltered from the sun, such as the northern side of a building; leave it thus five or six days, then take off and cook.

HOW TO SKIN A SKUNK.

We were hunting one day in New Jersey, northwest of Paterson, with a friend and two farmers living there, when one of them shot a skunk. We asked him how much he could get for the skin. He said it was not worth while to take it to town, but that he would eat the animal, as it was very good.

We thought at first that he was joking; but putting his gun and game bag to the ground, he looked at us earnestly and said, "Gentlemen, you seem to doubt; I will show you how it is done. We soon saw that we had been mistaken.

He made a fire, took hold of the skunk by the head with one hand, and with a stick in the other, held the skunk over the fire. He burnt off nearly all the hair, taking care to avoid burning the skin, commencing at the hind legs; then, with his **hunting** knife, he carefully cut off the bag containing the fetid matter, and skinned and cleaned it.

We then examined the skunk, and although it had not been washed, we could not find any part of it with a bad smell, and if we had not seen the whole operation, we certainly would not have thought that it was a skunk, the very name of which is repulsive.

The following week we dined with the farmer, ate some of that identical skunk, and found it very good.

HOW TO COOK AN OPOSSUM, AN OTTER, RACCOON, ETC.

Take out the leaves of sage, etc., which you put in the animal before exposing it to the weather. Pound well the liver and heart with about the same quantity of bacon, then mix that with two or three teaspoonfuls of chopped parsley, a pinch of grated nutmeg, salt and pepper; stuff the animal with that mixture, and also with six small onions fried in butter, and a bunch of seasoning composed of four sprigs of parsley, three of thyme, two cloves, two cloves of garlic, and two bay leaves, and sew it up again. Butter it well all over, place it on a spit before a very sharp fire; put three or four sage leaves in the dripping pan, and baste often with the drippings. Serve it when cooked with the gravy, throwing away the sage leaves.

It may also be served with a Mayonnaise or ravigote sauce.

VENISON.

If young, the hoof is not much opened, and the fat is thick and clear; when old, the hoofs are wide open.

To know if it is fresh enough, run a knife through the leg, or through the shoulder, and if it does not smell bad and stale, it is good. It is not as delicate when fresh as when it has been killed for five or six days. Many persons like it with a venison taste.

If fresh when you buy it, keep it from three to eight days before cooking it.

To improve a haunch of venison: after it is larded, place it in a crockery vessel for four days, with six onions cut in slices, a gill of sweet oil, same of claret wine, a salt-spoonful of allspice, four cloves, two sprigs of thyme, and a clove of garlic; spread the whole over it, basting twice a day with the same, and turning it over once a day; after which time you drain it, and it is ready to cook.

The same may be done for the shoulder or saddle, except that it must not be kept more than two days in the seasonings, and for cutlets, not more than twenty-four hours.

CUTLETS.

Take six cutlets, lard them well and put them in a stewpan, with salt, pepper, eight small onions, two carrots, four sprigs of parsley, two of thyme, two **cloves**, a bay leaf, a gill of broth, and same of water; **set it on a** good fire, and boil gently till **cooked.** Dish the cutlets so that every small end or bone rests on **the large end of** another, and serve with the sauce strained on them, or **with a** poivrade sauce.

HAUNCH.

Take off the thin skin around it and lard it well. Envelop it in buttered paper, two sheets in thickness, and tied with **twine;** place it on the spit before a sharp fire, and baste often with the drippings. Twenty minutes after, subdue the fire, or set farther from it; it takes about three hours to roast. Remove the paper about ten or fifteen minutes before taking from the fire, and place the haunch nearer it to make it take a fine color; then serve it with a poivrade sauce.

SHOULDER, OR SADDLE.

Cut the shoulder in fillets and lard them slightly. Put in a stewpan four ounces of butter and set it on a brisk fire; when hot, lay the fillets in, and when of a golden color, add the seasonings in which you have improved the saddle, or the same ones if you have not done it; then subdue the fire, wet with a little warm broth, simmer till cooked, dish the fillets, strain the sauce on them, and serve.

It may also be dressed entire, with the bones off; but it is more generally done in fillets.

It is very good served with an oil, or piquante sauce.

The same, stewed.—Cut the meat in square pieces, about two inches in size. Have in a stewpan, and on a good fire, a piece of butter the size of a duck's egg; when melted, sprinkle in, little by little, a tablespoonful of flour, stirring the while with a wooden **spoon;** when getting rather thick, add two ounces of bacon cut in dice, also half a pint of claret wine, same of warm water, salt, pepper, a pinch of allspice, two shallots chopped fine, or two green onions, four or five mushrooms, two cloves of garlic, and six onions; then lay the meat on the whole, and boil gently till cooked. Dish the meat, boil the sauce till of a brownish color, skim off the fat if there is too much of it, take out the cloves of garlic, turn the sauce on the meat, and serve hot.

When you have some left for the next day, warm it before serving it, if from a stew; but if from a roasted haunch, cut in slices and serve cold, with an oil sauce.

BEAR MEAT AND BUFFALO.

The meat of all large animals is better roasted than dressed in any other way.

Prepare, cook, and serve bear meat and buffalo meat like venison, or like à la mode beef.

SNAILS.

A GOOD many are now imported from Europe.

How to clean and prepare.—Throw them in boiling water, in which you have put some wood ashes; leave them in till they have thrown their cover wide open, which will take about fifteen minutes; then take them off, pull them out of the shell by the means of a fork, place them in lukewarm water, and leave two hours; next, rub them in your hands, and then soak in cold water; rub them again with your hands, in cold water, two or three times, changing the water each time, so as to take away most of their sliminess. Wash the shells in lukewarm water with a scrubbing brush, and drain them when clean.

Broiled.—Knead together and make a paste of a sufficient quantity of butter, parsley chopped fine, salt, pepper, and grated nutmeg; say about two ounces of butter, a tablespoonful of parsley, a saltspoonful of salt, a pinch of pepper, and the same of nutmeg (for two dozen). Put a piece of the above paste, the size of a kidney bean, in each shell, then the snails, and at the top again the same quantity of paste; lay them one by one, close together, in a crockery or cast iron kettle, the mouth of the snails up, and not one upon another; cover the kettle well, set it on a moderate fire, or in a moderately heated oven, and leave thus till cooked, which is easily seen by the parsley beginning to turn black, or as if fried. Lay them on a dish in the same order, and if there is any gravy in the kettle, put a part of it in each shell, and serve hot.

In eating them, be careful after having taken off the snail and swallowed it to turn down the shell, for there is some juice in the bottom of it which is delicious; the best way is to drink it as if from the bottom of a glass.

They could be broiled on a gridiron, but they are not as good as in a kettle; some of the juice is lost, and also the flavor.

Stewed.—Put in a stewpan four ounces of butter for fifty snails, and set it on a good fire; when melted, sprinkle in it a teaspoonful of flour, stirring awhile; then add a teaspoonful of parsley chopped fine, two sprigs of thyme, a bay leaf, a pint of white wine, and then the snails, which you have previously put back into their shells; cover the whole with warm broth, boil gently till the sauce is reduced and the snails are cooked, and serve them mouth upward, and filled with the sauce.

ASPIC OF MEAT.

Cut four middling sized onions in slices, lay them in a stewpan with a quarter of a pound of bacon (not smoked); then add about a quarter of a pound of each of the following meats: chicken, game (any kind), mutton and beef, also a calf's foot split in two, two ounces of rind of bacon, two sprigs of parsley, two of thyme, a clove of garlic, two carrots cut in two, one clove, and four small onions; wet with half a pint of water, and set on a brisk fire; cover the pan well. When nearly cooked, take the grease off with a ladle; add then boiling water enough just to cover the whole, and finish the cooking. Strain the juice, skim off the fat, if any, and let it cool; if it is not found clear enough when strained, beat well two whites of eggs, put them in the stewpan with the juice, set it on a sharp fire for about ten minutes, stirring the while, and take from the fire; add to it a few drops of lemon juice, and strain again.

Put in a mould some of the above juice, about two eighths of an inch in depth; place the mould on ice, and leave till the juice has turned into a jelly. Lay on that jelly some of the following meats, free from bones, and not allowing the pieces to touch the sides of the mould: chicken, game, tongues of beef, calf and sheep, of all or of either of them (the meats must be cooked beforehand). Cover the whole with **the remainder** of the juice, so as to have about the same thickness **at the top as** at the bottom. Place the mould **in a refrigerator** to cool, and turn into a jelly; **then** dip the mould in very warm water, turn over on a dish, remove the mould, and you have a fine *entrée*.

SANDWICHES.

We think this dish (if it can be **called a dish),** too well known to require any direction.

VEGETABLES.

GREEN vegetables especially must look fresh and have nothing rotten about them, or else they are not good.

When you cook vegetables, if green, put them in the water at the first boiling; if dry, such as beans, peas, etc., put them in cold water (it must be soft water), after having been soaked in lukewarm water for a few minutes.

Sauce for raw vegetables.—Some persons like to eat raw vegetables; the following sauce may be used in eating them; it certainly improves the taste:

Boil an egg hard, take the yolk and pound it, mix it well with two tablespoonfuls of sweet oil, one of vinegar, salt, pepper, and a teaspoonful of chopped parsley; a little mustard may be added.

ARTICHOKES.

The artichoke we refer to here is the plant somewhat resembling a thistle, having a large, scaly head, like the cone of the pine tree; the lower part of the leaves composing that head, with the broad receptacle underneath, is the eatable part.

How to eat them raw.—Quarter them, take off the

outer leaves and choke, and serve with oil, vinegar, mustard, salt, and pepper.

How to cook.—Clean them and take off the outer leaves, throw them in boiling water, with parsley, salt, and pepper; they are cooked when the leaves come off easily; then take from the fire and drain, taking care to put them upside down.

The same, fried.—When cooked as above, cut the upper part of the leaves, and then cut them in eight pieces, take the choke off, dip each piece in a thin paste made of flour, sweet oil, beaten egg, vinegar, salt, and pepper, and fry them with a little butter. Serve them with sprigs of fried parsley around.

The same, stewed.—When cooked as directed above, cut them in four pieces, and trim off the upper part of the leaves, take off the choke, and lay them in a stewpan; cover them with broth and set on a moderate fire; add then one ounce of butter for six artichokes, one sprig of parsley, and two mushrooms cut in slices; boil ten minutes, take the parsley off, and serve the artichokes with the mushrooms around; pour the sauce on the whole.

The same, with an oil sauce, or with a white sauce.—When cooked and cold, take off the choke, and serve with an oil sauce.

They may also be served with a white sauce, but they must be warm.

The Jerusalem artichokes are dressed like potatoes.

ASPARAGUS.

How to prepare and cook it.

Cut off most of the white part, so as to have the whole of one length if possible; then scrape the white end a little, soak them in water, and drain. Tie them in small bunches of about half a dozen; throw them in boiling water, with a little salt, and drain when cooked. Serve with an oil sauce.

Fried.—When cooked, make a thin paste with two tablespoonfuls of flour, two beaten eggs, and water; dip them in that paste, and lay them in a frying pan in which you have hot butter, and on a sharp fire; toss them gently, and serve, when you see the paste around them well fried.

The same, with milk.—For a bunch of asparagus, put two ounces of butter in a stewpan; when melted, add a pint of fresh milk, salt, and white pepper. Cut the eatable part of the asparagus in pieces about half an inch in length, and as soon as the milk boils, throw them into it, and serve when cooked.

They may be boiled in water before, according to taste.

The same, with sugar.—After they are cooked as above directed, put in a stewpan two ounces of butter, and set it on a moderate fire; cut the eatable part of the asparagus in pieces about half an inch in length, and put them in the pan when the butter is melted; season with two sprigs of parsley, one of thyme, a bay leaf, salt and pepper; stir all the time with a wooden spoon; put in just enough warm water to wet them; simmer thus ten minutes; then sprinkle into it two tablespoonfuls of crushed white sugar, and immediately mix in it two beaten yolks of eggs, and serve.

It takes about fifteen minutes for the whole process.

BEANS.

Green or string beans, dwarf or snap beans, French haricots, pole beans, kidney beans, horse beans, lima beans, etc.

How to prepare and cook when green.—Take the filanders off by breaking one end and pulling lengthwise; repeat the same for the other side, cut them in pieces half an inch long, soak them in cold water, and throw them in boiling water with a little salt. Boil them till cooked, which you will know by pressing one between your fingers to see if tender; take them from the fire, throw them in cold water to cool, and drain them.

How to serve them with broth.—Cook a quart of beans. Put two ounces of butter in a stewpan and set it on the fire; when melted, put the beans in with a teaspoonful of chopped parsley; stir five minutes; then add a gill of broth, salt, and pepper; simmer twenty minutes, and just in taking from the fire, mix in it two well beaten yolks of eggs, with the juice of half a lemon, and serve.

The same, with butter.—Put in a stewpan two ounces of butter, and set it on a good fire; when melted, put in it a quart of beans cooked in water, with a pinch of grated nutmeg, half a pint of milk, salt, pepper, and a teaspoonful of chopped parsley; keep stirring continually, boil ten minutes, take from the fire, mix in it two beaten yolks of eggs, and serve.

The same, with onions.—Put two ounces of butter in a stewpan and set it on the fire; when hot, put in it two onions cut in slices, and fry them. Then add salt, pepper, a pinch of grated nutmeg, a saltspoonful of chopped parsley, and a quart of beans cooked in water; also half a pint of boiling water; boil ten minutes, stir with a wooden spoon, take from the fire, sprinkle in it a few drops of vinegar, and serve.

The same, in salad.—Cook the beans in water, as directed above; then put a layer of them in a crockery vessel, the layer to be about one inch thick; then sprinkle on it salt and pepper; repeat the same process till all your beans are in; cover and leave thus three or four hours; then throw away the water, or drain if convenient; place the beans in a salad dish, with the sweet oil, vinegar, and parsley necessary; move like a salad, and serve cold.

GREEN BEANS, WITHOUT SHELLS.

How to prepare and cook.—Shell the beans; throw them in boiling water with a little salt, and an ounce of butter for a quart; when cooked, drain them. Put in a stewpan two ounces of butter, set it on the fire, and when melted, put in it a teaspoonful of chopped parsley, the beans, salt, pepper, and a teaspoonful of vinegar; toss gently now and then for a few minutes, and serve.

How to prepare and cook beans when dry.—Soak them in cold water (it must be soft water) for five or six hours, wash, and drain; then put them in a stewpan with cold water, and set on a good fire; boil till cooked, and drain them.

How to serve them with butter and parsley.—Have four ounces of butter in a stewpan, and on a good fire; when melted, put in it a quart of beans cooked as directed, with two sprigs of parsley, one of thyme, a bay leaf, a middling sized onion, with a clove stuck in it, a pinch of grated nutmeg, a teaspoonful of chopped parsley, salt, and pepper; stir with a wooden spoon; when hot, add half a pint of the water in which they were cooked; boil gently from twenty to thirty minutes. Throw away thyme, parsley, and bay leaf, and serve.

The same, stewed.—Put two ounces of lard in a stewpan and set it on the fire; when hot, put in it a quart of beans cooked as above, with a pinch of flour, same of nutmeg, same of chopped parsley, half a pint of broth, salt, and pepper; boil gently ten minutes, and serve.

COLORED DRY BEANS.

Soak a quart of them in cold water for six hours, wash and drain them. Put in a stewpan half a pound of bacon, and set it on the fire; five minutes after, put the beans in, with four **small** onions, salt, and pepper, boil gently till cooked, **and** drain. Put two **ounces** of butter in a stewpan on the fire; when melted, sprinkle in it a teaspoonful of flour, same of chopped parsley, then the beans without **the bacon and onions**; toss now and then for ten minutes, then add half a pint of claret wine, the same of the water in which they were cooked, boil gently twenty minutes; **then** put in it also the bacon and onions, boil five minutes longer, and serve the whole on the same dish.

WHITE OR COLORED BEANS, IN SALAD.

When cooked in water and drained, put a layer of them in a crockery vessel, about one inch in thickness; then sprinkle **on it** salt and pepper; repeat the same process till all your beans are in; then cover and leave thus four hours; put **the beans in a salad** dish after having drained them; add to them the oil, vinegar, chopped parsley, and salt necessary, **and serve them hot.**

BEETS.

Clean and wash well, but do not skin **them.** Put in a crockery vessel a **layer of** rye straw, moisten it slightly, place the **beets on it,** cover the vessel, and **place** it in a slow oven for five or six hours; cool **and skin** them.

Stewed.—When cooked, cut them in thin slices. Put butter in a stewpan, and when melted, sprinkle in it a pinch **of flour,** a teaspoonful of chopped parsley, salt, and pepper, then the beets; simmer twenty minutes, add a few drops of vinegar, and serve.

The same, in salad.—Cut them in thin slices when cooked, place them tastefully on a salad of chicory or endive, and serve like another salad.

CABBAGES, COLEWORT, COLLARD, SAVOY, &c.

How to prepare and cook them in water.—Take off the outer leaves, clean, cut in four pieces, free it from the stump, and throw it in boiling water with a little salt; add a little piece of nutmeg, boil about fifteen minutes, and drain.

How to serve with bacon.—When cooked put the cabbage in a stewpan with bacon, sausages, and a piece of breast of mutton; cover with cold water, season with three sprigs of parsley, a carrot, a clove, salt, and pepper; boil till the whole is well cooked, then throw away parsley, carrot, and clove, and drain; put the cabbage on a dish with the meat upon it, and serve warm.

The same, with milk.—Cook in water two middling sized cabbages, and when drained, cut them in several pieces. Put two ounces of butter in a stewpan, set it on a good fire, and when melted put the cabbages in it, with salt and pepper; sprinkle on them a teaspoonful of flour, add half a pint of good milk; keep stirring with a wooden spoon during the whole process; boil gently till the sauce is reduced, and serve.

The same, stewed.—Cook in water two large cabbages, and cut them very fine. Put in a stewpan about two ounces of butter, and set it on the fire; when melted put the cabbages in and stir five minutes; then add salt, pepper, and a pinch of flour; wet with a pint of broth, boil till cooked and the sauce reduced, and serve.

RED CABBAGES.

Prepare, cook, and serve them like other cabbages.

WHITE OR RED CABBAGES IN SALAD.

Take either a white or red hard cabbage; when all the outer leaves are taken off, see if it is clean, but do not wash it; if a cabbage is not clean do not use it for salad (as you want a hard one, and a hard one is always clean when the outer leaves are taken off). Then cut it in four pieces, trim off the stump and coarse end of the leaves; cut it as thin as possible, as in making **sourkrout, put it** in a crockery vessel, with salt, vinegar, and pepper sprinkled on, cover and leave thus from four to six hours; then **throw away** the water or vinegar, dress as **another** salad, and serve.

SPROUTS.

Prepare and cook them **in water** like cabbages. Put butter in a stewpan and set it **on the fire;** when hot, put the sprouts in, with **salt and pepper;** stir with a wooden spoon **for five or six minutes, and serve.**

SOURKROUT.

Soak in cold water for some time, changing the water three or four times; then put it in a stewpan with a pound of bacon, two ounces of sausages, and two ounces of lard to every quart of sourkrout, salt, and pepper; wet with water, boil from five to six hours, and serve with the bacon and sausages on it.

When cooked you **may drain it,** put it in a stewpan, wet with white **wine, boil five or ten** minutes, **and serve.** This is done very often **in Germany.**

CARDOON.

The white **part** only is good to eat. Clean well **and** scrape the sides; cut in pieces two inches and a half in length, and throw them in boiling water with a little salt; boil them till their sliminess comes off easily; then take from the fire, pour cold water in, and by the means of a towel remove the sliminess; soak in cold water and drain them. Lay a few slices of bacon in a stewpan, place the cardoons on them, and again lay slices of bacon on; season with two onions, two sprigs of parsley, one of **thyme**, a bay leaf, and a clove, salt, pepper, and the juice of half a lemon; **cover with water** and set on a good fire; boil **till cooked; take from the** fire and drain the cardoons only, throwing **away the** seasonings. Put the cardoons **back in the** stewpan, **in which** you have left the bacon; add two or three tablespoonfuls of **broth,** and two of Espagnole sauce; set on a slow fire, **and** simmer till the sauce is reduced to a proper thickness. Have at the same time **in a pan on the fire** a piece of ox marrow, **and** when melted **mix it well with** the sauce at the moment you take the cardoons from the fire, and serve hot either with or without the bacon.

CARROTS.

How to clean and prepare them.—Trim off all the small roots, wash them well, scrape them gently, taking care to scrape the skin only; then wash well, drain, and cut them in slices a quarter of an inch thick. (Some cooks cut them in fillets once in a while, as a change, but they have a better appearance in slices.)

How to serve them with fines herbes.—Prepare a quart of carrots, and throw the slices in boiling water to cook them well; then drain them. Put a piece of butter the size of two walnuts in a stewpan, and set it on a good fire; when hot sprinkle in it a teaspoonful of flour, stirring all the while; then add a pinch of grated nutmeg, salt, pepper, a teaspoonful of chopped parsley, and half a pint of broth; boil gently five minutes, then lay the carrots in, subdue the fire, simmer five minutes, and serve. Sprinkle a few drops of lemon juice on them just before placing the dish on the table, if it suits you.

The same, fried.—Prepare a quart of young carrots

(old ones are not very good fried). Have hot butter or lard in a frying pan, and on a good fire, and then lay the carrots in; toss now and then to have them fried on both sides; when cooked place them on a dish, sprinkle chopped **parsley**, salt, and pepper on them, and serve.

The parsley, salt, and pepper may also be put in the pan with the carrots, according to taste.

The same, stewed.—Prepare a quart of carrots, and throw the slices in boiling water for five minutes; take them out and drain. Put a piece of butter the size of two walnuts in a stewpan, set it on a good fire, and when melted add a teaspoonful of chopped parsley, salt, pepper, and then the carrots; wet with half a pint of warm broth; simmer till cooked, and serve.

The same, with sugar.—After having prepared a quart of carrots, you throw the slices in boiling water with a little salt for five minutes; take out and drain them. Put two ounces of butter in a stewpan, and set it on a good fire; when hot lay the carrots in, with a teaspoonful of chopped parsley, salt, and pepper, a pinch of grated nutmeg, and half a pint of warm broth; sprinkle in it, while stirring with a wooden spoon, a teaspoonful of flour; boil gently till cooked; then take from the fire, and sprinkle in it also a tablespoonful of well pounded loaf sugar; mix in the whole two yolks of eggs, and serve.

CAULIFLOWERS AND BROCCOLI.

How to prepare and cook them in water.—Clean and wash them well, throw in boiling water with a little salt; boil till cooked, and drain them.

How to serve with cheese.—Put them on a crockery dish when prepared; pour on a white sauce, in which you have mixed a little grated cheese; then dust the whole with fine bread crumbs; after which you take a soft brush or a feather, which you dip in lukewarm butter, and put a thin coat of it all over the cauliflowers; then place the dish in a quick oven for ten minutes, and serve as they are, i. e., in the dish in which they have been cooked.

The same, fried.—Take them from the boiling water when half cooked, and drain. Mix well two tablespoonfuls of flour with one beaten egg, a tablespoonful of vinegar, salt, pepper, and the quantity of milk necessary to make a paste thin enough to dip the cauliflowers in; then have hot lard in a stewpan on a sharp fire, and lay them in it; take them out when of a flaxen color, and serve.

Another way.—When half cooked, and drained as above, have in a stewpan on a sharp fire, two ounces of hot butter; add a teaspoonful of chopped parsley, salt, and pepper, and lay them in it. Fry them gently till of a fresh butter color, and serve.

The same, stewed.—When cooked in water and drained, put in a stewpan two or three ounces of lard, and set it on a good fire; when hot, put the cauliflowers in, with one gill of broth, salt, and pepper; simmer ten minutes, stir gently with a wooden spoon so as not to break them, and serve hot.

The same, with a tomato sauce.—Place them on a dish when cooked and strained, and immediately pour on them a tomato sauce, and serve. Do not allow them to cool.

Do the same with a white sauce.

The same, in salad.—After having cooked them in water, you allow them to cool in the drainer; then cut them in pieces, place them on a salad dish, and serve. It is dressed like another salad.

CELERY.

How to prepare and cook in water.—Clean, wash well,

cut off all the green leaves, split in four pieces, throw in boiling water with a little salt, boil from twenty to twenty-five minutes, and then drain it.

How to serve it fried.—Make a paste with two tablespoonfuls of flour, one of vinegar, a beaten egg, salt, and pepper; add to it the milk necessary to make a paste thin enough to dip the pieces of celery in, after being cooked in water; have hot lard in a stewpan on a sharp fire, and lay the celery in; fry it till of a golden color, dish it, dust it with fine sugar, and serve.

The same, stewed.—When cooked in boiling water, stew it the same as cauliflowers, simmering it fifteen minutes instead of ten.

The same, in salad.—Clean, wash well, cut off all the green leaves, split in four pieces, cut in pieces about one inch long, drain dry, and serve like another salad.

Soup celery is cooked and served like the other, except that you cut it in slices instead of pieces.

CORN (*sweet*).

The simplest and best way is to boil it, and then eat it with butter, salt, and pepper. When boiled with any meat soup, or with pot-au-feu, it is delicious to eat, and gives a good taste to the broth; it is also eaten with butter, salt, and pepper, as above.

WATERCRESS, STEWED.

Take only the top and the leaves around the stalk; clean and wash it well; throw it in boiling water with a little salt, and when cooked, drain it well, so as to extract all the water from it. Put a piece of butter the size of an egg in a stewpan; when melted, put the cress in, sprinkle on it a tablespoonful of flour (for three quarts); stir continually with a spoon, boil ten minutes, then add salt, pepper, a little grated nutmeg, and half a pint of broth; boil ten minutes longer, and serve either alone, or with hard boiled eggs on it; cut the eggs in two or four pieces.

The same, in salad.—Clean and wash it well, drain dry, or dry it in a towel, dress like another salad, and serve.

CUCUMBERS, FRIED.

Peel them, split them in four, take the seeds out, cut in pieces about one inch long, throw them in boiling water, with a little salt; boil till cooked, drain, and put them on a towel so as to dry them well; then put butter in a frying pan, and set it on a good fire; when hot, put in it some chopped parsley, salt, and pepper, two minutes after put the cucumbers in it, fry a few minutes, tossing them now and then, and serve.

The same, stewed.—Cook in boiling water, and dry them as above; then put them in a stewpan with a little butter kneaded with flour, add salt, pepper, and a pinch of grated nutmeg; moisten with broth, simmer to reduce the sauce; take from the fire, mix the yolks of two eggs in the sauce; add to it a few drops of vinegar, and serve them.

The same, in salad.—Peel and cut them in slices, and put them in a bowl; sprinkle salt on, cover and leave thus two hours; then drain and put them in the salad dish, add oil, vinegar, salt, pepper, and chopped parsley, and serve.

DANDELION.

Dandelion is a very healthy green in the spring, either cooked or raw.

Clean and wash them well several times, as it nearly always contains fine sand between the leaves; leave them in cold water about two hours, and drain; then throw them in boiling salt water, and boil twenty minutes if young, and thirty minutes if full grown; then put them in a drainer, press on them so as to extract all the water, after which you chop them fine; put about two ounces of butter in a stewpan (for two quarts), and set it on a good fire; when melted, sprinkle in it a teaspoonful of flour, also salt, and **pepper, then** put in the dandelion, and stir for **ten minutes, after** which time you wet it with broth; **keep stirring for** about fifteen minutes longer, **and serve.**

The same, in salad.—To serve in salad, it must be young, and as white as possible.

It is served just like another salad.

EGG PLANT, BROILED.

Split the egg plant in **two,** peel it, and take the seed out; put it in a crockery dish, sprinkle on chopped parsley, **salt, and** pepper; **cover the** dish, and leave thus about forty minutes; then take **it off,** put it on a greased and warmed gridiron, and on a good fire; baste with a little **sweet oil,** and seasoning from the crockery dish, and serve with the drippings when properly broiled. It is a delicious dish.

The same, fried.—Peel it, cut it in slices, put them in water with a little salt, for a quarter of an hour, take out, drain, and wipe it dry; make a light paste with a little water, one egg, and a little flour; dip the slices into it, **place** them in hot lard or butter **in a** frying pan on a good fire, turn over once, and serve hot **when fried.**

Another way.—When peeled and cut in slices about one inch thick, soak them in cold water with a little salt, for two hours, after which take off and drain. Have hot butter in a frying pan, on a good fire, and place the slices in, fry them properly, and serve without the butter.

The same, stuffed.—Split in two and peel, take the seed out, place it on a dish, sprinkle on it a little salt, and leave thus twenty minutes; soak at the same time a piece of bread without crust, in milk for twenty minutes also; then mix well that bread with chopped parsley, chopped bacon, a little butter, **salt** and pepper; fill the egg plant with that mixture, putting the two pieces together so as to make it appear as if it had not been split; **then put in a stewpan** two or **three thin slices** of fat bacon; place the egg plant **on them, put other slices** of bacon on; wet with a little broth, cover and put in a hot oven, and serve with the **sauce** when cooked. It takes about an hour.

Use as many egg plants as you wish, and the seasoning accordingly.

Another way.—Proceed as above in every particular, except that **you** use **a little** more butter to make your mixture, and no bacon; **also,** instead **of** putting slices of bacon in the stewpan, you use butter.

They may be cooked without joining the two pieces together, but be careful to have the mixture upward in the pan, and also on the table.

It takes about fifty minutes to cook.

ENDIVE, ALSO CALLED CHICCORY, SUCCORY, CURLED ENDIVE, ETC.

How to serve it with milk.—Take off all the green leaves, clean, cut in two or four, wash well in several waters, **and** throw **in** boiling water with **a** little salt; boil half an **hour,** take it out, throw in boiling water, leave two minutes, **and drain;** press on it in the drainer so as to extract all the water from it, after which chop it fine. Put about two ounces of butter in a stewpan; when melted, sprinkle in it a teaspoonful **of** flour, also salt and pepper; then put **in** the endive, say three or four heads, stir with a wooden spoon for ten minutes, after which time you beat two eggs **with milk, and** put them in the stewpan; keep stirring fifteen minutes longer, and serve.

The same, with broth.—Proceed as above in every particular, except that you add a little broth instead of eggs and milk.

The same, in salad.—Clean, wash, drain **dry, and serve** as directed **for** salads.

HOMINY.

Hominy is prepared in different ways; some make it in cakes, others like pap. The following **is**, however, the general way of preparing it: boil it for about three hours with water or milk, also butter, salt, and pepper; then mix with it some well beaten eggs, fry or broil, or even cook it in an oven and serve for breakfast.

LEEKS.

Clean, wash, and drain; throw them in boiling water with a little salt, boil fifteen minutes, and drain; press on them in the drainer, so as to extract all the water, then chop them fine. Put two ounces of butter in a stewpan; when melted, sprinkle in it a **teaspoonful** of flour, salt, and pepper, then add the leeks. Stir with a wooden spoon for **ten** minutes; after that beat two eggs with milk, and put them in a stewpan; keep stirring fifteen minutes longer, and serve.

LENTILS

Prepare, cook, and serve like white dry beans.

LETTUCE, COS LETTUCE, CABBAGE LETTUCE, CURLED SILESIA, WHITE OR GREEN LETTUCE, BUTTER LETTUCE, ETC.

How to prepare.—Take off the outer leaves, clean and wash well, throw them in boiling water with a little salt, boil ten minutes, and drain dry.

Stewed.—When **prepared, sprinkle on** the top **of**

each, salt, pepper, and a little grated nutmeg; then tie each head with a string. **Place in** a stewpan two **or three** slices of bacon, put the heads of lettuce in, season **with** two sprigs of parsley, **one of thyme,** a bay leaf, and **a clove, also salt, and** pepper; **cover with water,** and simmer about two hours in an oven; then take them from the pan, drain, pressing on them to extract all the water, and put them on a dish, the top upward. Have butter in a stewpan, and on a good fire; when melted, **sprinkle in** it a teaspoonful of flour, stirring with a wooden spoon; subdue the fire, add a little milk, and stir and simmer ten minutes longer; take from the fire, mix in it the beaten yolks of two eggs, **pour it on the lettuce,** which you have **kept** warm, and serve.

Another way.—When prepared, chop it fine. Put in a stewpan, **for four heads of** lettuce, three ounces of but**ter, and set it on the** fire; when melted, **put the** lettuce in with a little chopped chervil, **stir now and then** till cooked; then sprinkle in it a pinch **of flour,** wet with broth, boil ten minutes longer, keeping it stirred, and serve.

For a salad of lettuce, see salads.

MUSHROOMS.

Preserved mushrooms are used for sauces only.

The **first thing to consider** very attentively in mushrooms, **is, not to eat any that you** do not know to be good to **eat.** There are so **many** kinds of good and bad ones, that it is necessary to be very careful about even the edible ones, **or the** ones known as such when young; it is better and **safer** never to use them when old; they are considered old when the comb underneath is black before picking, **while when** young it is of a pink color.

How to clean and prepare them.—Cut off the lower part of the **stem**; skin them with a steel knife, commencing at the edge and finishing at the top; cut in pieces and put them in **cold** water, to which you have added a few drops of vinegar; leave them in it two hours, moving them occasionally; **then wash** well in two or three waters, and **drain.**

When cleaned and prepared thus, they are ready to be used in sauces, or to cook.

Broiled.—If you have large mushrooms, clean and prepare as above, except that you **do not cut** them; but when drained, put them upside down on a greased gridiron, and on a moderate fire; place a little butter around the stem upon **the comb,** and when done, place **them on** a dish which **you have warmed in advance, and in** the same position **they had on the gridiron; put again** around the stem **some** butter kneaded **with** a little chopped parsley, salt, **and** pepper, and serve.

They must **be served** warm.

As an ornament, **you may make,** with common white **note paper, as many** little **square** boxes as you have mushrooms **to** broil; grease them with butter, put the mushrooms in, set them on the gridiron, and on a moderate fire, and serve them in the boxes when done.

The same, stewed.—When cleaned and prepared as directed, and drained, throw a quart of them in boiling water, to which you have added a few drops of vinegar; boil five minutes, **take them out, put them in** cold water to cool, drain, and dry them in a **towel.** Put two ounces of butter in a stewpan and set it on a good fire; when melted, sprinkle in it a pinch of flour, add also a sprig of parsley, two small onions, a little piece of carrot, a bay leaf, salt, and pepper, cover with broth, and boil till the onions are cooked; then take from the pan, onions, parsley, and bay leaf, and put the mushrooms in instead; boil slowly about twenty minutes, take from the **fire,** add to the sauce the yolks of two eggs, well beaten with a few drops of vinegar, and serve warm.

Mushrooms are also cooked in omelets. (See Omelets.)

OKRA.

Okra is very little known here yet; it is pretty good in pickles; they make soup with it in the South and in the West Indies; in that case, make it like a vegetable soup.

ONIONS.

Stewed.—Clean a quart of small onions, throw them in boiling water, add two sprigs of parsley, one of thyme, a bay leaf, a clove, a little piece of nutmeg, a clove of garlic, salt, and pepper; boil twenty minutes, drain the onions only, and throw away the seasonings. Put two ounces of butter in a stewpan, and on a good fire; when melted, sprinkle in it a teaspoonful of flour; then add the onions, cover with half broth and half claret wine; boil gently till well cooked, and till the sauce is reduced, and serve.

It is a very good and very wholesome dish.

The same, in salad.—Clean small red onions; boil them in broth till cooked, drain, and when cold, put them in a salad dish; add oil, vinegar, salt, and pepper, and serve.

A little chopped chervil may also be added.

OYSTER PLANT. (*See Salsify.*)

PARSNIPS.

Fried.—Clean, wash in cold water, cut in slices or in fillets; throw them in boiling water with a little salt for ten minutes, and drain. Put butter in a frying pan and set it on the fire; when hot, put the parsnips in, sprinkle on them a little flour, stirring with a wooden spoon; then add a little broth, and white pepper; when done, place them on a dish, add some fine sugar, and serve.

The same, stewed.—After they are cleaned, washed, and cut in slices, boil them ten minutes as above, and drain. Put butter in a stewpan and set it on the fire; sprinkle a pinch of flour in it; when melted, add the parsnips, salt, and pepper, stir with a wooden spoon five minutes, cover with warm broth, simmer till cooked, and serve.

GREEN PEAS, WITH BACON.

Put four ounces of butter in a stewpan and set it on the fire; when hot, add four ounces of bacon cut in dice, fry it ten minutes; add then two quarts of peas, wet with half a pint of broth, same of water, season with two sprigs of parsley, one of thyme, and a bay leaf, four small onions, salt, and pepper; boil about forty minutes, throw away the seasonings, and serve peas and bacon together.

The same, boiled, or plain boiled, as it is sometimes termed.—Throw two quarts of peas in boiling water, with salt and pepper; boil till cooked, drain, and put them on a dish immediately, in order not to let them cool, put butter at the top, sprinkle a little salt and pepper on them, and serve.

The same, with sugar.—Put four ounces of butter in a frying pan and set it on a good fire; when hot, put two quarts of peas in it, with half a pint of warm water, two sprigs of parsley, and one ounce of fine sugar; simmer thirty minutes, take from the fire, mix in it the yolk of an egg, beaten with two teaspoonfuls of white sugar, take out the parsley, and serve.

PRESERVED PEAS.

They are cooked in the same way as green ones; except that, when you have opened the box, you throw them in boiling water, and boil them only three minutes; drain, cook, and serve, as green peas.

DRY PEAS.

Prepare, cook, and serve them, like white dry beans.

PINEAPPLE, IN SALAD.

Dust the bottom **of a** dish with white sugar, put a **layer of slices** on **and** dust again, repeating the same till the whole **is in;** then add over the **whole a pinch of** grated nutmeg, and French brandy **or** rum to suit **your** taste, and serve.

POTATOES.

How to prepare.—Cut off the germs or eyes, **if** any; if young and tender, take the skin off with a scrubbing **brush; if** old, peel them with a knife, or rather scrape the skin off; **for the part** immediately under the skin contains more nutriment than the middle; and then wash them.

How to cook them by steam.—Place them above a kettle of boiling water, in a kind of drainer made for that purpose, and adapted to the kettle; when cooked in this way, they are ready to be used, and are much better than when cooked in boiling water.

How to serve them with bacon.—Prepare two quarts of potatoes; cut them **in** pieces. Put in a stewpan half a pound of bacon cut **in** dice, and **set** it on the fire; when nearly fried, sprinkle **in** it a teaspoonful of flour, stirring **with a wooden spoon;** then add the potatoes, season **with** two sprigs of parsley, one of thyme, a bay leaf, salt, and pepper, add also a pint of warm water; boil gently till **cooked,** then take out parsley, thyme, and bay leaf, and **serve.**

The same, in balls.—Prepare and cook by steam a quart of potatoes; then peel, and mash them well; knead them with the same quantity of minced meat, also salt, pepper, a teaspoonful of chopped parsley, two ounces of butter, and the yolks of two eggs; when the whole is well mixed, **make balls as** large as a middling sized apple, beat them in well beaten white of eggs; then sprinkle a little flour on them, and throw them in boiling lard, which you must have boiling **just at the** same **time; take** them out when fried, and serve with parsley around.

The same, boiled.—Put two quarts of prepared potatoes in a stewpan and cover with water; season with two sprigs of parsley, one of thyme, a bay leaf, a little piece of nutmeg, four small onions, a small carrot, salt, and **pepper; set on a good** fire, and boil till cooked; drain the potatoes only. Put two tablespoonfuls of sweet oil in a frying pan on a sharp fire; when hot, fry the potatoes in it for about two minutes, and serve; adding vinegar, salt, pepper, and chopped parsley, as you serve.

The same, with butter.—Take one quart of potatoes, and prepare and cook them by steam, whole; then peel them carefully, and as fast as possible, in order not to let them cool; put on a dish and serve them, with butter, salt, and pepper on the table, so that every one may eat them according to taste.

Another way is: when they are on the dish, put some fried parsley around them; then pour on some brown butter, and serve hot.

DEMOCRATIC CAKE OF POTATOES.

Prepare and cook by steam a quart and a half of potatoes, peel, and mash them; mix with them the yolks of five eggs, half a lemon rind grated, and four ounces of fine, white sugar. Put four ounces of butter in a stewpan and set it on the fire; when melted, put the mixture in, stirring with a wooden spoon continually; as soon as it is in the stewpan, add the whites of the five eggs, well beaten; leave on the fire only the time necessary **to mix the** whole well together, and **take** off; when nearly cold, add, if handy, and while stirring, a few drops of orange flower water; it gives it a very good flavor; then put the whole in a tin mould, or in **a tart** dish, greased a little with butter; place in a quick oven for about thirty-five minutes, and serve.

The same, broiled.—Throw in boiling water **a** little salt, and about a quart of prepared potatoes; when cooked, take out and drain them; peel carefully, and cut them in slices half an inch in thickness; place the slices on **the** gridiron and set it on a slow fire; **rub** the upper part with a little butter, and as soon as **the** under part is broiled, turn each slice upside down and rub again with a little butter; when well broiled, place them on a dish, sprinkle a little salt on, and serve. Butter may be added, if you choose.

The same, fried.—**Peel, wash, and cut** in slices, or in square fillets, a quart of potatoes; have hot lard in a stewpan on a sharp fire; throw the potatoes in (observe that the potatoes must be entirely covered with lard—see direction **for frying—or oil)**; when fried, take them out gently with a skimmer, so as to let the grease drop in the pan; place them on a dish, sprinkle a little salt on them, and serve warm.

Sugar may be **used** instead of salt, according to taste.

Some cooks dip them in paste before frying, but **it is** not so good and sightly; they are much better without, and of a much more delicate flavor.

Another way.—Peel, wash, and drain dry, good pota**toes;** put them whole in hot grease, in a pan, and on a sharp fire (see direction for frying); when well fried, take **them out,** make a small hole inside, with a small, sharp pointed knife, to the depth of about two thirds of the thickness of the potato; fill that hole with butter maitre-d'hôtel, and serve warm on a warm dish.

The same, à la Franklin.—Prepare and cook in boiling water a quart of potatoes; peel, cut in slices, and keep them warm; then put four ounces of butter in a stewpan and set it on a good fire; when melted, fry in it, until of a golden color, four onions cut in slices; then add salt, pepper, a teaspoonful of flour, and one gill of warm water; simmer twenty minutes, pour on the potatoes, and serve.

The same, in maitre-d'hôtel.—Take two quarts of potatoes, prepare and cook them by steam, peel carefully, and cut them in thick slices; place them on a dish and keep warm. Put four ounces of butter in a stewpan and set it on a slow fire; add, when melted, a teaspoonful of chopped parsley, the juice of half a lemon, salt, pepper, and a pinch of allspice, stir ten minutes; afterward, put for five minutes on a sharp fire, keep stirring, then pour on the potatoes, and serve.

The same, in matelote.—Prepare and cook a quart and a half of potatoes, and peel and cut them in thick slices. Put in a stewpan a piece of butter the size of an egg, and set it on the fire; when melted, sprinkle in it a teaspoonful of flour, also the same of chopped parsley, salt, and pepper, then the potatoes, wet with half a pint of claret wine, same of broth; boil gently till the sauce is reduced, and serve.

The same, with milk or cream.—Peel and mash a quart of potatoes, when prepared and cooked. Put two ounces of butter in a stewpan and set it on a good fire; when melted, sprinkle in it a teaspoonful of flour, same of chopped parsley, a pinch of grated nutmeg, and salt; stir with a wooden spoon five minutes; then add the potatoes, and half a pint of milk or cream; keep stirring ten minutes longer, take from the fire, sprinkle in it two teaspoonfuls of fine, white sugar, and serve hot.

The same, in Provençale.—Put in a stewpan three tablespoonfuls of sweet oil, a teaspoonful of chopped parsley, two cloves of garlic chopped very fine, a pinch of grated nutmeg, the juice of half a lemon, salt, and pepper; set on a good fire, and when hot, put in it a quart of potatoes prepared and cooked by steam, and cut in thick slices; subdue the fire, simmer about ten minutes, and serve.

The same, sautées.—Take a quart of young and tender potatoes, peel them with a brush, and cut in slices. Put two ounces of butter in a frying pan on a sharp fire; when hot, put the potatoes in, and fry them till of a golden color; place them on a dish without any butter, sprinkle chopped parsley and salt on, and serve.

They may also be served without parsley, according to taste.

The same, with a white sauce.—Clean, wash, and throw a quart of potatoes in boiling water, with a sprig of thyme, two onions, a bay leaf, two sprigs of sweet basil, two cloves, salt, and pepper; when cooked, take the potatoes out carefully, peel, and cut them in two, place them on a warm dish, pour on them a white sauce, and serve warm.

Another way.—Put two ounces of butter in a stewpan and set it on the fire; when hot, add a teaspoonful of parsley chopped fine, and a little salt; five minutes after, put in it a quart of potatoes, prepared, cooked, peeled, and mashed, as directed; then pour on the whole, little by little, stirring continually with a wooden spoon, a pint of good milk; and when the whole is well mixed, and becoming rather thick, take from the fire, place on the dish, then set in a brisk oven for five minutes, and serve.

The same, in salad.—Cook them without water in an oven, or in hot cinders, if handy; then peel and cut them in thin slices; place them in a salad dish, season with chopped parsley, sweet oil, vinegar, salt, and pepper, and serve.

You may use butter instead of oil if you serve warm; you may also add slices of beets, and of pickled cucumbers, according to taste.

SWEET POTATOES.

Prepare, cook, and serve them like other potatoes—either boiled, fried, stewed, or in any other way.

PUMPKINS AND SQUASHES.

Peel, take out the seed, cut in pieces, and throw them in boiling water, with a little salt; drain when cooked, and afterward pass through a strainer. Put butter in a stewpan and set it on the fire; when melted, add chopped parsley, salt, and pepper, then the pumpkin, or squash; simmer ten minutes; after which, pour in it half a pint of milk, little by little, and stirring the while; leave ten minutes longer, that is, twenty minutes in all, and take from the fire; mix well in it the yolks of two or more eggs, according to the quantity of pumpkin you have, and serve warm.

Another way.—When cooked in boiling water as above, and drained, you put butter in a stewpan, and set it on the fire; when melted, add chopped parsley, a little grated nutmeg, salt, and pepper; then lay in the pieces of pumpkin or squash, stew for about six minutes, and serve warm.

PURSLAIN.

Clean, wash well, and throw in boiling water with a little salt, and boil till cooked, when take and drain. Put butter in a stewpan, set it on the fire, and when melted, lay the purslain in, stir a little, then sprinkle on, gradually, a pinch of flour, stirring the while; season with a pinch of chopped parsley, salt, and pepper; simmer about ten minutes, take from the fire, mix in it one or two beaten eggs, and serve.

In salad, it is prepared just like lettuce.

SALSIFY, OR OYSTER PLANT.

Scrape them, and throw one by one as you scrape them in cold water, with a few drops of vinegar; when they are all scraped, move them a little, take out of the water, and throw them in boiling water with a little salt, boil fifty minutes and drain; place them warm on a warm dish, and serve with brown butter, a maitre-d'hôtel, or white sauce.

Fried.—Make a paste with two tablespoonfuls of flour, a beaten egg, a tablespoonful of vinegar, salt, pepper, and the quantity of milk necessary to make the paste thin enough to dip the plants in, so that a thin coat only sticks to them; then, when they are cooked in water as above, you dip them in the above paste, and throw them in hot lard in a pan, and on a sharp fire; take them out when you see that the paste is fried enough, and serve with fried parsley around, and without any grease.

SKIRRET.

Prepare, cook, and serve like parsnips.

SORREL.

Take the sorrel, hold it by the stalk with one hand, and pull off the leaves with the other, one by one, so that only the stalk and fibres attached to it will remain after the pulling; the other part only is to be used, which you wash well, then drain and chop it fine, say a quart of it; throw it in boiling water, with a handful of chopped chervil if handy, and a little salt; when cooked, drain. Put a piece of butter the size of an egg in a stewpan, set it on a good fire, and when melted, put the sorrel in, sprinkle on it a tablespoonful of flour, stirring the while, and when all the flour is mixed, pour in also, little by little, and while stirring, half a pint of broth, or three quarters of a pint of milk, boil slowly ten minutes, and serve.

Eggs boiled hard and cut in four pieces may be put on the sorrel.

SPINAGE OR SPINACH.

Cook and serve like sorrel, omitting chervil, and adding sugar just before serving.

Eggs may be put at the top as for sorrel.

TOMATOES.

After they are washed, throw boiling water on them, take the skin off, and put them in a stewpan with butter, salt, and pepper; set it on the fire and simmer forty-five minutes; serve warm, with any kind of boiled or roasted meat.

The same, in salad.—Wash gently and wipe them dry; cut in slices, place them in the salad dish, season with sweet oil, vinegar, salt, and pepper; cover and let them stand thus two hours, turn over gently to mix well with the seasonings just before eating them.

Some onions may be added if you choose, but they must be prepared thus before: take some small red onions, chop them fine, put them in cold water for ten minutes, then wipe them dry in a clean coarse towel, and mix with the tomatoes.

TRUFFLES.

If they are preserved, as is generally the case, take

them out of the bottle or other vessel in which they are, and drain them; if not, then put a pound of them in a stewpan (after being wiped dry), with two sprigs of parsley, one of thyme, a clove of garlic, a bay leaf, a clove, four ounces of butter, two ounces of grated bacon, a little salt, same of white sugar, two small onions, and a small carrot; cover the whole with half broth and half claret wine; boil gently about one hour, take off parsley, thyme, garlic, bay leaf, clove, onions, and carrot, and serve.

TURNIPS.

Clean, scrape and wash well three pints of turnips, throw them in boiling water for ten minutes, take out and drain. Put four ounces of butter in a stewpan, and set it on the fire; when melted, sprinkle in a teaspoonful of flour, then put the turnips in with a pint of broth, salt, and pepper; simmer till cooked, and serve.

The same, with sugar.—Throw three pints of turnips in boiling water; boil them ten minutes, and drain. Proceed as for the above, except that you use two tablespoonfuls of sugar instead of flour.

Turnips may be served with a béchamel or poulette sauce, with or without sugar

Just before serving, you may also mix with them the beaten yolks of two eggs.

WILD CHICCORY.

Prepare, cook, and serve like dandelion.

CHESTNUTS.

To roast them, you have only to prick them with the point of a knife in any one place; and to boil them, they may be shelled before or after.

HOW TO PRESERVE TOMATOES.

Take good and well ripened ones, clean and wash them well, put them in a stewpan and set it on a moderate fire for a while; take from the fire, throw away the water coming from them, and then strain them into a vessel. Put what there is in the vessel back on the fire, and in the same stewpan, and let it reduce about half; take from the fire, pour in a crockery pot, and leave thus twenty-four hours; then put in bottles, cork well, and place them in a cold and dry place.

MUSHROOM CATSUP.

Clean and wash them well, stems and all; cut them in two or four pieces; then place the pieces in a crockery vessel, sprinkling salt on every layer of mushrooms, and leave thus twenty-four hours. Take them out and press them well, so as to take all the juice out, which you bottle at once, and cork. Put the mushrooms back in the vessel, and twenty-four hours after, press them again; and again put the juice in bottles, and the mushrooms in the vessel, and repeat this process again after another twenty-four hours. Then mix well together the juice of the three pressings; add to it pepper, allspice, one clove (or more, according to the quantity), broken in pieces; boil the whole, skim off the scum as long as you see any on the surface, and strain. Bottle when cool; put in each bottle two cloves and a peppercorn, cork air-tight, put in a cool and dry place, and it will keep for years.

GREEN WALNUTS IN SALAD.

The European walnut only can be used, and as soon as good to eat; that is, before the outer shell dries and opens.

Break the nuts in two, take out the kernels with a

pointed knife, and place them in a salad dish, with some juice of grapes not yet ripe; add salt and pepper, leave thus two or three hours, moving now and then, and serve. The eatable part will be found very good eaten that way.

To persons who have never eaten any, it may appear a strange dish, but let them try it.

SALADS.

HOW TO PREPARE CHICCORY, SUCCORY, ENDIVE, CURLED ENDIVE, LETTUCE, BUTTER LETTUCE, CABBAGE LETTUCE, COS LETTUCE, CURLED SILESIA, GREEN AND WHITE LETTUCE, ETC.

Take off the outer leaves, then detach and cut (or rather break with the thumb and fingers) in two, three or four pieces, all the large leaves, split the heart in four (we understand by the heart of a salad, the inside small leaves, when only a few of them remain), wash well and drain dry, taking care not to wilt the leaves, as it would give them an unsightly appearance.

If it were possible to clean the salad by merely wiping the leaves with a towel, it would be better than washing; but it must be washed if there is any earth or sand on it. Then it is ready to put in the salad dish; the pieces of the heart at the top.

HOW TO DECORATE A SALAD.

Place tastefully on the top of the salad some blossoms of the following plants: borage, Indian cress or nasturtium, marsh mallow, ox tongue or bugloss, periwinkle, wild chiccory, and also the petals of roses and of pinks. Place the salad thus decorated, on the table, at the beginning of the dinner. You may put a few of each, or only of those you can procure. It is as agreeable to the eye during the dinner, **as it is to the** palate when you eat it.

HOW TO MAKE THE SALAD.

When the time comes to eat the salad, place near the person that makes it, oil, vinegar, salt, and pepper; then the oil necessary is poured on it first, the pepper after; put in the spoon the quantity of salt you want to use, pour vinegar on it, dissolve it by moving it in the spoon with the fork and then move the salad.

The salad may be made by the waiter, on the sideboard; that is, when the time comes to eat it, the waiter takes it from the table and makes it.

The salad should be made by an experienced person, who can judge at a glance what quantity of oil, vinegar, salt, and pepper, is necessary. The quantities cannot be given, as it depends on the quantity of salad; it requires about two tablespoonfuls of sweet oil, to one of good vinegar.

Chopped parsley and **cives must be offered at the same** time with the salad, as many persons **like that** seasoning.

Salads of cabbages (red and white), cauliflowers, celery, dandelion, **fetticus, or** corn salad, purslain, **and** watercress, are made like **the above.**

SOUP CELERY IN SALAD.

Clean, wash well, and scrape it carefully; cut it in **thin slices, place them in a salad dish, sprinkle on salt,** pepper, vinegar, **and a little mustard;** leave thus from four to six hours; then throw the vinegar away, send **to** the table, and decorate and make it like another salad. It will require very little salt and pepper, as most of it remains when you throw away the vinegar.

9*

APRICOTS, ORANGES, PEACHES, PEARS, STRAWBERRIES, RASPBERRIES, BLACKBERRIES, CURRANTS, AND LIKE BERRIES, IN SALAD.

Dust the bottom of a dish with white sugar, put a layer of slices of apricots, oranges, peaches, or pears, or a layer of the others entire, and dust again; repeat the same till the whole is in, then add over the whole a pinch of grated nutmeg, and French brandy or rum to suit your taste, and serve.

SALAD OF CHICKEN, FOWL, PARTRIDGE, PRAIRIE HEN, PHEASANT, ETC.

Take a roasted chicken or partridge, etc.; when cold, cut it in pieces as for fricassee, place them on a dish with pickled cucumbers cut in slices, and a little chopped parsley; add the sweet oil, vinegar, salt, and pepper necessary; move well, and serve.

Some boiled eggs may be put around the dish, and also a cabbage lettuce cut in four pieces.

A few sprigs of green parsley may also be placed around the dish.

COCOANUT IN SALAD.

Peel it carefully and soak it in brandy for twenty-four hours. A little sugar may be added.

EGGS IN SALAD.

Cut hard boiled eggs in slices, add chopped parsley, sweet oil, salt, vinegar, and pepper; move, and serve.

SALAD MACÉDOINE.

This salad ought to be called "compound salad," as it is made of a little of everything that can be served in salad, i. e., fish, meat, green and dry vegetables, &c. When the whole is mixed you add chopped parsley, sweet oil, vinegar, **salt** and pepper; you move **till** your arms are sore, and you have a salad macédoine. Every **one** has a right to try it.

SALMON AND TURBOT.

Cut in slices, place them in a salad dish, with hard boiled eggs cut in two, or with some lettuce, and serve as directed for salads.

EGGS.

With asparagus.—Cut in pieces about a quarter of an inch long, a gill of the tender part of asparagus, throw it in boiling water with a little salt; boil fifteen minutes and drain. Beat eight eggs just enough to mix the yolks with the whites; put them in a stewpan, season with a pinch of grated nutmeg, salt, and pepper; add also a tablespoonful of warm water, set on a slow fire, stir till they are becoming thick; then add four ounces of butter, stir five minutes longer; then add the gill of asparagus; simmer about fifteen minutes longer, and serve.

The same, boiled.—Put the eggs in boiling water, as much as possible at the first boiling; leave five minutes; take out and put them immediately in cold water to cool; then shell them without breaking them, serve thus on a purée of celery, mushrooms, or sorrel.

The same, with brown butter.—Break gently in a plate or dish, and without breaking the yolks, eight eggs; sprinkle salt and pepper on them. Put two ounces of butter in a frying pan, and on a good fire; when turning brown subdue the fire. Put also, and at the same time, the same quantity of butter in another frying pan, and on a good fire, and when hot, place the eggs in without breaking the yolks; then spread over the eggs the brown butter you have in the other; take from the fire when you see the whites becoming hard; put them on a dish, pour on them a tablespoonful of vinegar which you have warmed in the pan after having used the brown butter, and serve.

The same, fried.—Put half a pound of lard in a frying pan, **and on a** good fire; **when hot,** break gently, one by **one** (being careful not to break the yolk), the quantity of eggs you can put **in** the pan without allowing them to adhere together; **turn** them upside **down once** with a spoon or skimmer; **take** from the pan with a skimmer as soon as the white part becomes hard, and serve with fried parsley around, or on a garniture of vegetables.

The same, mashed.—Beat six eggs just enough to mix the whites and yolks together; put two ounces of butter in a stewpan, and set on the fire; when melted take from the fire, add salt, pepper, and a pinch of grated nutmeg, then the eggs, also a tablespoonful of broth; put back on a very slow fire, stir continually till cooked, and serve warm.

The same, in matelote.—Put a bottle of claret wine in a stewpan and set it on a good fire; add to it two sprigs of parsley, one of thyme, a clove of garlic, a middling sized onion, a clove, a bay leaf, salt, and pepper; boil fifteen minutes; then take all the seasonings out and have your wine boiling gently; break one egg in by letting it fall gently in order to have it entire, and then take it out immediately with **a skimmer,** and place it on a dish; **do** the same with eight eggs; keep them in a warm (but not hot) place. After which put in the wine, without taking it from the fire, four ounces of butter kneaded with a tablespoonful of flour; boil till reduced to a proper thickness, pour it on the eggs, and serve.

The same, with onions.—Cut in dice three middling sized onions; put them in a stewpan with four ounces of butter, and set it on a moderate fire; when the onions are turning yellow, sprinkle on them a teaspoonful of flour, salt, and pepper; add a gill of warm water, boil gently till reduced to a proper thickness. Have ready the quantity of eggs **you want,** which must be boiled hard, and cut in four pieces; put them in the stewpan, leave only **one** minute longer on the fire, and serve.

The same, with green peas.—Throw a gill of green peas in boiling water with a little salt, boil them twenty minutes, and drain. Beat eight eggs just enough to mix the yolks with the whites; put them in a stewpan, and set it on the fire; season with a pinch of grated nutmeg, salt, and pepper; add a teaspoonful of warm water, then the green peas, keep stirring for five minutes; then add four ounces of butter, simmer fifteen minutes longer, and serve.

The same, sur le plat.—Butter the bottom of a crockery dish with two ounces of butter; break in it gently six eggs, without breaking the yolks; sprinkle salt, pepper, and a little grated nutmeg on them, put the dish on warm cinders, and when the white is hard, take off and serve.

They must be served in the crockery dish.

The same, poached.—Fill a kettle with water, about two thirds full, add **to it a** gill of vinegar, and a little salt; put it on the fire, and take it off at the first boiling; immediately break the eggs in, gently; take them out as soon as the white is hard, place them on a purée of celery, or of sorrel, **and serve warm.**

The same, in the shell.—Put eggs in boiling water for two minutes, if you like them soft or underdone, and three minutes, if you like them quite done. After the two minutes of boiling, take from the fire, and leave them in **the water half a** minute longer, then take them out, and serve them on the table, enveloped in a napkin.

Cooked in this way **they** are eaten either in the shell by the means of an egg cup, or in a glass.

Another way of cooking **them is to** put them **in boil**ing water, and take the water immediately from the fire; **leave them** in it five minutes.

The same, à la neige, or snow-like.—Break ten eggs and separate **the** yolks from **the whites; beat** the whites till they are turned into a **thick foam**; then sprinkle in them four ounces of fine white sugar, **and a** tablespoonful of essence of vanilla, stirring the while **to mix** well. Then put in a stewpan a pint of milk, a tablespoonful of orange flower water, and two ounces of sugar; set it on a good· fire, and as soon as it boils, take a tablespoonful of your beaten eggs, and let drop gently in the pan; do the same for the whole, as rapidly **as possible;** take them out with a **skimmer as soon** as you see them hard, and place in a dish; **then** take the **milk from the** fire, beat the yolks of the eggs in a vessel with a **little of the** milk from the stewpan, put that mixture in a stewpan, and this back on the fire; **stir** with a wooden spoon **till it** is becoming thick, take **off** and **pour on the whites, and serve** thus when cold.

OMELETS.

How to beat the eggs.—Break in a bowl the quantity of eggs you want, or as many as there are persons at the **table; beat** them well with a little milk, or at least a little water if you have no milk; add also a little salt and pepper.

How to place on the dish.—When the omelet is cooked, you slide it gently from the pan into the dish, and when half of it is in the dish, you turn your pan upside down so as to fold the omelet; it is more tender and tasty. Do not turn it over in the pan so as to fry both sides, except when directed.

With apples.—Peel two or three apples, cut them **in** thin, round slices, **fry them** with a little butter, and take **them from the** pan; **then put** a little more butter in the pan, and when hot, pour in it six beaten eggs, in which you have mixed the slices of apples; turn over once, and serve as directed.

With asparagus.—Cut **the eatable part of** the asparagus half an inch in length, throw them in boiling water **with a** little salt, drain them when cooked, and chop them fine; **beat** them **with eggs and a** little milk; have hot butter **in a** frying **pan on** a good fire; **pour** the eggs in, tossing continually till done, and serve **on a dish as** directed.

With bacon.—Put two ounces of butter in a frying pan; when melted add two ounces of bacon cut in dice; when turning brown and very hot, pour in eight eggs, beaten as directed above; toss the pan almost all the time till done, and serve as directed.

With ham.—Proceed as with bacon in every particular, and use ham instead of bacon.

With fin herbes.—Beat as directed six eggs, with two tablespoonfuls of parsley, and one of cives chopped fine. Put four ounces of butter in a frying pan, and set it on a good fire; when hot, pour the eggs in, toss now and then till done, and serve as above directed.

When about half done, drop a piece of butter the size of a walnut under the omelet, to prevent it from adhering to the pan.

With kidneys.—Roast a calf's kidney, and chop it fine; beat it with eggs as directed. Put butter in a frying pan, and set it on a good fire; when hot, pour the eggs in, toss now and then till done, and serve.

With mushrooms.—Cut mushrooms in pieces, and beat them with eggs as directed for omelets; have hot butter in a frying pan on a good fire, pour the eggs in, toss the pan till done, and serve.

Au naturel.—Put two ounces of butter in a frying pan; when hot pour in it six eggs, beaten as directed for omelets, toss the pan all the time till done, place on a dish, and serve.

Grated cheese may be added on the omelet; in that case, when the cheese is on it, put in a quick oven for two or three minutes, and then serve.

The cheese may also be beaten with the eggs.

The best cheese for omelets is Gruyère.

With sorrel.—Put two ounces of butter in a frying pan, and set it on the fire; when melted, pour in it six beaten eggs, toss almost continually till done, turn it over once to fry both sides, and when cooked, serve it on a purée of sorrel.

SOUFFLÉE.

Mix well the yolks of eight fresh eggs with about four ounces of fine white sugar; beat well the whites of the eight eggs; afterward mix well together yolks, whites, and the rind of half a lemon chopped very fine. Put four ounces of butter in a crockery dish, place it on a moderate fire; when the butter is melted, pour the eggs in, mix well the butter, and as soon as you see the whole well mixed, place in a very hot oven for five minutes; take it out, dust with fine sugar, and serve hot.

With sugar.—Mix well the yolks of eight eggs with two ounces of fine white sugar and a pinch of salt, and beat well the whites; then mix well yolks, whites, and the rind of half a lemon, having the latter chopped very fine. Put four ounces of butter in a frying pan, and set it on the fire; when melted, pour the eggs in, and toss now and then till done; dust a dish with fine white sugar, put the omelet on, then dust again the upper side with the same; have ready a red hot shovel, or any other flat piece of iron, pass it over the top of the omelet, so as to color it while melting the sugar, and serve warm. The whole process must be performed quickly.

With rum.—Make an omelet with sugar as above, and when on the table, pour a gill or so of rum on it, set fire to it, and let it burn as long as it can, taking slowly but continually with a silver spoon the rum from the sides, and pouring it on the middle while it is burning, and until it dies out by itself; then eat immediately.

With truffles.—Slice four ounces of truffles, beat them with six eggs, a little milk, and a little salt and pepper. Put in a frying pan four ounces of butter, and set it on a good fire ; when melted pour the eggs in, toss almost continually till done, and serve as directed for omelets.

A la Washington.—Make four omelets of four eggs each, one with apples, one with asparagus or sorrel (according to the season), a third with fines herbes, and the fourth, au naturel ; you serve them on the same dish, one lapping over the other. It makes a fine as well as a good dish

This omelet, or rather these omelets were a favorite dish to the Father of his country ; they were very often served on his table when he had a grand dinner.

PASTRY, TARTS, PIES, ETC.

WHAT IS NECESSARY TO MAKE GOOD PASTRY.

To make good paste, and consequently good pastry, always use the best wheat flour, properly sifted, the best fresh butter, fresh eggs, fine, white salt, a marble table, or a very clean and very smooth board; be in a cool place in summer, and in a moderately warm one in winter; use cold water in summer, and lukewarm water in winter.

PASTE A.

Take half a pound of butter, put it in a pail of very cold water for half an hour, and take it out; make a paste with it and a pound of flour, also two eggs, half a pint of the water in which the butter was, and about a quarter of an ounce of fine salt; knead the whole properly with the fingers; then dredge your table or board with flour, take a rolling pin and roll it thin, fold it over once and roll again thin; repeat the same process five times in summer and six in winter, and leave it thus half an hour in summer and an hour in winter, before using it.

PASTE B.

Take three quarters of a pound of butter, and put it in a pail of very cold water for half an hour. Make a paste with it and one pound of flour, four eggs, half an ounce of fine salt, and a little water; knead the whole well; roll it with a rolling pin to a thickness of half an inch, then break it in pieces with your fingers; knead again and break it again. Then knead and roll it thin; leave it thus half an hour in summer and an hour in winter, before using it.

PASTE C.

Put a pound of butter in a pail of very cold water for half an hour. Take one pound of flour, two eggs, a quarter of an ounce of fine salt, a little water, and two ounces of the butter from the pound above mentioned, and knead the whole well together; spread with a rolling pin; then divide the remaining fourteen ounces of butter in eight parts, take one of them and spread it on the paste, then fold it over once, and roll again thin; repeat this process seven times more, and then fold the paste over twice; roll thin again, repeat this last process once, and half an hour after, it is ready for use.

PASTE D.

Work into a paste two pounds of flour with a little water, four eggs, half an ounce of salt, half a pound of butter, and four ounces of fine, well boiled beef **suet**; spread it on the board, fold it over once, and roll it thin; fold and roll again four times more; half an hour after, it is ready for use.

PASTE E.

Beat well together the yolks of six eggs and half a pound of fine, white sugar; whisk to a froth the six whites; mix the whole with six ounces of the best flour (which flour you must have previously dried in an oven, and sifted before using it); when the whole is properly mixed, it makes a light paste, and is ready for immediate use.

CHOCOLATE BISCUIT.

Pound well two ounces of chocolate, mix it properly with paste E, put it in a well buttered mould or moulds, and place them in a moderately heated oven; watch carefully till baked, which you easily tell by the color it assumes.

CINNAMON, LEMON, ORANGE, OR VANILLA BISCUIT.

Proceed as for chocolate biscuit in every particular, except that you use cinnamon, lemon, etc., enough to give the taste, instead of chocolate; for lemon or orange, you mix with the paste about the fourth part of a rind, well grated.

Many names are given to these biscuits, according to fancy; they are called biscuits en caisse, à la cuiller, à la royale, etc.; these names mean nothing.

They may be baked in moulds, in small square paper boxes, buttered, or on slips of paper only; it is very easily done.

FILBERT BISCUIT.

Take eight ounces of sweet almonds and four ounces of bitter ones; throw them in boiling water for five minutes; take out and skin them, put them in a mortar with a few drops of orange flower water, or well beaten whites of eggs; when reduced to a paste, mix well with it four ounces of flour (the flour must be prepared as for paste E); also with eight ounces of fine, white sugar, the yolks of two eggs well beaten, and the whites of four eggs whisked to a froth; when the whole is properly mixed, put it in a well buttered mould, which place in a moderately heated oven; watch it carefully, take out when cooked, which is easily known by the color it assumes.

Biscuits with hazelnuts, peach, or other kernels, may

be made in the same way; that is, using them instead of almonds.

ANCHOVY CAKE.

Knead four ounces of flour with two ounces of butter, a little salt, and a little water. Clean four anchovies and put them in vinegar for five minutes; then cut them in small pieces, put them in a bowl, and cover them with sweet oil; leave them thus ten minutes. Roll the paste thin, then place a little more than half of it on a tart dish, raising it all around with the thumb and forefinger; cover that paste with the anchovies, and these with the remainder of the paste, after having cut it in square pieces; spread some of the oil in which were the anchovies, on it, bake in a warm oven, baste now and then with a little of the oil, and serve warm.

LEMON CAKE.

Mix well with some paste A, the rind of half a lemon well grated, also four ounces of fine, white sugar, and a teaspoonful of orange flower water; butter a mould, put the mixture in it, and put it in a moderately heated oven for about an hour.

LIGHT CAKE.

Take half a pound of flour, knead it with a little lukewarm water and yeast, put it in a warm place, and when it has swelled about three times its bulk (when first made) it is ready for use.

Knead to a paste, one pound and a half of flour with the same quantity of butter, also fifteen eggs, salt, and about half a pint of milk; then mix this again with the paste made with yeast, and when the whole is properly kneaded, put it in a warm place for about ten hours. After which, make a ball with three fourths of the paste, put it in a tin dish; then make another ball of the other fourth, place it on the top of the larger one, moistening with a little milk or water the parts joined, in order to make them stick together; put them in a rather brisk oven, and ten or fifteen minutes after, place a piece of paper over the top ball—a kind of cap to prevent its baking too fast, as it is much smaller than the lower one; it takes about forty-five minutes to bake it.

It may be served cold as well as warm.

If found too large with the above quantities, make it smaller, or make two or more out of it.

PLUM CAKE.

Mix well in a vessel a pound of sugar with a pound of butter; then mix again with it eight eggs, one by one; then mix again with it half a pound of raisins, also half a pound of flour, and a liquor glass of rum; when the whole is well mixed, bake in an oven.

RICE CAKE.

Mix well with some paste A, six eggs and six ounces of rice (the rice must have been cooked previously in milk); add also a little salt, and four ounces of fine, white sugar; then butter well a piece of paper, place the paste on it, and put it in a warm oven. Take out when baked, which takes about an hour, dust it with sugar, put again in the oven for two minutes, and serve warm.

SAVOY BISCUIT, OR SPONGE CAKE.

Mix well with some paste E, a little of the rind of a lemon, well grated, and a little piece of vanilla, well pounded. Butter a mould well, and dredge the butter slightly with fine, white sugar; place the paste in the mould, and put it in a moderately heated oven. It takes about fifty minutes to bake; after which, take it out, let cool a little, turn over a dish, remove the mould, put again in the oven five minutes only, and it is done.

You may put half the quantities above mentioned, or double them, according to the size of your mould or moulds.

TEA CAKE.

Mix with some of the paste A, four ounces of sugar and a little water; spread the paste, and roll it to a thickness of about three eighths of an inch; cut it in small pieces, and of different shapes, put them on slightly buttered sheet iron pans, or on pieces of buttered paper, glaze the top with a very little yolk of egg well beaten with water, dust with fine white sugar, bake in a slow oven, and eat warm.

FARCE, FOR MEAT PIES.

Take four ounces of fillet of veal, four ounces of round of beef, and eight ounces of beef suet; see that the whole is free from fibres, or thin skin; chop the whole as fine as possible; chop also very fine a little parsley, a little piece of bay leaf, and the same of thyme; pound the whole well, and mix together meat, suet, and spices; add to it while pounding, and little by little, the whites of two eggs, and one yolk, beaten together; when well mixed, it forms a kind of thick paste, then add a liquor glass of French brandy, and one gill of white wine, to every pound of meat. Add to it water or broth, and work it at the same time till you bring it to a rather liquid farce; add, then, salt, pepper, and a little grated nutmeg, and it is ready for use.

This farce may also be made with game, poultry, or birds, raw, roasted, or cooked in any way, and in the same proportions as above; that is, you mix it with the same quantity of beef suet, and proceed as above in every other particular.

FARCE, FOR FISH PIES.

Clean as directed for fish, and cut in pieces about two inches long, a pound of fresh fish—cod, eel, sole, or turbot. Put it in a stewpan with two sprigs of parsley, one of thyme, half a bay leaf, one clove, salt, pepper, one clove of garlic, and half a glass of white wine; cover with water, and set it on a good fire; boil till cooked, let cool, take the fish out, take the bones out, and chop it very fine; then pound it well, with six ounces of butter, a little chopped parsley, one beaten egg, salt, pepper, and a little grated nutmeg; bring it to a rather liquid farce, by adding a little water, and mixing well, and then it is ready for use.

APPLE PIE, OR ANY OTHER FRUIT PIE.

Quarter, peel and core as many apples as you want, envelop them with some of paste A; put them in a tin or sheet iron pan, and in a warm oven; twenty minutes after make a few holes at the top with a fork to let the vapor out; put back in the oven till done, which you easily tell by the color and the appearance of the pie. There are some kinds of apples that require a longer time than others to cook. Dust the pie with sugar when taking it from the oven, and serve warm or cold.

Any other fruit pies are made in the same way, also rhubarb pie.

These pies may also be made with marmalades of fruits, or with the fruits cooked before in any way; in that case, take some of paste B to make them.

Tarts or pies may also be made with sweetmeats; for these take some of pastes B or C, roll it thin, put it on a buttered tin or sheet iron pan, or even on a piece of tered paper; spread the marmalade on it, and cover with another piece of the same **paste, but** as thin as possible; you join the two pastes together by merely wetting both all **around,** and pressing them **gently** together with the fingers; **bake in** the oven like other pies.

All these tarts or pies may be made with any kind of sweatmeats, and of every shape. Many names are given them, not according to the way they are made, but merely according to the shape; the whole depends upon the fancy of the maker; some are called tartlets, others **ladies'** slippers, etc., etc.

HOW TO FILL AND COVER THE MOULD, TIN PAN, OR SHEET IRON PAN FOR MEAT PIES.

Bring some of paste D to a thickness of one sixteenth of an inch, and line the bottom and sides of the mould or pan with it; place the meat inside, and pour on it some farce for meat pies, to fill the hollow **places;** then cover with a piece of the same paste, and which you join with the paste of the sides, by merely **wetting with** water **the two** pastes, **and** pressing them together **with the** fingers. Make a few holes at **the top with a fork** or something **else** to let the vapor out **while** baking, and place **in a properly** heated oven.

If the meat **is cooked before** putting it in the paste, it will take from one to two hours to bake the pie, according to its size; **and if** the meat is raw, it **will take from two** to three hours.

Meat **pies may** be eaten **warm** or cold, according to taste.

BIRD PIE.

By birds, are **understood all,** from the partridge or pheasant to the smallest **of birds;** turkey is very seldom prepared in pie.

Clean and prepare as directed for birds; cut them in

two or four pieces, or use them whole, according to their size; fry the birds in butter, with salt, pepper, a pinch of allspice, and a little chopped parsley; when half done, take from the fire, and place in the mould as soon as they are cold.

CHICKEN PIE.

Cut a chicken as for fricassee; you may take the bones out if it suits you, and proceed as for bird pie in every other particular.

HAM PIE.

Cook the ham in water and seasonings, as directed for ham, only take it from the fire an hour before it is entirely cooked; let cool, bone it, cut it in slices, and proceed as directed for pies.

HARE PIE AND RABBIT PIE

Clean and cut in pieces a hare, or half of it; take the bones out, lard the pieces, fry them half done, with butter, salt, pepper, a piece of allspice, and a little chopped parsley; let cool, put in the mould or pan, as directed, and leave two hours in the oven.

LAMB PIE.

Take one pound or more of lamb, according to the size you want to make the pie; cut it in pieces and take the bones out, fry with butter, salt, pepper, chopped parsley, and a pinch of allspice; take from the fire when half done, let cool, put in the mould or pan, as directed, and bake.

MINCE PIE.

Chop fine any kind of meat, game, poultry, or butcher's meat you may have left from a dinner, of either, or of all of them; add to every pound of it a quarter of a pound of mince meat for sausages, and mix the whole well; then fry the mixture with butter, chopped parsley, and a pinch of allspice; leave on the fire about twenty-five minutes, wet with broth during the process, and also add a pinch of flour; take from the fire and let cool; put in the mould as directed, and leave about two hours in the oven.

Mince pies are made of any size, from half a pound to eight or ten pounds; when very large, leave it longer in the oven.

Mince pies are very **good for** breakfasts, lunches, or suppers.

VEAL PIE.

Take a piece of veal and proceed as for lamb pie.

FISH PIE.

Clean as directed for fish in general, about three pounds of any kind of fish (you may use of one or of many kinds at the same time, as it suits you); cod, eels, soles, or turbot, are said to be superior, but every kind of fish is very good when well prepared. Cut the fish in pieces about two inches long; fry it with butter, chopped parsley, a pinch of allspice, salt, pepper, and a few drops of lemon juice; take from the fire when half done, and let cool. Place the fish in the mould, or pan, as directed for meat pie, fill the hollow places with farce for fish pies, and proceed as for meat pies in every other particular.

VOL-AU-VENT.

Bring to a thickness of three quarters of an inch, some of paste C; give it a round form, and of the size of the dish you want to serve it on; put the paste on a sheet iron pan; then with the point of a knife you cut the paste at the top, about three fourths of its thickness, and three quarters of an inch from the edge, and the cut describing a circle; beat yolks of eggs with water, and glaze slightly with them the inside of the circle, which is at the same time the upper part of the paste; **then put** it in a rather quick oven, seeing carefully that it bakes even; turn the pan round occasionally, as the oven might be warmer on one side than on the other; take it out when well raised, and of a fine color. Then with a knife take off the cover carefully (we understand by cover, the upper part inside the circle you have cut at the top before baking), and by the means of a spoon, remove the inside paste which is not baked, leaving only the bottom and sides untouched; then fill the empty place with butcher's meat, game, fish, or fruit, cooked beforehand—the meat must be roasted, boiled, or stewed; the fish must be boiled or stewed; and the fruit must be cooked in a stewpan, with sugar enough to sweeten it—and put the cover back on the whole; after which process you serve the vol-au-vent warm.

As can be seen by the above receipt, a **vol-au-vent** may be served in some hundreds of ways.

It may also be served without a cover.

BABA.

Make a light paste with about four ounces of flour, milk, and a little yeast; when raised, knead it with twelve ounces of flour, and let it raise again; knead it again with nine ounces of butter, and eight eggs, using the eggs one after another, and mixing the whole well; add also then six ounces of raisins, and a liquor glass of brandy; bake it in a moderately heated oven.

CUSTARD AND FLAN.

Put a pint of milk on the fire, and let reduce one half. Take twelve ounces of flour, same of butter, and knead to a paste, with the yolks of four eggs, and also with the milk;

leave thus half an hour; then mix again with the whole four ounces of fine, white sugar, and a few drops of essence of rose; then put the mixture in a crockery dish, and the dish in a moderately heated oven; watch it carefully till done, which you will know by the color it assumes.

Another way.—Make a light paste with a pint of milk (after having given it one boil), one pound and a half of flour, same of butter, five beaten eggs, a few drops of any essence, and a little salt; put it in a crockery dish, and the dish in a rather hot oven. It will take about forty minutes to cook it.

FRITTERS.

Boil till reduced one third, a quart of milk; let cool a little, and mix in it flour enough to make a thin paste; chop fine the rind of half a lemon, and mix it with the paste, also a little sugar, and the yolks of two eggs; spread the paste on a table, let cool about two hours; then cut it in small pieces, either round, square, or of any other shape; dip each piece in well beaten eggs, lay them in hot lard in a stewpan, and on a good fire, fry them till of a fine golden color, place on a dish, dust them with sugar, and serve warm.

FRITTERS WITH APPLES.

Make a thin paste with flour and lukewarm water; then add to it the yolks of one or two or more eggs, with a teaspoonful of sweet oil to each, then the white or whites of your eggs, after having well beaten them, and mix the whole well.

Peel, core, and cut apples in slices, put the slices in French brandy with a little sugar, also some rind of lemon chopped fine, and leave thus three or four hours; then take the slices out, dip each in the above paste, lay them in hot lard in a stewpan, and on a good fire; fry till of a fine golden color, take from the pan, drain, and place them on a dish, dust with fine, white sugar, and serve them warm.

Fritters with peaches, pineapples, strawberries, raspberries, and any other kind of fruit, may be made like the above. The only difference is, that you quarter peaches, etc., and that you use strawberries, etc., entire.

MACAROONS.

Throw in boiling water for five minutes ten ounces of sweet almonds, and two ounces of bitter ones; skin them well; put in a mortar, and grind them to a paste, adding a few drops of the white of eggs during the process. Grind well also a pound of white sugar, with the quarter of a rind of lemon well grated; then mix well together almonds, sugar, and the whites of two eggs. Make balls of any size with it; put the balls on a piece of paper, beat the yolk of an egg with half a gill of water, and glaze the top of the balls with it by the means of a pencil, or a goose feather; put them in a slow oven; it will take about fifteen minutes to cook them.

The same, with chocolate.—Proceed as for the above in every particular, except you add to the mixture two or more ounces of pounded chocolate.

MERINGUE, OR FRENCH KISSES.

Whisk to a froth the whites of ten eggs, then mix well with them half a pound of fine white sugar, and a few drops of essence of lemon; the best way to mix well is to sift the sugar on them slowly, and continue whisking the eggs till all the sugar is in; when properly done, it forms a rather stiff froth. Butter very slightly a sheet of white paper, pour your mixture on it by means of a spoon. You may make four, six, eight, ten, etc.; dust each cake with fine, white sugar, place in a slow oven for about ten minutes, or till it becomes brown; then take from the oven, and put each cake upside down on a tin sheet; this is easily done with a flexible knife; then with a spoon take out part of the inside, and dust it slightly with fine, white sugar; when cold it is ready for use, and may be kept two or three days in a very dry closet.

When you are to serve them, fill each with the following cream: beat well the yolks of ten eggs with one glass of good milk; mix one glass of milk with five ounces of fine, white sugar, and one spoonful of fecula; put in a stewpan the two mixtures, and set it on a slow fire; stir continually with a wooden spoon till it begins to become thick, then add to it the whites of the ten eggs, well beaten with two ounces of fine, white sugar; keep stirring two minutes longer, take from the fire, and let cool; add a few drops of essence to flavor it, and also about an ounce of isinglass dissolved in a little water, and serve.

APPLE MERINGUE.

There are many ways to make apple meringues; but the easiest and best is to fill the cakes with apple jelly, instead of cream, and proceed as for meringue in every other particular.

NOUGAT.

Throw a pound of sweet almonds in boiling water for five minutes; skin them well, and when cool, cut them in four or five pieces lengthwise; then melt a pound of fine, white sugar with two spoonfuls of water, in a copper or crockery pan, and on a good fire, stirring all the time with a wooden spoon; when well melted, put the almonds in; keep stirring about five minutes longer, take from the fire, add a little of the rind of a lemon well grated, oil the mould, put it on the corner of the range in a warm, but not too hot place; put the almonds and sugar in the

10*

mould, and little by little take off when of a brown color, turn on a plate, remove the mould, and serve.

PANCAKES.

Make a thin paste with one pound of flour, four eggs, two tablespoonfuls of sweet oil, one of French brandy, a little salt, the necessary quantity of lukewarm water and milk, about half of each; let it remain thus two or three hours at least; then put about an ounce of lard, butter, or oil in a frying pan, and set it on a brisk fire; when hot, put some of the paste in it with a ladle, spread the paste so as to cover the bottom of the pan; fry on both sides, place it on a dish, dust it with fine, white sugar on both sides, and serve warm.

Buckwheat and other pancakes are made in the same way.

PUDDINGS.

Every one knows how to make puddings. It is unhappily (for the constitution in general, and stomach in particular) too well known by all cooks or *soi-disant* cooks. We are of opinion that no one, and above all, children, ought to eat any kind of pudding, no matter how good it may taste.

Pudding eating is an English custom, but before following a custom of another country, people ought to consider if that custom or fashion (whatever it is) has not been introduced in that country by necessity, which is the case for pudding eating in England, and in some parts of Holland.

In England, where the fog is perpetual, or nearly so in many parts, and where it exists at least eight or nine months of the year in others, the stomach requires to be filled with something very heavy, something that will stay there till the next meal, and very often longer than that.

It is well known that in England, farm hands, or other persons working in the open air, eat six times a day, and have pudding at least three times; they drink home brewed beer, which is very heavy, and very rich also; let any one here, in this pure, clear atmosphere, eat six times a day, have pudding three times, with a pint of home brewed beer every time, and see how they will feel in the evening. We beg of all that may doubt our observations to try the experiment.

Pastry in general, no matter how light it may be made, lies heavier on the stomach than any other food, and is very difficult of digestion. There are thousands of persons that have never had any indigestion but from pastry. Children like pastry very much; this is very easily understood as their young stomachs digest very rapidly, they crave food oftener than grown persons. Pastry being easier to have at any time than anything else, it is given to them; and from habit in youth, arises the liking when grown up. The stomach being accustomed to it from infancy, may digest it better, but it is always at the expense of the whole system; the stomach must work hard, too hard in digesting it; whence come dyspepsia, weakness, and finally consumption, or debility, or any other sickness of the same kind.

RISSOLÉS.

Cut round or square pieces, about two inches in size, of paste A; fold it around to make a border; place on each piece a little marmalade of apricots; have hot lard or grease in a frying pan, and on a good fire; lay the pieces gently in, and take them out when of a golden color.

They must be served hot, and dusted with sugar.

Any other marmalade may be used.

WAFFLES.

Make a thin paste with eight ounces of flour, six ounces of sugar, two eggs well beaten, a few drops of orange flower water, half a liquor glass of brandy, and the milk necessary; warm the mould on both sides; grease both sides with butter; put some of your paste in it, close it gently, set it on the fire, turn over to warm both sides equally, dust them with sugar when done, and eat either warm or cold; it takes hardly one minute to make one, with a good fire.

BLANC-MANGER.

Throw in boiling water two ounces of sweet almonds and the same of bitter ones; when the skin comes easily off, take from the fire and drain. Then skin and pound them well with the same quantity of sugar, lay the whole in a pan with about a pint of water, set on the fire, and when on the point of boiling, take off and strain. Put in a stewpan about a pint of milk, with your strained juice, nearly an ounce of isinglass, a little of the rind of a lemon, well grated, and a little nutmeg, well grated also; set on a moderate fire, simmer just enough to melt the isinglass; then strain, put in a mould, set it on ice, and use when cool.

FONDUE.

Beat well six eggs, and put them in a stewpan with two ounces of Gruyère, well grated, and about one ounce of butter; set on a brisk fire, and leave till it becomes rather thick, stirring all the time with a wooden spoon; take from the fire, add pepper, and stir a little; turn over on a warm dish, and serve.

This is a very favorite dish in Italy, and also in Switzerland where it originated.

CHARLOTTE RUSSE.

Line the bottom and sides of a round mould with pieces of Savoy biscuit; fill it with well whipped cream; turn the mould over on a dish; put fifteen minutes on ice, and serve after having removed the mould.

APPLES IN CHARLOTTE RUSSE.

Quarter, peel, and core about a quart of apples. Put butter in a stewpan, and set it on the fire; when melted, put your apples in with sugar, and a little grated nutmeg; then take from the fire, put in an oven, and when cooked, drain them; put them back on the fire for ten minutes, stirring the while, and take off. Butter slightly a round mould; line the bottom and sides with croutons; fill the mould with the apples; cover with slices of the soft part of bread; put in an oven for about twenty-five minutes—the oven must not be too hot—then take off, turn over on a dish, remove the mould, and serve hot.

CREAM FOR ENTREMETS.

With burnt sugar.—Put two ounces of sugar in a small tin pan, with a tablespoonful of water, set on the fire, and boil till burnt, and of a light brown color; take off, and put it in a stewpan with a pint of milk, four ounces of white sugar, a few drops of rose or orange flower water; boil ten minutes, stirring occasionally; take from the fire, beat the yolks of two eggs, and one entire, put in the pan and mix the whole well, then strain, after which you put the mixture in small cream pots for that purpose: place them in a hot but not boiling bain-marie, and as soon as it thickens take them out, dust them with fine white sugar, let cool; place them on ice for about fifteen minutes, and then it is ready to be served.

With chocolate.—Put in a stewpan and on a moderate fire, six ounces of chocolate, three tablespoonfuls of water, three ounces of white sugar, stir now and then with a wooden spoon till melted; then pour in it, little by little, a quart of good fresh milk; boil ten minutes, take from the fire, and mix in it one egg well beaten with the yolks of five others; strain through a fine sieve, put in cream pots or cups, place them in hot but not boiling bain-marie, take off as soon as it thickens, dust with fine white sugar, let cool, place on ice for about fifteen minutes, and use.

With coffee.—Put a quart of milk in a stewpan with six ounces of white sugar, and half a pint of very strong coffee; set on the fire, and proceed as for chocolate cream above in every other particular.

With eggs.—Beat well six eggs with a little fecula, then add a pinch of grated cinnamon, and two or three tablespoonfuls of fine white sugar, beat again well, pour the whole in a crockery dish, dust with sugar, set it in a quick oven, and serve when done.

With lemon or orange.—Put in a stewpan a quart of good fresh milk, with the rind of half a lemon cut in pieces and six ounces of white sugar; set on the fire, and proceed as for chocolate cream in every other particular.

With tea, vanilla, or other essences.—You proceed as for chocolate cream in every other particular, except you use instead of six ounces of chocolate, half a pint of very strong tea, or a small piece of vanilla, or a few drops of essence. Many different kinds of creams are made in this way.

DESSERT CREAMS.

How to prepare the milk.—Put in a vessel about a quart of milk with a pinch of gum arabic, which you have previously dissolved in a few drops of water; whip to a froth with a whisk (this you must do in a cool place, if in summer time), and use it at once; it cannot be kept even on ice. If you want to color the cream, do it with a trifle of carmine.

CHOCOLATE CREAM.

Pound well two ounces of chocolate with three ounces of white sugar; melt the whole in two tablespoonfuls of warm water; let cool, put on ice till nearly frozen. During this process, prepare a quart of milk as directed above; whisk the whole well together, and serve.

COFFEE CREAM.

Melt four ounces of white sugar in two tablespoonfuls of strong warm coffee, let it cool, place on ice, and finish it with chocolate cream.

LEMON AND ORANGE CREAM.

Take a piece of loaf sugar weighing about four ounces, grate fine on it one third of the rind of a lemon or orange; pound the piece of sugar well, melt it then in two tablespoonfuls of warm water; let cool, put on ice, and finish it as chocolate cream.

CREAM WITH ORANGE FLOWER WATER, ESSENCE OF ROSE, OR ANY OTHER ESSENCE.

Melt four ounces of sugar in two tablespoonfuls of warm water, let cool, place on ice till nearly frozen; then add to it a few drops of essence, whisk it well with a quart of prepared milk, and serve.

RASPBERRY AND STRAWBERRY CREAM.

Melt four ounces of white sugar in two tablespoonfuls of juice of raspberries or strawberries, place on ice, and finish it as chocolate cream.

VANILLA CREAM.

Pound well a little piece of vanilla, with four ounces of white sugar, and melt in two tablespoonfuls of warm water, and then finish it as chocolate cream.

ICE CREAM.

How to make the syrup.—Clean well some currants about half ripe, and about one fourth of raspberries; mash them well in a vessel, leave them thus twenty-four hours, and then strain through a sieve or a towel, into a vessel. Weigh the juice, add to it a pound of loaf sugar to every half pound of juice, put the whole in a kettle, set it on a good fire, and when boiling, skim it carefully; one minute's boiling is enough; pour it in an earthen vessel, let cool, and bottle it: it is then ready for use.

Do the same with blackberries, cherries, raspberries, strawberries, etc.

How to make the ice cream.—Have in a pail or bucket some ice broken in small pieces; mix well in a vessel some of the above syrup with clear water, about half of each; fill your moulds or other vessels with it, put them in the pail of broken ice, move them to accelerate the freezing, and serve when well frozen.

COMPOTES FOR DESSERT.

How to make syrup for compotes.—*Common syrup.*—Put a pound of loaf sugar in a crockery stewpan, with a pint of water, a wine glass of brandy, and a pinch of well grated cinnamon; set it on a slow fire, boil gently for ten minutes, skimming off the foam; then take from the fire and let cool; bottle it; cork it well and keep to use it when wanted. It may be kept for months in a cool and dry place.

Apple syrup.—Peel quarter, and core four or six apples, of the pippin variety; cook them well in about a pint of water, a wine glass of brandy, and a pinch of grated cinnamon; when well cooked, put them in a coarse towel, and press the juice out; put it in a stewpan and set it on a good fire; add a pound of loaf sugar, take the foam off with a skimmer a little before it boils, and boil about five minutes; take from the fire, let cool, bottle it, corking well. It may be kept for months.

Pear syrup is made in the same way.

COMPOTES OF APPLES.

Quarter, peel, core, and cook apples in a stewpan, with a little water and sugar; when done, put them on a plate, pour some apple syrup on them, and serve.

OF APRICOTS AND PEACHES.

Cut the apricots or peaches in two, and take the stone out. Throw them in boiling water for two minutes; take them out; throw them in cold or ice water, and take them out immediately; then peel them. Put a pint of water in a crockery pan and set it on a good fire; when boiling, put the apricots or peaches in, with some sugar; boil a little, and skim off the foam; take out, place them on a dish, dust with sugar, pour some common syrup on them, let cool, and serve.

OF BLACKBERRIES, CURRANTS, RASPBERRIES, STRAWBERRIES, ETC.

Make common syrup as above directed, and when ready to be taken from the fire, throw the blackberries, etc., in it; boil one minute, and serve.

OF CHERRIES.

Cut off the stalks of the cherries about half their length, wash well, and drain them; put them in a crockery stewpan with just enough water to wet them, and also a little sugar—about three ounces to every pound of cherries; place them on a dish when cooked, pour on them some common syrup, and serve warm or cold, according to taste.

OF ORANGES.

Peel four oranges; the under skin or pith must also be carefully taken off with a sharp knife; divide each orange as divided by nature (that is, open it in two, first, then detach each piece one after another, and without breaking them). Put a pint of common syrup in a crockery stewpan and set it on a brisk fire; at the first boiling, subdue the fire; put the oranges in and simmer about three or four minutes; take from the fire, let cool, turn on a plate, and serve.

OF PEARS.

Peel the pears, cut the stalk half its length, put them

in a crockery stewpan, with a little sugar, a few drops of lemon juice, a pinch of grated cinnamon, and a little water; set on a moderate fire, and at the first boiling add two gills of claret wine. Simmer till cooked, then put the pears only on a dish; put the stewpan back on the fire, add the juice and water in it about the same quantity of pear syrup; boil about fifteen minutes, pour the whole on the pears, and serve warm or cold.

OF PINEAPPLES.

Peel and cut in slices, put them in a crockery pan, with a little water and sugar, set on a good fire, and finish and serve like apricots.

OF PLUMS.

Throw the plums in boiling water and take them out when half cooked; put them in a crockery stewpan, with a little water and a little sugar; simmer till cooked, place them on a dish, pour some common syrup on, and serve when cold.

OF QUINCES.

Quarter, peel, and core the quinces; throw them in boiling water for five minutes; take out and drain them; put them in a crockery stewpan, with four ounces of sugar for every pound of quinces, a few drops of lemon juice, a little water, and a pinch of grated cinnamon; set it on the fire, simmer till cooked, place them on a dish, pour some common syrup on them, and serve cold.

JELLIES FOR DESSERT.

With apples or quinces.—Peel, core, and cut in small pieces, two quarts of good apples or quinces; put them in a stewpan, with a clove well pounded, and the juice of half a lemon; cover with water, set it on a moderate fire, and boil gently till well cooked. Put them in a jelly bag, under which you place a vessel to receive the juice; when the juice is all out, put it in a pan for that purpose, with half a pound of loaf sugar to every pound of juice, and boil to a jelly. Put the jelly in pots, let cool; cut a piece of white paper the size of the inside of the pot, dip it in brandy, put it over the jelly, cover the pot well, and place in a dry and cool closet.

What remains in the bag may be used to make a compote.

Watch the process carefully, skimmer in hand, to skim and stir now and then, lest it should burn.

With apricots, peaches, plums, etc.—After having taken the stone out, and cut them in four pieces, you proceed as for apples in every other particular.

With blackberries, currants, grapes, raspberries, or other berries.—Press the blackberries well in a coarse towel, to have all the juice, which you put in a stewpan, with as many pounds of loaf sugar as of juice, and finish as directed for apple or quince jelly.

MARMALADES OF APRICOTS, PLUMS, QUINCES, ETC.

Peel and stone two pounds of apricots; crack the stones, throw about two thirds of the kernels in boiling water, and leave them in till the skin comes off easily; skin them well, and cut them in small pieces lengthwise. Place the apricots in a pan, with about a pound and a half of sugar; set on the fire and boil twenty minutes, stirring the while with a wooden spoon; five minutes before taking from the fire, put also the kernels in the pan; then put in pots or bowls as soon as out of the fire.

With marmalade of quinces, sweet almonds may be used.

SWEETMEATS.

With blackberries, cherries, currants, raspberries, **etc.**—

Mash the blackberries, etc., well; put a fine sieve over a vessel and strain them through it; place what is in the vessel in a stewpan for that purpose, with the same weight of loaf sugar; set it on the fire, skim it carefully; it takes about half an hour to cook; then put in pots and let cool; cut a piece of white paper the size of the inside of the pot, dip it in brandy, put it over the fruit, cover the pots, and place them in a dry and cool closet.

With grapes.—Proceed as for blackberries in every particular, except that you put half a pound of loaf sugar to every pound of juice.

With peaches, or plums.—Throw peaches or plums in boiling water for one minute; take off, and at the same time throw them in cold water to cool quickly; then skin them immediately, cut in two pieces and take the stone out, put them in a stewpan, and finish like blackberries above.

With pears.—Quarter, peel, and core the pears; put them in a stewpan with half a pound of loaf sugar to every pound of fruit, and the rind of a lemon well grated; set on the fire, and finish like blackberries.

CURRANTS, BLACKBERRIES, OR OTHER FRUIT FOR DESSERT.

Beat well the white of an egg with a little water; dip the fruit in, and roll it immediately in some fine crushed sugar; place it on a dish, and leave it thus five or six hours, and serve.

A more sightly and exquisite plate of dessert than a plate of currants dressed thus, cannot be had.

Besides all our receipts, any kind of fruit may be served for dessert, according to the season; also, any kind of cheese; also, fruits preserved in liquor.

BILLS OF FARE.

To make models of bills of fare is not difficult, but to follow them is nearly impossible; hardly one in a hundred would suit any one.

Bills of fare vary according to the season of the year, and therefore to the produce in the market.

We will try to give another, and we think a better, way of making them to suit everybody, every purse, and at any time.

A dinner, no matter how grand, is composed of three courses, and seven kinds of dishes.

The first course comprises dishes of four kinds, viz.; soups, relevés, hors-d'œuvre, and entrées.

The second course comprises dishes of two kinds, viz.: rots and entremets.

The third course comprises dishes of one kind, the dessert.

The number of dishes of each kind is generally according to the number of guests.

It may also be according to the importance of the occasion for which the dinner is given; to the honor the giver or givers wish to show the personage or personages invited; to the amount of money they are willing to spend, &c.

A dinner may be composed of:

FIRST COURSE.

1 or 2 Soups. 1 or 2 Relevés of Meat.
1 or 2 Relevés of Fish. 1 to 4 Hors-d'œuvre.
1 to 8 Entrées.

SECOND COURSE.

1 or 2 Rots. 1 to 10 Entremets.

THIRD COURSE.

1 to 30 plates of Dessert.

The size of the relevés and rots should be according to the number of guests.

By the above **everybody** can see that for a dinner **they want** one or two soups; one to four entrées; one **to thirty,** or even more plates of dessert, &c.; therefore select as many **or as** few dishes of each or of any kind as you please for your dinner.

It will be just as easy to select dishes for a small dinner **as for a grand one;** for instance, you select a soup, an entrée or rot, **or both;** of fish or of meat, or of both; one or more entremets, and one or more plates of dessert.

We have divided the following table in seven parts, each part being **in the order the** dishes of which must be served, and representing **the seven** kinds of dishes composing a dinner.

By this means you select the dish or dishes which suit **you, and which** you can procure in **any or** all of the seven parts, and your bill of fare is made, and more to your liking than any steward on earth can do.

THE FIRST PART, OR SOUPS, IS COMPOSED OF:

Broth,
Consommé,
Juliennes,
Potages,
Potages purées,
Soups.

THE SECOND PART, OR RELEVES.

Beef:
  à la mode,
  boiled, served warm,
  fillet, broiled or roasted,
  corned, a large piece.
Capon, boiled,
Chicken, "
Ham, "
Lamb:
  fore quarter,
  hind quarter,
  in galantine,
Matelote,
Mutton, a leg boiled or stewed,
Perch, boiled,
Pies, Meat,
Pike, boiled,

Pork (fresh):
  a leg roasted,
  any large piece roasted,
  (salted), any large piece boiled or stewed,
Salmon, stewed or roasted,
Shad, broiled or stewed,
Sturgeon, " "
Trout, " or roasted,
Tunny, broiled,
Turbot, boiled or broiled,
Turkey, boiled, roasted, or stewed,
Veal:
  breast, with green peas, or with onions,
  in galantine,
Venison, haunch of,
Wild Boar, stewed.

THE THIRD PART, OR HORS-D'ŒUVRE.

Anchovy,
  Cake,
Artichokes, raw,
Cervelas of all sorts, found at pork butchers,
Cucumbers (fresh), with vinegar and salt,
  (pickled), cut in slices,
Eggs in the shell,
Escalops of Salmon or Veal,
Herrings, salted or red,
Melons,
Mushrooms, broiled or in boxes,
Olives, preserved,
Ox tongue, smoked,

Oysters, raw,
Potatoes, à la Franklin,
Radishes (black):
  black, served in slices with salt and vinegar,
  spring, served with butter,
Sardines,
Sausages of any kind:
  fresh, fried,
  smoked,
Tunny, salted, smoked, or pickled,
Walnuts, in salad; the European nut only can be served in this way.

THE FOURTH PART, OR ENTREES.

Angel Fish, with brown butter or white sauce,
Aspic of Meat,
Barbel, boiled, broiled, or in matelote,
Bass, boiled, stewed, or in matelote,
Bear meat, stewed,
Beef:
    à la mode,
    braised,
    fillet, with cucumbers, or mushrooms, sauté, or a piece left from the day before,
    loin,
    ribs, braised, stewed, with cucumbers or mushrooms,
    steaks, broiled, fried, or fancy,
    boiled, broiled, fried, in gratin, in miroton, or maitre-d'hôtel, with piquante, Robert, or tomato sauce, and in salad,
Black Fish, boiled, fried, stewed, or in matelote,
Blue Fish, boiled, fried, stewed, or in matelote,
Bream, boiled, fried, or stewed,
Buffalo meat, stewed,
Cabbages, with bacon,
Calf:
    brain, boiled, or with mushrooms,
    ears,
    feet,
    head, in poulette, stewed, or with oil,
    heart,
    kidneys,
    liver, sauté, or stewed,
    lights,
Calf—pluck,
    sweetbreads,
    tail,
    tongue,
Capon, boiled, or with rice,
Carp, boiled, broiled, stewed, or in matelote,
Chicken, broiled, in blanquette, or fricassee, Marengo, with onions, or peas, sauté, or in tartar,
    broiled, in fricassee, or salad, with oil, piquante or poivrade sauce.
Clams,
Codfish (fresh), boiled, broiled, or fried,
    (salted), boiled, in bechamel, or brown butter, with caper sauce, or croutons, in maitre-d'hôtel, with milk, oil, or potatoes, and cold,
Conger, boiled, or in poulette,
Crabs,
Croquettes of fowl,
Dab fish, boiled, or broiled,
Duck, in salmis, with turnips, or cold,
Eels, or eel pout, broiled, or in poulette,
Eggs, boiled, or poached,
Fish, boiled, broiled, or stewed,
Flounders, fried, or stewed,
Frogs,   "   "
• Giblets, in fricassee, or stewed,
Goose or Gosling, in salmis, with turnips, or cold,
Haddock, boiled, or broiled,
Halibut, boiled, stewed, or with cream,
Hare, in civet, or cold,
Herring (fresh), boiled, or fried,

BILLS OF FARE.

Lamb:
    chops, broiled, sautées, in papillotes, with vegetables, or in the oven,
    feet,
    head,
    heart,
Lamprey, boiled, or in poulette,
Leveret, sauté,
Lobster, in salad, or omelet,
Mackerel (fresh), broiled, with butter, in maitre-d'hôtel, or stewed,
    (salted),
Muscles,
Mutton,
    breast, broiled, or in the oven,
Mutton Chops, broiled, with crumbs, sautées, in papillotes, with vegetables, or in the oven,
    leg, with beans, or eggs, and piece left,
    saddle,
    shoulder, boiled, stewed, with beans, or pieces left from the day before,
Ox:
    brain,
    heart,
    kidneys,
    liver,
    tail,
    tongue,
Oysters, **broiled, fried**, or stewed,
Partridge, **broiled**, with cabbage, in **salmis**, fricassee, or salad,
Peas, with bacon,
Perch, **stewed, or** in matelote,
Pheasants, broiled, with cabbage, in salmis, fricassee, or salad,

Pigeon, broiled, fried, with green peas, or stewed,
Pig:
    brain,
    ears,
    feet,
    head,
    kidneys,
    liver,
    tail, boiled, or broiled,
    tongue,
Pickerel, **boiled, or** in matelote,
Pike, in matelote,
Porgy, boiled, stewed, or in matelote,
Pork cutlets,
Potatoes, with bacon, or in balls,
Prairie Hen, broiled, with cabbage, in salmis, fricassee, or salad,
Rabbit, fricandeau, in gibelotte, with green peas, or in civet,
Salad of Fowl, Game, Salmon, or Turbot,
Salmon (fresh), broiled, or piece left,
    (salted),
    (smoked),
Salted pork, **boiled**,
Sheep:
    brain,
    feet, broiled, or in poulette,
    heart,
    kidneys, broiled, or with champagne,
    liver,
    tail,
    tongue,
Sheepshead, boiled, broiled, **or** with cream,
Smelts, fried, or stewed,
Snails, broiled, or stewed,

Sole, in Normande, or in maitre-d'hôtel,
Sourkrout,
Sturgeon, broiled,
Sweetbreads,
Tench, boiled, broiled, stewed, or in matelote,
Tripe (double), broiled, or stewed,
Trout, stewed,
Troutlet, in matelote,
Tunny, stewed,
Turkey, in salad, or pie, or cold,
Turtle Steaks,
Veal:
    blanquette,
    breast, in matelote, or stewed,
    cutlets, broiled, with crumbs, in fines herbes, or in papillotes,
    fricandeau,
    loin, with a garniture, or stewed,
    shoulder, stewed, or a piece left,
Venison:
    cutlets,
    shoulder, stewed, or cold,
Vol-au-vent, with meat,
Weak Fish, boiled, stewed, or in matelote,
White Fish of the lakes, stewed, or in matelote,
Whitings, boiled, broiled, or stewed,
Wild Boar, stewed.

THE FIFTH PART, OR ROTS.

Barbel, fried,
Bass, "
Bear Meat, roasted,
Beef:
    fillet, broiled, or roasted,
    ribs, roasted,
Birds (small), roasted,
Black Birds, "
Buffalo Meat, "
Calf's Liver, roasted, or in the oven,
Capon, roasted,
Carp, fried,
Chicken, roasted, or stuffed,
Crape, roasted,
Duck, "
Eel, fried, or roasted,
Fig-peckers, roasted,
Fish, fried, or roasted,
Fox, roasted,
Goose or Gosling, roasted,
Guinea Fowl, "
Haddock, fried,
Halibut, fried,
Ham, roasted,
Hare, "
High-holders, roasted,
Kid, roasted,
Lamb, hind quarter, roasted,
Lapwings, "
Meadow Larks, "
Mutton:
    breast, roasted,
    fillet, "
    leg, "
    shoulder, "
Opossum, "
Ostrich, "
Otter, "
Partridge, "
Peacock or Hen, roasted,
Pelican, "
Perch, fried,
Pheasant, roasted,
Pickerel, fried,
Pigeons, roasted,

Pig's Kidneys, in brochette,
Pike, fried, or roasted,
Plover, **roasted,**
Pork:
    chime, roasted,
    shoulder, "
Prairie Hen, "
Quails, "
Rabbit, "
Raccoon, "
Reed Birds, "
Salmon, "
Shad, "
Sheep Kidneys, **in brochette,**
Sheepshead, **fried,**
Skunk, roasted,
Snipe, "
Sole, fried,
Squirrel, roasted,

Sturgeon, roasted,
Sucking Pig, roasted,
Tench, "
Thrush, "
Trout, "
Turkey, roasted, **or stuffed,**
Tunny, roasted,
Veal:
    breast, roasted,
    loin, "
    rump, "
    shoulder, "
Venison, haunch, **roasted,**
Weak Fish, fried,
White Fish of the lakes, fried,
Wild Boar, roasted,
Woodchuck, "
Woodcock, "
Yellow Birds, "

THE SIXTH PART, OR ENTREMETS.

Artichokes, fried, stewed, or with oil, or white sauce,
Asparagus, **fried,** with milk, with oil, or white sauce,
Beans, with bacon, broth, onions, in salad, green, dry beans, with butter, stewed, lima beans, or colored,
Beets, stewed, or in salad,
Cabbages, with milk, in salad, stewed, and red in salad,
Cardoon,
Carrots, with fines herbes, fried, or stewed,
Cauliflowers, with cheese, fried, stewed, in tomato or white sauce, or in salad,
Celery, fried, stewed, or in salad; soup celery in salad,
Cucumbers, fried, or stewed,
Dandelion, stewed, or in salad,

Eggs, with asparagus, in **brown** butter, fried, mashed, in matelote, with onions, green peas, or sur-le-plat,
Egg Plant, broiled, fried, stewed, or stuffed,
Endive, Chiccory, or Succory, with milk, or broth, or in salad,
Fetticus, in salad,
Leeks,
Lentils, with butter, stewed, or in salad,
Lettuce, Cos-lettuce, &c., stewed, or in salad,
Mushrooms, stewed,
Omelets, with asparagus, bacon, fines herbes, ham, kidney, mushrooms, au naturel, with sorrel, truffles, or à la Washington,
Onions, stewed, or in salad,

Parsnips, fried, or stewed,
Peas, preserved and cracked, boiled,
Potatoes, boiled, broiled, with butter, cake, fried, à la Franklin, in maitre-d'hôtel, matelote, with milk, in proven ale, sautées, with white sauce, or in salad,
Potatoes (sweet), dressed in every way like other potatoes,
Purslain, stewed, or in salad,
Salads of any greens,
Salsify, with butter, or in salad,
Skirret,
Sorrel, stewed,
Spinage,
Sprouts,
Sweet Corn,
Tomatoes, boiled, or in salad,
Turnips, stewed, or in béchamel,
Watercress, stewed, or in salad,
Whitings, fried,
Pastry—Baba,
    biscuits, with chocolate, cinnamon, filbert, lemon, orange, savoy, or vanilla,
    cakes, lemon, light, or plum,

Pastry:
    pies, any kind of fruit pies, tarts, or tartlets,
Sweet Dishes:
    asparagus, with sugar,
    blanc-mange,
    cake of rice,
    carrots, with sugar,
    Charlotte, apples in, Russe,
    croquettes of rice,
    creams, burnt sugar, chocolate, coffee, eggs, essences, lemon, orange, tea, or vanilla,
    custard,
    eggs, snow-like, called also œufs à la niege,
    fondue,
    fritters, with apples, peaches, pineapples, raspberries, strawberries, &c.,
    meringue,
    omelets, soufflé, with sugar, rum, or apples,
    pancakes,
    peas, with sugar,
    rissolés,
    turnips, with sugar,
    vol-au-vent of fruits,
    Waffles.

THE SEVENTH PART, OR DESSERT.

Baba,
Biscuits,
Charlotte Russe,
Cheese of every kind,
Compotes of
    apples,
    apricots,
    blackberries,
    cherries,
    currants,
    oranges,

Compotes of
    peaches,
    pears,
    pineapples,
    plums,
    quinces,
    raspberries,
    strawberries,
Creams:
    chocolate,
    coffee,

Creams.
    essence,
    ice,
    lemon,
    orange,
    raspberry,
    strawberry,
    vanilla,
Fritters of
    apples,
    peaches,
    pineapples,
    raspberries,
    strawberries, &c.
Fruit:
    of any kind, according to the season,
    preserved in liquor,
    prepared with eggs and sugar,
Jellies of
    apples,
    apricots,
    blackberries,
Jellies of
    currants,
    grapes,
    peaches,
    plums,
    quinces,
    raspberries,
    strawberries,
Macaroons,
Marmalades of
    apricots,
    plums,
    quinces, &c.,
Oranges, in salad,
Sweetmeats of
    blackberries,
    cherries,
    currants,
    grapes,
    peaches,
    pears,
    plums,
    raspberries, &c.
Waffles.

Some dishes are served either as relevés or as entrées, others as entremets, or as dessert, according to taste.

There are so many kinds of fruit at nearly every season of the year, that it is very easy to have as many plates of them as are wanted for dessert.

BREAKFAST.

We are of opinion that everybody ought to eat as little meat as possible, and drink no wine, beer, or any other liquor at breakfast, no matter what the sex or age, except when prescribed by the physician in case of sickness, debility, etc.

The food may be selected from the following:

Bread and Butter,
Eggs,
Omelets,
Fried Fish,
Fried Potatoes, or other vegetables,
Sardines,
Fruit, according to the season.

As for meat, in case some should be eaten, it ought to be cold, such as fowl or veal, cooked the day before.

Muffins, and other cakes or pastes, served warm, are very bad for the stomach and teeth.

The beverage ought to be either coffee, with milk, chocolate, cocoa, choca, or cold water, but do not by any means drink tea at breakfast.

Although cold meat is not by far so injurious as warm meat for breakfast, it ought, nevertheless, to be as little partaken of as possible, and especially by the young.

We do not understand by breakfast a meal taken under that name in the afternoon; then it should be called *dinner*, or at least *lunch;* at such a meal, the following dishes may be served:

Calf's head, served cold,
Cervelas of any kind, found at pork butchers,
Headcheese,
Mutton Chops,
Veal Cutlets,
Eggs, cooked in any way,
Fried Fish,
Fruit, according to the season,
Galantine of Birds,
    " Veal,
Ham,
Cold Meat, of any kind,
Oysters,
Omelets,
Paté de foie gras,
Meat and Fruit Pies, served cold,
Salad of Chicken,
    " Partridge, and other birds,
    " Lobster,
Sandwiches,
Sardines,
Sausages, of any kind, fresh or smoked,
Smoked Tongue,
Smoked Fish or Meat,
Fried Vegetables,
Drinks according to taste.

LUNCH.

What we have described above for breakfasts taken in the afternoon, may be served for lunch, no matter at what hour it is taken.

SUPPER.

This being the last meal taken before going to bed, all persons should be careful about what they eat then, especially if they take no bodily exercise, or retire soon after it.

Some persons are not aware that their rest depends nearly, if not entirely, on what they have eaten at supper.

What is served for a lunch, or for a dessert, may be served for a supper.

EVENING PARTIES.

Lemonade is a good drink in the evening.

Bavaroises, bichofs, creams, punch, wines, and fruit, are served at evening parties, besides the supper.

INDEX.

A la crême fish, 81.
A la mode beef, 66.
Allemande sauce, 45.
Anchovy, 90.
    butter, 46.
    cake, 215.
    sauce, 45.
Angel fish, ray, and skate, 80, 81, 90.
Apples, 213.
Apricots, 202.
Artichokes, 169.
    Jerusalem, 170.
Asparagus, 170.
    fried, 171.
    with milk, 171.
    " oil, 170.
    " sugar, 171.
Aspic, 167.
Baba, 222.
Bacon, 25.
Bain-marie, 11.
Baking, 7.
Barbel, 82.
Barley, lemonade, 18.
    sugar, 18.
Bass, 82.
Batter, for frying, 20.
Bavaroise, with chocolate, 22.
    " coffee or tea, 23.
Bay leaf, 23.
Beans, 171.
    green, 173.
    in salad, 172, 174.
    Lima, 171.
    colored, 173.
    purée, 62.
Bear meat, 164.
Béchamel sauce, No. 1, 46.
                  No. 2, 47.
Beef, to select, 66.
    to make tender, 66.
    to broil or roast, 66.
    cow beef, 66.
    bull beef, 66.

Beef, à la mode, 66.
    braised, 67.
    fillet, 67.
        broiled, 68.
        roasted, 68.
        with cucumbers, 68.
        " mushrooms, 69.
        sauté, 69.
        left for the next day, 69.
    loin, 70.
    ribs, broiled, 70.
        roasted, 70.
        stewed, 71.
        braised, 71.
        with cucumbers, 71.
        " mushrooms, 71.
    steaks, broiled, 71.
        fried, 72.
        fancy, 72.
    boiled, 73.
        served warm, 73.
        broiled, 73.
        fried, 73.
        in gratin, 73.
        " miroton, 74.
        " maitre-d'hôtel, 74.
        with piquante, Robert, or tomato sauce, 74.
        in salad, 74.
    soup, 31.
Beets, 174.
Bichof, warm, 23.
    cold, 23.
Bills of fare, 239.
Beignet, 223.
Birds, preserved, 23.
Biscuits, with chocolate, 214.
        " cinnamon, 214.
        " filbert, 214.
        " lemon, 214.
        " orange, 214.
        " Savoy, 216.
        " vanilla, 214.
Blackberries, 202.

INDEX.

Blackbirds, 153.
Black fish, 82.
Blanc mange, 228.
Blanquette, 102, 140.
Blue fish, 82.
Boiling, 7.
Brain, 74, 109, 122.
Braised beef, 67.
Braising, 11.
Bread, 25.
    farce, 58.
    sauce, 46.
Breakfast, 247.
Bream, 82.
Breast, 103, 117.
Broccoli, 178.
Broiling, 7.
Broth, 25.
    chicken, **42.**
    herb, 42.
    made quickly, 31.
    for sauces, 30.
    " soup, potage, or purée, 30.
    another, 31.
    turtle, 43.
    veal, 42.
Brown butter, 47.
Buffalo meat, 164.
Butter maitre-d'hôtel, 47.
Buttered paper, 21.
Cabbages, 175.
    garniture, 58.
    soup, 39.
    in salad, 175.
    sourkrout, 176.
Cakes, anchovy, 215.
    lemon, 215.
    light, 215.
    plum, 216.
    rice, 216.
    sponge, 216.
    tea, 217.
Calf's brain, 109, 110.
    ears, 110.
    feet, 110, 111.
    head, to prepare, 111.
    to cook, 111.
    in poulette, 112.
    with oil, 112.
    kidneys, 112.
    lights, 112.
    liver, 113, **114.**
    pluck, 115.
    sweetbreads, **115.**
    tail, 115.
    tongue, 116.
Caper sauce, 48.
Capon, to select and clean, 134.
    boiled, 135.
    with rice, 135.
    roasted, 135.
    in galantine, 148.
Caramel, 19.
Cardoon, 176.
Carp, 82.

Carrots, to clean, 177.
    with fines herbes, 177.
    fried, 177.
    stewed, 178.
    with sugar, 178.
    purée of, 63.
Cat fish, 88.
Catsup, 25.
Cauliflowers, to clean, **178.**
    with cheese, 178.
    fried, 179.
    stewed, 179.
    in salad, 179.
    with sauce, 179.
Celery, 179.
    soup, in salad, 201.
    dried, 21.
    purée of, 63.
Charlotte russe, **229.**
    apple, 229.
Cheese, 39.
Chelmon, 88.
Chestnuts, 197.
    purée of, 63.
Chiccory, 200.
Chicken, to clean, **134.**
    to select, 136.
    broth, 42.
    broiled, 136.
    in fricassee, 136.
    Marengo, 138.
    with **onions,** 139.
    with peas, **139.**
    roasted, 138.
    sauté, 138.
    stuffed, 138.
    in tartar, 139.
    with oil, piquante, or poivrade sauce, 140.
    boiled in fricassee, 140.
    " in salad, 202.
    " blanquette, 140.
    " galantine, 148.
    preserved, 23.
Choca, 17.
Chocolate, 17.
Chops, 118, 126.
Clams, 97.
Coal fish, 88.
Cocoa, 17.
Cocoanut, in salad, **202.**
Cod fish, 91, 92, 93.
Coffee, 15, 16.
Colored beans, 173.
Common syrup, 234.
Compotes, 234.
    apple syrup, 234.
    pear " 234.
Conger, 93.
Cooking, 7.
Corn (sweet), 180.
Corn salad, 201.
Consommé, 30.
Coulis of fish, 48.
    lobster, 49.

INDEX. 253

Coulis of veal, 48.
Courses, 240.
   first, 240.
   second, 240.
   third, 240.
Crabs, 97, 98.
Creams for entremets, 230.
   " dessert, 232.
   sauce, 49.
Croquettes of fowl, 140.
   rice,
Croutons, 20.
   garniture, 58.
Crumbs, 20.
Cucumbers, 24, 181.
   pickled, 24.
   sauce, 50.
Currant sauce, 49.
Curry, 11.
Custard, 222.
Cutlets, 105, 129.
Dab fish, 82.
Dandelion, 181, 182.
Dessert, 246.
   compotes, 334.
   creams, 230.
   fritters, 232.
   fruit with egg and sugar, 238.
   other fruit, 218.
   jellies, 236.
   marmalades, 237.
   sweetmeats, 237.
Diet, 25.
Dinner, 239.
   kinds of dishes, 239.
Doree or Dory, 88.
Draining, 12.
Ducks and Ducklings, 141
   to select, 141.
   roasted, 141.
   in salmis, 142.
   with turnips, 142.
   cold, 142.
   in galantine, 148.
   preserved, 23.
Ears, 110, 131.
Eel, 80.
Eggs, with asparagus, 204.
   boiled, 204.
   with brown butter, 204.
   fried, 205.
   mashed, 205.
   in matelote, 205.
   with onions, 205.
   " green peas, 206.
   poached, 206.
   sur le plat, 206.
   in the shell, 206.
   snow-like, 207.
Egg plant, 182.
   boiled, 182.
   fried, 182.
   stuffed, 183.
Endive, with broth, 184.
   " milk, 183.

Endive in salad, 184.
Entrées, 242.
Entremets, 245.
Escalops, 88, 108,
Espagnole sauce, 50.
Essence of spinage, 50.
Evening parties, 249.
Fancy words and expressions, 15.
Farces and garnitures, 58.
   bread, 58.
   cabbage, 58.
   croutons, 58.
   matelote, 59.
   mushrooms, 59.
   papillote, 60.
   quenelle, 60.
   salpicon, 60.
   truffle, 61.
   vegetable, 61.
Farce for fish pies, 218.
   " meat pies, 217.
Fecula, 36.
Feet, 110, 122, 131.
Feticus, 201.
Figpeckers, 158.
Fillet, 67, 119.
Fines herbes, 26.
Fish, 26, 80.
   sauce, 51.
   to keep, 15.
   quality, 27.
   to select, 80.
   to clean and prepare, 80.
   same family or kind, 81.
   how it can be cooked, 81.
   to know when cooked enough, 81.
   stuffed, 81.
   à la creme, 81.
   in matelote, 88.
   " escalops, 88.
   " Normande, 96.
   " poulette, 93.
   " maitre d'hôtel, 92, 95, 96.
   " salad, 203.
   salted, 92, 94, 96.
   smoked, 96.
   to improve, 82.
   boiled, 82.
   broiled, 82.
   fried, 84.
   roasted, 85.
   stewed, 86.
   that may be boiled, broiled or stewed, 88.
   anchovy, 90.
   angel 90.
   barbel, 82, 83, 84, 88.
   bass, 82, 84, 87, 88.
   black, 82, 84, 87, 88.
   blue, 82, 84, 87, 88.
   bream, 82, 84, 87.
   carp, 82, 83, 84, 87, 88.
   cat, 88.
   chelmon, 88.
   coal, 88.

Fish: cod, 91, 92, 93.
    conger, 83.
    crocodile, 88.
    dab, 82.
    doree, 88.
    eel, 83, 85, 88, 93.
    flat 87.
    flounder, 84, 87.
    flying, 88.
    frog, 93.
    gar, 88.
    gold, 88.
    growler, 88.
    gurnard, 88.
    haddock, 82, 83, 91.
    hake, 88.
    halibut, 81, 83, 84, 87.
    head, 88.
    herring, 84, 94.
    king, 88.
    lamprey, 83.
    loach, 88.
    mackerel, 95, 96
    mullet, 88.
    perch, 82, 84, 87, 88.
    pickerel, 82, 84, 88.
    pike, 81, 82, 84, 85, 88.
    pilchard, 88.
    pilot, 88.
    porgy, 82, 84, 87, 88.
    ray, 90.
    roach, 88.
    salmon, 81, 83, 85, 87, 88.
    shad, 81, 83, 85, 87.
    sheep's head, 81, 91.
    skate, 90.
    smelts, 84, 88.
    sole, 84, 96, 97.
    sprats, 84.
    sturgeon, 81, 84, 86, 87.
    sucker, 88.
    sun, 88.
    tench, 82, 83, 84, 87, 88.
    trout, 83, 85, 87.
    troutlet, 88.
    tunny, 81, 83, 85, 87.
    turbot, 81, 82, 83.
    weak, 82, 84, 87, 88.
    whiting, 82, 84, 87.
    white fish of the lakes, 84, 87, 88.
    small, 84.
    clams, 97.
    crabs, 97.
    lobster, 98.
    muscles, 99.
    oysters, 100, **101.**
    shrimps, 101.
Flan, 222.
Flounder, **84.**
Fondue, **228.**
Fowl, 202.
Fox, 159, **101.**
French kisses or meringues, 224.
Fricandeau, 106.
Fricassee, 136, 156.

Fritters, 223.
Frogs, 93.
    fried, 93.
    stewed, 94.
Fruit, 27, 218.
    with eggs and sugar for dessert, 238.
Frying, 8.
    directions for, 8.
    grease,   " 20.
    batter,   " 20.
Galantines, 147, 148.
Game, 151.
    to **preserve, 151.**
    to clean, 151
    bear, 164.
    blackbird, 158.
    buffalo, 164.
    ducks, 141.
    figpecker, 158.
    fox, 159.
    goose, 143.
    grouse, 152.
    hare, 152.
    hedgehog, 133.
    high-holders, 158.
    lapwings, 158.
    leveret, 153.
    meadow lark, 158.
    opossum, 159.
    ostrich, 153.
    otter, 159.
    partridge, 154.
    peacock, 156.
    pelican, 156.
    pheasant, 146.
    pigeon, 143.
    plover, 158.
    prairie hen, 154.
    quail, 156.
    rabbit, 157.
    raccoon, 159.
    reed bird, 158.
    robin, 158.
    skunk, 160.
    snipe, 159.
    squirrel, 160.
    thrush, 158.
    turkey, 144.
    wild boar, 133.
    woodcock, 159.
    woodchuck, **159.**
    yellow birds, **159.**
Gar-fish, 88.
Garlick, 26.
Garnitures, 58.
Gibelotte, 157.
Giblets, 149.
    in fricassee, **149.**
    stewed, **150.**
Glazing, 12.
Gold fish, 88.
Goose and gosling, 143.
Grape, 238.
Grease for frying, 20.

INDEX.

Grouse, 152.
Growler, 88.
Guinea fowl, **143**.
Gurnard fish, **88**.
Haddock, 82.
Hake, 88.
Halibut, **83**.
Ham, **to prepare, 130**.
    boiled, **130**.
    roasted, **130**.
Hare, to select, **152**.
    in civet, **152**.
    roasted, **153**.
    left for the **next day, 153**.
    pie, **220**.
Hazelnut butter, **51**.
Head, **111, 132**.
Head fish, **88**.
Heart, **75**.
Herb broth, **42**.
Herring, **94**.
High-holders, **158**.
Hominy, **184**.
Hors-d'œuvre, **241**.
Ice cream, **233**.
Indian sauce, **51**.
Indigestion, **24**.
Italian sauce, **51**.
Isinglass jelly, **48**.
Jellies, **236**.
Julienne, **33**.
Juice, **52**.
Kale, **175**.
Kid, **127**.
Kidney, 75, 112, **123, 132**.
King fish, 88.
Kitchen utensils, **13**.
Lait de poule, **43**.
Lamb : chops, **126**.
    fore quarter, **126**.
    hind quarter, **126**.
    roasted, **127**.
    left for the **next day, 127**.
    in galantine, **148**.
    feet, **127**.
    head, **127**.
Lamprey, **83**.
Lapwings, **158**.
Lard, **21**.
Larding, **12**.
Leeks, **184**.
Leg, **120**.
Lemon, 214, **215**.
Lemonade, **18**.
    barley, **18**.
Lentils, in salad, **184**.
    purée of, **63**.
Lettuce, **184**.
    stewed, **184**.
    in salad, **200**.
Leveret, **153**.
    sauté, **153**.
Light cake, **215**.
Lights, **112**.
Lima beans, **171**.

Liver, **76, 113**.
Loach, **88**.
Lobster, in salad, **98**.
    " omelet, **99**.
    sauce, **49**.
Loin, **70**.
Lunch, **248**.
Macaroni, **34**.
Macaroons, **224**.
Macédoine, **202**.
Mackerel, **95**.
Maître-d'hôtel sauce, **52**.
Marengo chicken, **138**.
Marinade sauce, **52**.
Marmalades, **237**.
Matelote, **88, 89**.
    garniture, **59**.
Mayonnaise sauce, **53**.
Meadow lark, **158**.
Meats, 26, 27.
    to keep, **14**.
    to cook, **13**.
    quality, **27**.
Melons, **241**.
Meringue, or **French kisses, 224**.
    apple, **225**.
Mince pie, **220**.
Minced beef, **73**.
Mint, **19**.
Miroton, **74**.
Mixing, **8**.
Mock turtle soup, **40**.
Monaco potage, **34**.
Muffins, **248**.
Mullet, **88**.
Muscles, **99**.
Mushrooms, **185**.
    purée of, **64**.
    catsup, **198**.
    farce, **59**.
Mutton, to select, **117**.
    breast, broiled, **117**.
        in the oven, **117**.
        roasted, **118**.
    chops, broiled, **118**.
        with crumbs, **118**.
        sautées, **118**.
        in papillote, **119**.
        " the oven, **119**.
        with vegetables, **119**.
    fillet, roasted, **119**.
    leg, **120**.
        boiled, **120**.
        roasted, **120**.
        stewed, **121**.
        with beans, **121**
        left over, **121**.
    saddle, **122**.
    shoulder, **122**
Nougat, 225.
Oil sauce, **53**.
Oiled paper, **21**.
Okra, 187.
Omelets, 208.
    to whisk the eggs, **208**.

Omelets, to dish, 208.
   apple, 208.
   asparagus, 208.
   with bacon, 209.
     " ham, 209.
   fines herbes, 209.
   with kidneys, 209.
     " mushrooms, 209.
   au naturel, 209.
   with sorrel, 209.
   soufflée, 210.
   with sugar, 210.
     " rum, 210.
     " truffles, 210.
   à la Washington, 211.
Onions, 187.
Opossum, 159, 161.
Orangeade, 18.
Oranges, 202.
Osmazome, 12.
Ostrich, 153.
Otter, 159, 161.
Ox brain, 74.
   heart, 75.
   kidneys, 75.
   liver, 76.
   tail, 76.
   tongue, 77.
     smoked, 78.
   double tripe, 78.
Oysters, 100, 101.
   sauce, 53.
Oyster plant, 195.
Panado, 43.
Pancakes, 226.
Pap, 24.
Paper, buttered, 21.
   oiled, 21.
Papillote, 60, 119.
Parsley, dried, 21.
   fried, 22.
   white, 22.
Parsnips, fried, 187.
   stewed, 188.
Partridge, to select, 154.
   broiled, 154.
   with cabbage, **154**.
   roasted, 155.
   in salmis, 155.
     " fricassee, 156.
     " salad, 202.
     " galantine, 148.
   preserved, 23.
Paste A, B, C, D, **E, 212, 213**.
   for frying, 20.
Pastry, 212—228.
Peacock, 156.
Peach, 202.
Pear, 202.
Peas, green, 188.
   preserved, 188.
   dry, 189.
   purée of, 64.
   soup, 37.
Pepper, white, 22.

Perch, 80.
Pheasant, 23, 154, 202.
Pickerel, 82.
Pickled cucumbers, 24.
Pickles, 25.
Pies, 212.
   to cover, 219.
   fruit, 218.
   meat, 219—221.
   apple, 218.
   bird, 219.
   chicken, 220.
   fish, 221.
   ham, 220.
   hare, 220.
   lamb, 220.
   mince, 220.
   rabbit, 220.
   veal, 221.
Pig's ears, 131.
   feet, 131.
   head, 132.
   kidneys, 132.
   tail, 132.
   tongue, 132.
   sucking, 133.
Pigeons, to select, 143.
   boiled, 143.
   fried, 143.
   with green peas, 144.
   roasted, 144.
   stewed, 144.
Pike, 82.
Pilchard, 88.
Pilot fish, 88.
Pineapple, 189.
Piquante sauce, 53.
Plover, 158.
Pluck, 115.
Plum, 216.
Poached eggs, 206.
Poivrade sauce, 54.
Porgy, 82.
Pork, to select, 128.
   to improve, 128.
   chine, 128.
   cutlets, 129.
   leg, roasted, 129.
   salted, 131.
   other parts, 131.
Potages, 32.
Potatoes, to prepare, 189.
   to cook, 189.
   with bacon, 189.
   in balls, 189.
   boiled, 190.
   broiled, 191.
   with butter, 190.
   cake, 190.
   fried, 191.
   à la Franklin, 192.
   maître-d'hôtel, 192.
   matelote, 192.
   with milk, 192.
   in Provencale, 193.

INDEX.

Potatoes : purée, 65.
   sautées, 193.
   with white sauce, 193.
   in salad, 193.
   sweet, 194.
Pot-au feu, 29.
Poulette sauce, 54.
Poultry, 134.
   to clean, 134.
   capon, 135.
   chicken, 136.
   duck, 141.
   duckling, 141.
   goose, 143.
   gosling, 143.
   guinea fowl, 143.
   pigeon, 143.
   turkey, 144.
Prairie hen, 154.
Preface, 3.
Preserves (compotes, jellies, marmalades), 234, 236, 237.
Printanier potage, 34.
Provençale sauce, 54.
Puddings, 226.
Pumpkins, 194.
Punch, 19.
Purées, 62, 65.
Purslain, 194.
Quails, 156, 157.
Quenelles, 60.
Quinces, 236.
Rabbit, 157.
   in gibelotte, 157.
   " civet, 157.
   pie, 220.
Raccoon, 159, 161.
Radishes, 241.
Raspberries, 202.
Ravigote sauce, 55.
Ray, 90.
Red herring, 94.
Reed birds, 158.
Relevés, 241.
Rhubarb pie, 219.
Ribs, 70.
Rice, 32, 216.
Rissolés, 227.
Roach, 88.
Roasting, 8.
Robert sauce, 55.
Robins, 158.
Rots, 244.
Roux sauce, 55.
Sago potage, 36.
Salads, 200.
   to prepare, 200.
   to decorate, 200.
   to make, 201.
   apricot, 202.
   bean, 172, 174.
   beef, 74.
   beets, 174.
   blackberries, 202.
   cabbages, 175.

Salads : cauliflowers, 179.
   celery, 201.
   chicken, 202.
   chiccory, 200.
   cocoanut. 202.
   cucumbers, 181.
   currants, 202.
   dandelion, 182.
   eggs, 202.
   endive, 200.
   fettieus, 201.
   lentils, 184.
   lettuce, 200.
   lobster, 98.
   Macédoine, 202.
   onions, 187.
   oranges, 202.
   partridge, 202.
   peaches, 202.
   pears, 202.
   pheasants, 202.
   prairie hens, 202.
   pineapples, 189.
   potatoes, 193.
   purslain, 184.
   raspberry, 202.
   salmon, 203.
   succory, 200.
   strawbery, 202.
   tomato, 196.
   turbot, 204.
   walnuts, 198.
   watercress, 181.
   wild chiccory, 200.
Sage, 21.
Salmis, 142, 155.
Salmon, 81.
Salpicon garniture, 60.
Salsify, 195.
Sandwiches, 168.
Sardines, 84.
Sauces, 45.
   Allemande, 45.
   anchovy, 45.
   butter, 46.
   bread, 46.
   broth for, 30.
   béchamel No. 1, 46.
       "   No. 2, 47.
   brown butter, 47.
   butter maitre d'hôtel, 47.
   caper, 48.
   coulis of fish, 48.
       " of lobster or shrimps, 49.
       " of veal, 48.
   cream, 49.
   cucumber, 50.
   currant, 49.
   Espagnole, 50.
   essence of spinage, 50.
   fish, 51.
   hazelnut butter, 51.
   Indian, 51.
   Italian, 41.
   juice, 52.

Sauces: maître d'hôtel, 52.
marinade, 52.
Mayonnaise, 53.
oil, 53.
oyster, 53.
piquante, 53.
poivrade, 54.
poulette, 54.
Provençale, 54.
ravigote, 55.
Robert, 55.
roux, 55.
suprême, 56.
tartar or cold, 56.
tomato, 56.
truffle, 56.
white, 57.
Sausages,
Sautéing, 9.
Savory, 26.
Savory cake, 216.
Seasoning, 9.
Semoulina, 36.
Shad, 81.
Sheep, brain, 122.
" feet, 122.
" kidneys, 123.
" tails, 124.
" tongues, 124.
Sheepshead fish, 81.
Shrimps, 101.
sauce, 49.
Simmering, 10.
Skate, 90.
Skirret, 195.
Skunk, 159, 160.
Smelts, 84.
Smoked tongue, 78.
Snails, 165.
Snipes, 159.
Sole, 84, 96, 97.
Sorrel, 195.
purée of, 64.
Soups, 29.
hints for, 27.
plates, 29.
beef and mutton, 31.
broth for, 30.
made quickly, 31.
cabbage, 39.
cauliflower, 39.
cheese, 39.
consommé, 30.
milk, 40.
mock turtle, 40.
onion, 41.
ox tail 41.
pot-au-feu, 29.
rice, 32.
turtle, 43.
Juliennes, 38.
potage à la Condé, 32.
à la Crécy, 32.
with carrots, etc., 33.
" celery, 33.

Soups:
potage with chestnuts, 33.
" fecula, 36.
" frogs, 33.
" lettuce, 34.
" macaroni, 34.
à la Monaco, 34.
printanier, 34.
with pumpkin, 35.
" rice, 35.
" sago, 36.
" semoulina, 36.
" sorrel, 36.
" tapioca, 36.
" tomatoes, 36.
" vermicelli, 38.
purée with beans, etc., 37.
" " green beans, 37.
" " carrots, 38.
Sourkrout, 176.
Sparrowgrass, 170.
Spinage, 106.
Sponge cake, 216.
Sprats, 84.
Sprouts, 176.
Squash, 194.
Squirrel, 164.
Steaks, 44, 71.
Stewing, 10.
Stirring, 27.
Straining, 13.
Strawberry, 202.
Stuffing, 81.
Sturgeon, 81.
Succory, 200.
Sucker, 88.
Sucking pig, 133.
Sun fish, 88.
Supper, 249.
Suprême sauce, 56.
Syrup for compotes, 234.
Sweetbreads, 115.
Sweetmeats, 237.
Sweet potatoes, 194.
Tail, 76, 115, 124, 132.
Tapioca potage, 36.
Tartar sauce, 56.
Tarts, 212.
Tea, 17.
cake, 217.
Teal, 141.
Tench, 82.
Thrush, 158.
Thyme, 21.
Time to keep fish, 15.
to keep meat, 14.
to cook meat, 13.
Toasts, 22.
Tomatoes, 196.
in salad, 196.
sauce, 56.
to preserve, 198.
Tongue, 77, 116, 124, 132.
Tripe, double, 78.
Trout, 83.

INDEX.

Troutlet, 88.
Truffles, 196.
    sauce, 56.
    garniture, **61**.
Tunny, 81.
Turbot, **81**.
Turkey, to select, **144**.
    to clean, 134.
    boiled, 145.
    roasted, 145.
    stewed, 146.
    stuffed, 145.
    left for the next day, **147**.
    in salad, 202.
    " galantine, 147.
    preserved, 23.
Turnips, 197.
    purée of, **65**.
Turtle, broth, **43**.
    steaks, 44.
Vanilla, 214.
Veal, 102.
    blanquette, **102**.
    broth, **42**.
    breast, stewed, 103.
        with green peas, **103**.
        roasted, 103.
        with onions, 104.
        in matelote, 105.
    cutlets, broiled, 105.
        with crumbs, 105.
        " fines herbes, 106.
        in papillote, 105.
    fricandeau, 106.
    loin, stewed, 107.
        with a garniture, **107**.
        roasted, 107.
    rump, roasted, 108.
        in escalops, 108.
    shoulder, roasted, 108.
        stewed, 108.
        left over, 109.
    pie, 109.
    in galantine, **148**.
Vegetables, 169.
    quality, 27.
    green and dry, **169**.
    sauce for, 169.
    artichokes, 169.
        Jerusalem, **170**.
    asparagus, 170.
    beans, 171.
    beets, 174.
    broccoli, 178.
    cabbage, 175.
    cardoon, 176.
    carrot, 177.
    cauliflower, 178.

Vegetables:
    celery, 179.
    soup, 180.
    corn salad, 201.
    corn, sweet, 180.
    cucumber, 181.
    dandelion, 181.
    egg plant, 182.
    endive, 183.
    feticus, 201.
    leek, 184.
    lentil, 184.
    lettuce, 184.
    mushroom, 185.
    okra, 187.
    onion, 187.
    oyster plant, **195**.
    parsnip, 187.
    pea, 188.
    potato, 189.
    pumpkin, 194.
    purslain, 194.
    radishes, 241.
    rhubarb, 218.
    salsify, 195.
    skirret, 195.
    sorrel, 195.
    sourkrout, 176.
    sparrowgrass, 170.
    spinage, 196.
    sprouts, 176.
    tomato, 196.
    truffle, 196.
    turnip, 197.
    watercress, **180**.
    wild chiccory, **197**.
    garniture, 61.
Venison, to select, 162.
    to improve, 162.
    cutlets, 162.
    haunch, 163.
    shoulder, or saddle, **163**.
    cold, 164.
Vermicelli, potage, **37**.
Vol-au-vent, 221.
Waffles, 228.
Walnuts, in salad, 193.
Watercress, 180, 181.
Weak fish, 82.
White fish, of the lakes, 84.
White sauce, 57.
Whitings, 82.
Why this book is small, 27.
Wild boar, 133.
Wine in sauces, 13.
Woodchuck, 159, 161.
Woodcock, 159.
Yellow birds, 158.

THE NEW AMERICAN CYCLOPÆDIA.

EDITED BY
GEORGE RIPLEY AND CHARLES A. DANA.

PUBLISHED BY
D. APPLETON & COMPANY, New York

In 16 Vols. 8vo, Double Columns, 750 Pages each.

Price, Cloth, $3.50; Sheep, $4; Half Mor., $4.50; Half Russia, $5 per Volume.

EVERY one that reads, every one that mingles in society, is constantly meeting with allusions to subjects on which he needs and desires further information. In conversation, in trade, in professional life, on the farm, in the family, practical questions are continually arising, which no man, well read or not, can always satisfactorily answer. If facilities for reference are at hand, they are consulted, and not only is the curiosity gratified, and the stock of knowledge increased, but perhaps information is gained and ideas are suggested that will directly contribute to the business success of the party concerned.

With a Cyclopædia, embracing every conceivable subject, and having its topics alphabetically arranged, not a moment is lost. The matter in question is found at once, digested, condensed, stripped of all that is irrelevant and unnecessary, and verified by a comparison of the best authorities. Moreover, while only men of fortune can collect a library complete in all the departments of knowledge, a Cyclopædia, worth in itself, for purposes of reference, at least a thousand volumes, is within the reach of all—the clerk, the merchant, the professional man, the farmer, the mechanic. In a country like ours, where the humblest may be called to responsible positions requiring intelligence and general information, the value of such a work can not be over-estimated.

PLAN OF THE CYCLOPÆDIA.

The New American Cyclopædia presents a panoramic view of all human knowledge, as it exists at the present moment. It embraces and popularizes every subject that can be thought of. In its successive volumes is contained an inexhaustible fund of accurate and practical information on Art and Science in all their branches, including Mechanics, Mathematics, Astronomy, Philosophy, Chemistry, and Physiology; on Agriculture, Commerce, and Manufactures; on Law, Medicine, and Theology; on Biography and History, Geography and Ethnology; on Political Economy, the Trades, Inventions, Politics, the Things of Common Life, and General Literature.

The Industrial Arts and those branches of Practical Science which have a direct bearing on our every-day life, such as Domestic Economy, Ventilation, the Heating of Houses, Diet, &c., are treated with the thoroughness which their great importance demands.

The department of Biography is full and complete, embracing the lives of all eminent persons, ancient and modern. In American biography, particularly, great pains have been taken to present the most comprehensive and accurate record that has yet been attempted.

In History, the New American Cyclopædia gives no mere catalogue of barren dates, but a copious and spirited narrative, under their appropriate heads, of the principal events in the annals of the world. So in Geography, it not only serves as a general Gazetteer, but it gives interesting descriptions of the principal localities mentioned, derived from books of travel and other fresh and authentic sources.

As far as is consistent with thoroughness of research and exactness of statement, the popular method has been pursued. The wants of the people in a work of this kind have been carefully kept in view throughout.

It is hardly necessary to add that, throughout the whole, perfect fairness to all sections of country, local institutions, public men, political creeds, and religious denominations, has been a sacred principle and leading aim. Nothing that can be construed into an invidious or offensive allusion has been admitted.

DISTINGUISHING EXCELLENCES.

While we prefer that the work should speak for itself, and that others should herald its excellences, we cannot refrain from calling attention to the following points, in which we take an honest pride in believing that the New American Cyclopædia surpasses all others:—

I. IN ACCURACY AND FRESHNESS OF INFORMATION.—The value of a work of this kind is exactly proportioned to its correctness. It must preclude the necessity of having other books. Its decision must be final. It must be an ultimatum of reference, or it is good for nothing.

II. IN IMPARTIALITY.—Our work has undergone the examination of Argus eyes. It has stood the ordeal. It is pronounced by distinguished men and leading reviews in all parts of the Union, strictly fair and national. Eschewing all expressions of opinion on controverted points of science, philosophy, religion, and politics, it aims at an accurate representation of facts and institutions, of the results of physical research, of the prominent events in the history of the world, of the most significant productions of literature and art, and of the celebrated individuals whose names have become associated with the conspicuous phenomena of their age—doing justice to all men, all creeds, all sections.

III. IN COMPLETENESS.—It treats of every subject, in a terse and condensed style, but fully and exhaustively. It is believed that but few omissions will be found; but whatever topics may, through any oversight, be wanting, are supplied in an Appendix.

IV. IN AMERICAN CHARACTER.—The New Cyclopædia is intended to meet the intellectual wants of the American people. It is not, therefore, modelled after European works of a similar design; but, while it embraces all their excellences, has added to them a peculiar and unmistakable American character. It is the production mainly of American mind.

V. IN PRACTICAL BEARING.—The day of philosophical abstraction and speculation has passed away. This is an age of action. *Cui bono* is the universal touchstone. Feeling this, we have made our Cyclopædia thoroughly practical. No man of action, be his sphere humble or exalted, can afford to do without it.

VI. In Interest of Style.—The cold, formal, and repulsive style usual in works of this kind, has been replaced with a style sparkling and emphatically readable. It has been the aim to interest and please, as well as instruct. Many of our writers are men who hold the foremost rank in general literature, and their articles have been characterized by our best critics as models of elegance, force, and beauty.

VII. In Convenience of Form.—No ponderous quartos, crowded with fine type that strains the eyes and wearies the brain, are here presented. The volumes are just the right size to handle conveniently; the paper is thick and white, the type large, the binding elegant and durable.

VIII. In Cheapness.—Our Cyclopædia has been universally pronounced a miracle of cheapness. We determined, at the outset, to enlarge its sphere of usefulness, and make it emphatically a book for the people, by putting it at the lowest possible price.

Such being the character of the New American Cyclopædia, an accurate, fresh, impartial, complete, practical, interesting, convenient, cheap Dictionary of General Knowledge, we ask, who can afford to do without it? Can the merchant, the statesman, the lawyer, the physician, the clergyman, to whom it gives thorough and complete information on every point connected with their several callings? Can the teacher, who is enabled, by the outside information it affords, to make his instructions doubly interesting and profitable? Can the farmer, to whom it offers the latest results of agricultural research and experiment? Can the young man, to whom it affords the means of storing his mind with useful knowledge bearing no any vocation he may have selected? Can the intelligent mechanic, who wishes to understand what he reads in his daily paper? Can the mother of a family, whom it initiates into the mysteries of domestic economy, and teaches a thousand things which more than saves its cost in a single year? In a word, can any intelligent American, who desires to understand the institutions of his country, its past history and present condition, and his own duties as a citizen, deny himself this great American digest of all human knowledge, universally pronounced the best Cyclopædia and the most valuable work ever published?

www.ingramcontent.com/pod-product-compliance
Lightning Source LLC
Chambersburg PA
CBHW032206230426
43672CB00011B/2524